The New Prohibition
Voices of Dissent
Challenge the Drug War

Foreword by Governor Jesse Ventura (Ret.)

Edited by Sheriff Bill Masters

libertybill.net

Accurate Press
St. Louis, Missouri

The New Prohibition
Voices of Dissent Challenge the Drug War

©2004 by Bill Masters

ISBN 1–888118–10–5 paperback $14.95
Printed in the United States of America

Published by Accurate Press,
a division of Accuprint, Inc.
P.O. Box 86, Lonedell, MO 63060 U.S.A.
http://www.accuratepress.net
1-800-374-4049

Acknowledgements

First I want to thank those who contributed their work to this volume. While the debate over drug policy reform is moving steadily into the mainstream, it continues to take a lot of courage to speak out on this issue. A diversity of views is expressed in these pages: the only constant is a perspective of questioning the *status quo*. The views of any one author should not be assumed to represent the views of other authors. At the same time, readers are encouraged to read the essays with an open mind, and not let disagreement on some issues lead to premature dismissal of other arguments.

I also want to thank all the people who contributed to this book in other ways. Ari Armstrong served as Assistant Editor. Richard Lamping provided conceptual ideas, communicated with contributors, and helped to proofread the material. Jennifer Armstrong created the cover design and page layout. The following people assisted with proofreading: Fred Boucher, Juanita Feigenbaum, Dawn Lamping, Brian Schwartz, Sharon Armstrong, and Edward Peters II.

Finally, I want to thank all those in law enforcement across the country who are doing what they can to restore the title "Peace Officer" as the highest badge of honor for those in our profession.

Sheriff Bill Masters

Contents

Contents

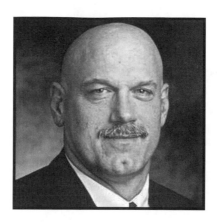

Foreword

BY JESSE VENTURA

Jesse Ventura became the 38ᵗʰ governor of Minnesota in 1998, winning as a Reform Party candidate with a campaign budget of less than $400,000. After graduating from high school in 1969, Ventura joined the Navy and was trained as a SEAL (Sea, Air, Land). Following his honorable discharge in 1973, he attended North Hennepin Community College on the GI bill. After his 11-year career in professional wrestling, Ventura became an actor, appearing in films such as Predator. *Ventura served as Mayor of Brooklyn Park, Minnesota, from 1990 to 1995, citing crime reduction as a major issue, and then hosted a radio talk show. He is a member of the Make a Wish of Minnesota Board of Advisors, the Screen Actors Guild, and the American Federation of Television and Radio Artists. He is also the author of three books, including* Jesse Ventura Tells It Like It Is.

It sure is nice to see someone isn't buying into all the government baloney on "winning the war on drugs." That's why I'm so pleased to see a book like this making its way into the mainstream.

Maybe now the message will get out there: the so-called "war" isn't working, and it's time to take a new approach!

Legalization? Maybe, maybe not, but we shouldn't rule anything out. The bottom line is that our country is losing billions of dollars in revenue because we're too shortsighted to learn from our past.

My mother lived through Prohibition, and she told me that there are obvious similarities between alcohol then and drugs today: in both cases, the gangsters get rich while the government wastes money fighting a losing battle.

As you read the viewpoints in this book, take these essays to heart and keep an open mind about what is really going on in our country. And maybe you'll be able to convince our lawmakers to throw conventional thinking out the door and start using common sense.

Governor Jesse Ventura

Section I:

PERSPECTIVES FROM LAW ENFORCEMENT

1. Shoveling Hay in Mayberry

BY BILL MASTERS

Bill Masters has served as sheriff of San Miguel County, Colorado (county seat, Telluride), since 1980. He is the author of Drug War Addiction: Notes from the Front Lines of America's #1 Policy Disaster.

When I first moved to Telluride, the town was still a mining community, filled with hard-rock miners who worked hard and played hard. There was a lot of drinking going on at night, but basically the town was a safe place where women could walk unescorted and children could play on the streets, even on Main Street.

I was 23 years old but looked 16. I had moved to Telluride to spend a season skiing and working in the mountains. I got a job as a ski lift operator for the brand new ski resort that had just started up the year before. It was a fun time. Because of the ski area, the town was attracting more and more newcomers, whom the local population called "hippies," no matter what they looked like or acted like.

The local police force consisted of just one town marshal, an odd character named Everett, who dressed like a Wild West gunslinger: big cowboy hat, leather vest, a low-slung gun belt, and holster which held a large revolver. He was about 5'6" tall and must have weighed about 140 pounds. The "hippies" had a saying about the local lawman: "Everett is mean, but he is fair; he gives shit to everyone."

Everett would drive around town in an old police cruiser that had a massive 400-cubic-inch engine, which enabled him to speed down Main Street and catch up with any lawbreaker who might try to outrun him—this in a town that had only a mile and a quarter of paved streets. In the car he always kept a mean mutt that, he claimed, he had "trained as a police dog; it will bite anyone carrying dope." Most people believed it would just bite anyone.

The dog would station himself under the patrol car if the marshal was on a call or walking the streets and then jump out snarling and barking at anyone who happened to walk too close to the marked cruiser.

The townspeople were pretty much divided over Everett's performance as a lawman. The "hippies" hated him and the "miners," who were never big law-and-order fans, at least tolerated him.

Everett soon became the center of controversy. He raided the first known Passover Seder ever to be held in Telluride after learning that the participants might be consuming wine without the proper liquor license. He came into the ceremony with his "posse," a group of local citizens many claimed to be vigilantes, with guns drawn. Some "hippies" who had recently been elected to the town board were attending the Seder, and at the next board meeting they fired Everett, ending his Telluride law enforcement career.

The town board struggled with its police responsibilities for a while and hired a number of different people to be the marshal. They eventually hired a young police officer from Arizona as chief and later me as a deputy. It was a real Andy and Barney kind of operation. Even though the chief was a conservative Mormon and I was a Barry Goldwater fan, we were branded as the "hippie marshals."

We tried to take the job seriously, but we constantly bore the brunt of the town's jokes. The favorite one the miners would pull would be to go over to Everett's home while he was at work (he had found employment working for the mining company) and let his dog out of its pen. The dog, not knowing any better, would walk uptown until he found the patrol car, which was now being used by the "hippie marshals," and take up his usual post under the car. The chief or I would try to get into the big cruiser, trying to look serious in our new uniforms and badges, only to be chased away by Everett's mean-ass dog.

During those days the police phone rang at my house. One night I got a call from a downtown business owner who stated, in a voice filled with panic, that there were a bunch of tough guys on Main Street trying to start a fight. I drove downtown and found a group of ten or so young punks, fueled by booze or whatever, giving everyone who walked by a hard time in an effort to provoke, as we cops say, a "violent or disorderly response."

As I walked up to them, they turned their attention to the lone baby-faced officer. I gathered up what little bravado I had and ordered them to move on. And they just laughed. But just as I was going toe-to-toe with a couple of them, figuring I was going to lose all my front teeth, there was a wavering in their ranks. A couple of guys from the back of the group were pulling on the ones in the front facing me off. The group slowly started to move on down the street. Just as I was feeling pretty tough, I looked over my shoulder and saw that the sidewalk behind me had filled with miners, hippies, realtors, and construction workers, all patrons from a café across the street. They had seen I was in trouble and had come out to help, saying, "We got your back; just tell us what to do."

It was that kind of community. Maybe I was just the local deputy Barney, but I was their deputy Barney, and they weren't going to let anything happen to me.

The Drug Warrior

During my early days as sheriff, the only illegal drug found around Telluride, as in most of America, was a little bit of marijuana. I took the drug laws seriously, and we started arresting more and more people for small amounts of drugs. The old jail had only two cells that didn't really work for more than an overnight sobering-up, so the county started paying a neighboring community 70 miles away to house our increasing number of prisoners.

I encouraged a state and federal drug task force to investigate drug dealing in the county. We were able to get court orders allowing us to tap several phones of suspected dealers, and after spending over half a million dollars—a lot of money in those days—we seized several ounces of cocaine and arrested the "kingpin" of a drug ring. He was let out of jail by a local judge after serving only eight months of an eight-year sentence.

Together with various drug task forces, I arrested the owner of the cable TV company, two city council members, a deputy district attorney, a chief of police, one of my own deputies, realtors, construction workers, high school kids, housewives, and the editor of the local newspaper, all on drug charges, right here in Mayberry.

I arrested one big land developer for distributing cocaine. He was from Ohio and had contributed heavily to a young, up-and-coming Republican senator's campaign. After his arrest he called on the senator, and the next thing I knew I had the FBI calling on me asking why I was harassing this upstanding citizen.

Every time I needed more money for the sheriff's office, I would play the tough guy. Not on the hard ones, the burglars or thieves or—God forbid!—the conservative supporter of mine caught driving home drunk. No, I was the tough guy on the easy ones, the dopers. Busting these people, I found, was not rocket science. In fact, it was easy.

In addition, when the Board of County Commissioners questioned my budget, I immediately accused them of being soft on drugs and even un-American. And it worked! I intimidated brave liberals and budget-slashing conservatives into always giving me what I needed. Drug dogs, more police cars, more deputies, a new jail, dispatch centers—all, to a degree, in the name of the drug war.

The county spent untold money on investigating and incarcerating drug dealers, but not one penny on treatment.

The conservative and religious community applauded my efforts—until we started arresting their sons and daughters and seizing their cars.

The patrons of the café that had stood behind me on that dark night, just a few years before, now hanged me in effigy and then set fire to the uniformed mannequin.

Glenn Frey even wrote a song about it, one I've quoted before:

You read it in the headlines,
you hear it every day,
they say they're going to stop it,
but it never goes away.
They bring it into Miami,
run it through LA,
they hide it up in Telluride,
man it's here to stay.

After I became sheriff, I learned during elections that the candidate who played the toughest on drugs won! I shamed my Democratic opponents if they wavered for a moment on the issue, and I beat them. Some elections were close, but I always won.

We arrested as many people as we could and started a DARE program in the schools. The drug problem just got worse. We began seeing more marijuana and cocaine, then ecstasy, meth, and heroin.

One dealer I busted told me, "Sheriff, you just don't get it. The only reason I am dealing dope is because there is money in it. If I didn't make money, I wouldn't do it. And sheriff, every time you bust somebody, my risk, my price, and my profit increase."

Nevertheless, in spite of all the community turmoil, I didn't care; the law was on my side. Some DEA agents even gave me an award for "outstanding contributions to the field of drug law enforcement." Accepting it like a Boy Scout achievement badge, I hung the award on my office wall, where it still hangs today.

Justice that Works

One day I was out politicking, talking to an old boy that I assumed would agree with me. I was complaining to him about the increasing drug problems in the county, the drug dealing, the community turmoil caused by all the arrests. After listening to my tirade in silence for a few minutes, he slowly turned to me and drawled, "You know, Sheriff, I don't want to tell you your business, but it sounds to me like you've been shoveling hay into the wrong end of the horse."

That comment bothered me. Obviously, if we were handling the problem the correct way we would have a stronger, safer, and healthier horse, but we aren't and we don't.

I began to look closely at the problem. I realized that we in law enforcement took on the burden of controlling drugs, convincing our lawmakers that we could handle it and that people would stop using drugs if we threatened them with arrest and long prison terms. However, in fact, the opposite has occurred.

Since the real beginning of the drug war in the early 1970s, when drugs were largely found in cities and on college campuses, the availability, potency, and quantity of drugs have increased. Anyone who says differently is a liar or a fool. Drugs are now available in every town, village, government school, and prison in the nation. By all measurable criteria, law enforcement has failed to stop drug use in this country, and we will continue to fail.

Law enforcement resources to the tune of $50 billion a year are spent in vain, investigating, arresting, and incarcerating drug users and sellers, at the expense of investigating, arresting, and incarcerating real criminals.

In the year before the terrorists struck and killed 3,000 people at the World Trade Center, American law enforcement officers arrested 750,000 people for possession of marijuana—and only one foreign terrorist.

Were those poor souls trapped in the towers in their final moments safer because some pot smokers were in jail? Was it effective government policy to maintain drug units in almost every police department in the nation, investigating drug users, while foreign terrorists took flying lessons in our own schools and practiced slicing the throats of flight attendants in neighborhood gyms?

Now we are aware of the FBI's Phoenix memorandum and the Minneapolis FBI agent's vain attempts to investigate terrorists before September 11th. Some agents tried to sound the alarm, ring the bell that said these known criminals—the same ones who bombed the World Trade Center before, who attacked our warships and embassies, who killed our sailors and Marines and innocent civilians world-wide—were going to hijack a plane and use it in a suicide attack in this country.

We know that no action was taken on the Phoenix memorandum's central recommendation: to compile information on the visa applications filled out by foreign students seeking admission to aviation schools.

It seems so simple. However, the administration in the Justice Department said that with hundreds of foreigners in flight schools around the country, officials at FBI headquarters regarded the proposed anti-terrorist investigative plan as a "sizable undertaking."

But I think arresting three quarters of a million American citizens every year for possession of a relatively harmless plant—now *that* is a sizable undertaking.

What was the response to these misguided law enforcement priorities? Did the administrators transfer thousands of agents from the Drug Enforcement Administration into the immigration service or some other anti-terrorist organization to track down the foreign terrorists living in our country? Did they lead and marshal the forces of law enforcement into a tight group focused on the challenges ahead, leaving the old and inefficient practices behind?

No, the American law enforcement response began by strip-searching little old ladies at the airport and running ads on TV that said "I smoked pot today and helped the terrorists."

If American pot users support terrorism, then American law enforcement practices and policies are enabling the same terrorists to commit their evil deeds. Blaming the pot smoker for terrorism is nothing more than spin, an attempt to deflect blame away from the American law enforcement community that blindly ignored the warning signs of the pending murderous crime.

Further, the only reason drugs are so valuable and therefore attractive to criminals as a method of making money, be it for terrorism or greed, is the fact that drugs are illegal. The profit in drug dealing, like any business, comes from the risk the businessperson must take, whether selling pot or tomatoes. Since drugs are against the law, the risk of arrest and rip-offs by rivals (thefts that cannot be reported to the police) is great, and the profit potential is tremendous. What costs only pennies per unit to produce is sold to consumers for a fortune.

Then, of course, everyone is shocked when bums, criminals, and terrorists are attracted to the opportunities to make money that our own policies are creating for them.

Ultimately, though, those committing the crimes must be the ones held responsible. This is really the root of the problem, why we continue shoving hay into the wrong end. We have repeatedly blamed certain crimes on drug use instead of allowing individuals the freedom to decide what goes into their bodies, but then holding them completely responsible for their actions that harm or endanger others. Any justice system that suppresses the virtues of both freedom and responsibility will be ineffective.

The only reason why drugs and crime have expanded to reach every Mayberry village in the country is our blind obedience to misguided laws and police tactics that just do not work. It is time to admit our own folly and stop our addiction to the drug war.

2. Prohibition: The Enemy of Freedom

BY RICHARD MACK

Richard Mack served on the Provo, Utah, police force from 1979 to 1988. He worked as an undercover narcotics officer in 1982 and also served as a juvenile crime specialist and resource officer for the Provo School District. Mack was promoted to sergeant in 1985 and later became a detective. In 1988 Mack moved back to his hometown of Safford, Arizona, and successfully ran for sheriff of Graham County, a position he held until 1996. Currently Mack lives in Provo and works as an author and law-enforcement consultant.

Benjamin Franklin, one of the Founders of this great country, warned us to never surrender liberty for the false promise of increased security. Avoiding that advice is nothing new and has been tried time after time throughout history. Propaganda urging us to surrender our liberty is certainly raising its head in America today.

Prohibition did not work in the 1920s, it has failed today, and it will never provide peace and safety—quite the contrary. The prohibitionists scream for more laws and government controls. "It's for the children." "We've got to send a message to pushers." "We've got to get tougher on crime." Or, "Our goal is zero tolerance." All the while the loss of freedom worsens, taxes and manpower are wasted, and fellow human beings are inhumanely warehoused in prisons, where their problems are only exacerbated. Prisons are infested with drugs, too.

The answers to today's social calamities do not lie on the path we've been traveling. We will not find the solutions in more laws, taxes, bureaucracy, or political strategies, but rather by returning to those principles upon which this country was based. The answer is still freedom, responsibility, personal accountability, fairness, and respect. Cracking the whip through a police state only breeds contempt and destroys trust and liberty.

A century and a half ago a lawyer from the backwoods served as president and issued a warning about the dangers of prohibition: "Prohibition goes beyond the bounds of reason in that it attempts to control a man's appetite by legislation and makes crimes out of things that are not crimes. A prohibition law strikes a blow at the very principles upon which our government was founded." The 16th president of the United States made some egregious errors during a most difficult time (the Civil War), but Abraham Lincoln nailed the danger of prohibition squarely on the head. Prohibition does not work! That is, unless you're using it to create more corruption and a huge black market in which organized crime flourishes and the police state crescendos.

Serving as a "Narc"

In 1982, I was an undercover narcotics officer. I lived within the drug culture for six months. I hated every minute of it. In my daily routine, I was surrounded by addicts and ex-cons. I was way out of my comfort zone. But I learned a lot. The first thing I learned was that most of these people were basically good. For the most part I liked them, and at least one of them, Ted, is still a personal friend today.

There was one guy I hoped would drop off the end of the earth, though. We called him "Crazy Mike." He was from Chicago, and he always bragged about blowing things up, including a former boyfriend of his girlfriend. He served some time for that.

At one point during my undercover assignment, rumors started floating around the bars that I was a cop. Crazy Mike heard it and asked me about it. "I don't think you are and I can't see how it could be true," he assured me, "but if I ever find out you are a cop, I'll put a bomb in your car."

This threat just gave me another reason to stay away from Crazy Mike, a guy I didn't like anyway. But he was actually the exception. I really cared for most of the people I associated with while serving as a "narc," even though under normal circumstances I never would have socialized with any of them.

I was making cases against the majority of the people I associated with. Obviously, not all of them used or dealt drugs, but most of them did. My friend Ted smoked pot occasionally, but he never sold it as far as I could tell, and he drank frequently. I saw him drunk once or twice, and he chased girls a lot. (His fancy sports car seemed to help with that.)

Ted was an electrician and traveled quite a bit to jobs. He always contacted me when he got back into town, at the roach-infested, trashy apartment that I stayed in. (It was only about a mile from my real home, so it wasn't too hard for me to sneak home at night to see my wife and kids.) Ted was my golf buddy, and we golfed every chance we got. Our friendship was authentic, and I enjoyed his company.

When I finished my undercover assignment, he was out of town. A few days after the arrests were made of the dozens of people I had built cases against, Ted walked back into town and nearly got tarred and feathered. Some of the "bar" people thought Ted might have been in on my assignment, as he was constantly around me. He was furious. He called me at the police station and chewed me out pretty good.

I was patient as he let off some steam because I wanted to talk with him, too. "Ted," I said firmly. "Ted," I said once again. I finally got his attention and he stopped to listen to me. "Ted, I am really sorry you nearly got beat up when you came back to town. I'm relieved that you didn't. No, there is not a warrant out for your arrest, so you don't have to worry about that. Yes, I lied to you about what I did for a living and what my real name was. But Ted, one thing I didn't lie about was our friendship, and I still consider you a good friend of mine. Now, my wife and I would like to have you over for dinner tomorrow night."

There was a moment of silence and then he said, "Ah, what the hell. You know I can't turn down home cooking." He came for dinner and then took my kids for a ride in his fancy car. Then we all went to my softball game. The kids really enjoyed Ted and his car. They did comment on how much he smoked, though.

Ted and I were different. He smoked, he drank, at times he used marijuana, and his morals were not in line with my Mormon background. But he was a good man. He cared about his children, and he was a hard worker. He was loyal and understanding, and he had a great sense of humor.

Spinning Our Wheels

So I had to ask myself a question: should I have arrested Ted, too? I arrested about twenty others for mere possession of marijuana, so why not

Ted? (I actually never had the physical evidence to make a case against Ted, but he nevertheless used pot and presented me with a philosophical dilemma.) Why were we arresting people, some really decent people, for smoking marijuana? Should we arrest all the "Teds" in the country? Take his sports car, ruin his career, give him an arrest record and some jail time, and maybe overall just teach him a lesson?

I couldn't see it then, and I can't see now how arresting Ted or thousands more like him is going to be beneficial to anyone. Not to me, not to my family, and certainly not to my community. Why don't we leave people alone? Going after people for what they might do is wrong. We must never punish people in anticipation of their acts.

Leave people alone unless they in some way create a victim. Let people make their own choices, run their own lives, and, as stupid and loathsome as their behavior may be, leave them alone. Government leaving people alone. What a novel idea! It is not the government's job to protect us from our own stupidity!

Another aspect of my undercover education was learning how badly we (law enforcement) are spinning our wheels in the enforcement of drug laws. We have not even scratched the surface, yet we continue to make it a top budget priority and dedicate millions of police hours and billions of taxpayer dollars so we can have more wheels spinning. This scheme creates more government jobs and bureaucracy but has little effect on reducing the drug market.

Abuse and Corruption

The detrimental results from the "spinning wheels" of the drug war include the destruction of American idealism. When you have approximately 600,000 police officers (both federal and local) who dedicate a good portion of their time attempting to determine what citizens have in their pockets, glove compartments, and homes, there is bound to be abuse. This abuse has resulted in the unethical and unlawful confiscation of personal property: homes, cars, boats, bank accounts, etc.

Where does this property go after it is confiscated? Usually it goes to supplement and augment the budgets of the police agencies that did the confiscating in the first place. No police officer or police administrator in this country should have to be told that such a practice is a huge compromise of standards and ethics. It is flat-out wrong! Yet those who purport to "protect and serve" continue this confiscation policy with impunity.

The war on drugs is routinely used as a rationalization for many government abuses. "We have to do this to you so we can better protect you and take care of you." Yes indeed, if you allow it, the government will take care of you, and you'll get all the fringe benefits Big Brother has to offer.

In the March 14, 1994, issue of *Time*, there were two articles that every American should have found disturbing. The first, "How to Achieve the New World Order," by Henry Kissinger, suggested subtly, that we must compromise American idealism in order to fit into the modern global society. I am fed up with compromising American principles of liberty to fit into anything else, whether it is Kissinger's "New World Order," Bush's "Homeland Security," or the government's so-called "War on Drugs." They all mean the same thing and come with the same price tag: "Surrender liberty for safety!"

Time's other frightening article was, "Who Should Keep The Keys? The federal government wants the power to tap into every phone, fax, and computer transmission." Why do they want this? So they can take care of you! So they can protect and serve you! The article explained that the government needs these powers to have the capability "to keep tabs on drug runners, terrorists, and spies." Now, don't you feel better? Don't you feel safer?

Perhaps the real question is, do you feel free? And even more importantly, does your government make a conscious effort to protect individual rights? Do the leaders of your government agencies make certain, above all else, that they stay within Constitutional limitations? Or do your government leaders grab for every piece of power they can get their greedy little hands on, the Constitution notwithstanding?

A Double Standard

Another aspect of my undercover lab experiment into the "social behavior of the American drug culture" was the education I received about the effects of alcohol in comparison to marijuana.

One of the rules for my tenure as an undercover agent was never to get drunk or out of control. When you're "under," you've got to know what you're doing. I was to do everything I could to "fit in" with my new surroundings. So I smoked, and my virgin lungs would not allow me to inhale, so I became very proficient at simulating. This ability came in handy for the times the marijuana joints were passed around.

I also drank, mostly beer, and this was another major problem, as I hated beer with a purple passion. To this day I cannot understand how anyone ever took a second swallow of that stuff. Have you ever tried to act like you enjoyed something while at the same time hiding your body's gagging reaction? I did that for six months. It never got any easier, either (although I will say Hamm's beer went down the easiest). Most of the beer I poured out every chance I got—in bathrooms, outside, into someone else's drink, and even on the floor of a dark corner of a bar. I got rather creative with that process.

I did smoke marijuana a few times, but dozens of times I hid it in my hand and simulated smoking. Marijuana was everywhere. It was routinely passed around in every bar. At some bars we would go outside and share a joint among four or five of us. The few times I could not simulate the smoking of marijuana, when using a pipe or "bong" (an apparatus that helps the smoke get deeper into your lungs for a better high), I actually felt the effect of the marijuana high and I found myself wondering what in the heck the big deal was. The marijuana made me somewhat dizzy, and I do mean somewhat; it was certainly minimal, and it made me a little happy and I got the "munchies." I certainly knew what I was doing and was completely aware of my surroundings, my job, and that I had a wife and three beautiful children waiting for me at home.

I saw people who smoked pot all day and others who drank all day. The pot smokers were much more in control of their physical and mental faculties than the drinkers were. In all my twenty years of law enforcement I have never seen a person who has smoked marijuana to be in a condition of staggering, slobbering, and throwing up. Too many times, however, I have seen booze drinkers in such a condition, and much worse. I am aware of numerous instances annually in which consumers of alcohol have drunk themselves to death. There has never been one documented case where this has occurred with marijuana use. Government propaganda claims that marijuana is ten times more carcinogenic than tobacco. Yet there has never been, not once, a single case documented of a person dying from the use of marijuana.

The Principle of Freedom

I do not and never will condone or encourage the use of marijuana, alcohol, tobacco, or, to a large degree, prescription drugs. They are all dangerous and harmful. However, when the alternative is forcing American citizens at the point of a gun to not possess pot and threatening users with jail and the confiscation of homes, cars, and bank accounts, I no longer can condone such tyranny. What a person smokes most certainly does not justify SWAT teams with Uzis raiding his home. And it does not justify arrests and jail time. We will never arrest away our nation's drug problem.

On October 10, 2002, United States Drug Czar John Walters stated at a press conference in Las Vegas that if marijuana were decriminalized, "it would do tremendous harm to the war on drugs." I pray that I am not the only one who has a problem with this picture.

First, Czars are from Russia, and the word actually is derived from "Caesar." Neither of these offices should have any application in the "land of the free." Isn't it sad that bureaucratic appointments have become so legion that they ran out of titles for them and were thus forced to seek job titles from despotic regimes?

Second, if the legalization of marijuana in some way "harms" their precious "war on drugs," then so be it. What they have been doing certainly has not worked. The "drug czar" seems more concerned about protecting the drug war bureaucracy, which feeds on more jobs and more money, than about actually solving the problem. This bureaucratic force perpetuates the mythology that "we will do better next year if we can just acquire more agents and more money to more adequately go after the drug pushers." They've been saying that for over 30 years.

The most important aspect of the legalization debate is the principle of freedom, a concern that is apparently lost in the shuffle. Can anyone seriously look at this issue, no matter how you line up on the use of marijuana, and agree that our police should be attempting to stop citizens from using pot at the point of a gun? If we as Americans support this type of draconian enforcement, then is it any wonder that few of our individual liberties and God-given rights are left inviolate? Such enforcement is the product of a police state and threatens to destroy the America as envisioned by the Founders. Is this the price we are asked to pay for the drug war? If it is, then the false promise of security and the war on drugs have become the real enemies of Constitutional American liberty.

3. Gangster Cops in the Drug War

BY JOSEPH McNAMARA

Joseph McNamara served as a patrolman in Harlem before earning his doctorate in public administration at Harvard. In 1973 he became chief of police in Kansas City, Missouri. From 1976 to 1991 he served as chief of police in San Jose, California; he was then appointed a research fellow at the Hoover Institution. McNamara has written three best-selling detective novels and a criminology textbook. A version of the following essay was originally published by California Lawyer, *Volume 20, Issue 5, May 2000.*

On February 29, 1999, New York Mayor Rudolph Giuliani told TV interviewer Larry King that Amadou Diallo's death was a tragic accident, but unfortunately people also died every week in tragic automobile accidents. The following day, across the country, Los Angeles Mayor Richard Riordan, commenting on the Los Angeles Police Department's questionable report on LAPD gangster cops running amuck, said he had never been more proud of the department. Both mayors were straining to restore credibility to their damaged police departments. The two politicians were also defending their own legacies as crime fighters, as well as the confrontational police cultures they had nurtured. Although the geography is different, the political spin is similar.

The LAPD scandal involved an "elite" anti-gang unit. Rafael Perez, a former member of the unit, was convicted of stealing cocaine from the police evidence room. In return for a lesser sentence, Perez told of extensive criminal activity in the department. Cops had shot people without cause, planted guns on them, and then celebrated the shootings over beer at barbecues. Perez depicted how cops had framed people and testified against those victims to ensure that they received long prison terms. He also detailed the same kind of drug-related police crimes that have plagued New York and other cities. Cops committed armed robberies of drug dealers, taking their money and selling their drugs themselves.

The LAPD report was widely criticized for blaming the scandal on a few rotten apples, when allegations from the convicted cop and a number of citizens were that numerous LAPD cops had perpetrated a wave of corruption and gangsterism. The city faced a plethora of lawsuits against its police department. It is difficult to understand why the mayor said he had "never been prouder" of the department.

The New York case that Mayor Giuliani wanted to see forgotten involves Diallo, who was unarmed and had committed no crime, but was killed in his own hallway in a barrage of 41 police bullets. His death at the hands of four plainclothes officers from the "elite" NYPD Street Crimes Unit certainly is not comparable to a traffic accident.

My father, brother, uncles, cousins, and I collectively served more than 150 years in the NYPD. None of us would have shot Diallo. If we had, a jury would have convicted us of breaking the law, because in those days both the formal and informal peer values of policing held that you did not shoot unless you were sure the bad guy was going to shoot at you. The jury that acquitted the four New York policemen who killed Diallo reflected the new political and police morality. The cops had been way too aggressive and had made a fatal mistake, but their aggression flowed from police department policy. Therefore, they had committed no crime.

I left the NYPD after 17 years to become police chief of two of America's largest cities, Kansas City and San Jose, over the next 18 years, during which time I observed a sea change in American policing. Spurred on by fiery political rhetoric of a war on drugs and crime, the NYPD, LAPD, and other departments unleashed plainclothes police to "hunt" drug violators and other criminals in minority neighborhoods. The NYPD Street Crimes Unit bragged, "We own the night." Its LAPD counterpart, CRASH (Community Resources Against Street Hoodlums), was equally macho. Some of its members wore death-head logos on their unit jackets and similar tattoos on their arms, aping the intimidation methods of the street gang members they were supposed to police.

Both of these bellicose units were formed, in part, because there are no victims or witnesses in drug crimes as there are in murders, rapes, and assaults. Thus, many cops, with encouragement from their superiors to produce the arrests demanded by city hall, began to regard everyone in certain neighborhoods as suspects. In 1968, in *Terry v. Ohio*, the U.S. Supreme Court approved letting officers frisk people under questioning for suspicious actions in the interest of the officers' safety. The court permitted an external "pat down" for weapons, but not a search for drugs. Nevertheless, millions of times a year in the name of the war against drugs, police officers do illegally search people and, when they discover drugs, perjure themselves so that the evidence is admissible. These police felonies have become so commonplace that they have found their way into police jargon. In the NYPD, cops joke about "testilying" instead of testifying. In the LAPD, it is laughed at as "joining the liars' club."

These aggressive tactics have not conquered the drug problem, but throughout the nation they have provided an umbrella under which some cops have become badge-carrying gangsters, committing thousands of crimes such as murders, kidnappings, armed robberies, stealing and selling drugs, and framing people. The results have been devastating to the victims, to minority communities, and to honest cops.

Guilty cops, after being caught in predatory felonies, rationalize their conduct. They dehumanize the "enemy." New York cops call their victims "mutts" and "scum," while members of the LAPD refer to them as "assholes" or "dirtbags." The rogue cops universally talk about a sense of street justice permeating their departments. "The end justified the means. These were bad guys. We did what we had to do to get them," as one convicted sergeant put it.

The public does not realize that police drug gangsterism is not just a local problem, but has become a national epidemic. The police code of silence and tendencies of police chiefs and mayors to put a damage-control spin on scandals have obscured the magnitude of police drug-related crimes. Assurances that only a few cops are involved and that action has been taken so that it can "never happen again" reassure citizens. But the ugly truth is that the confrontational style of policing illustrated by New York and Los Angeles permits the gangster cops to go on with their crimes for years. One of the great ironies is that some of the worst gangster cops are far from rotten apples. They have outstanding arrest records and own more commendations than their fellow officers do. Otherwise-honest cops and even supervisors hesitate to report the gangster cops, because all too often the message from city hall is one of law and order and denial of police misconduct. Whistle-blowers are more likely to be fired than rewarded.

Thankfully, the nation in recent years has enjoyed welcome decreases in crime, and fewer police officers have been slain in the line of duty. A booming economy, the decline of the crack cocaine market, and demographics probably had as much to do with it as the police. And crime decreased in large cities such as San Jose and San Diego, which rejected abrasive police methods in favor of working in partnerships with neighborhood groups to reduce disorder and crime. In any event, lawbreaking by law enforcers is not an option in a free society. Where police crime flourishes it can only create disrespect for law and police, and create more crime.

No one knows how many hundreds of millions of dollars have been paid out in successful lawsuits against police abuses. Bad policing ends up in human tragedies. These are not accidents but the inevitable result of wrong-headed styles of policing. The problems in Los Angeles may finally force ambitious politicians everywhere to avoid "in your face" policing. The first step in avoiding unnecessary police shootings and police gangsterism is for politicians to drop the war rhetoric and to train police officers to understand that they are not soldiers with a duty to kill the "enemy," but peace officers with a duty to protect and serve the communities in which they work.

4. End Prohibition Now

BY JACK COLE

Jack Cole retired as a detective lieutenant after a 26-year career with the New Jersey State Police. For 12 of those years Cole worked as an undercover narcotics officer. He is currently the executive director of Law Enforcement Against Prohibition (www.leap.cc). The following essay is based on a presentation Cole made at a policy conference in Belgium held October 15–16, 2002.

The policy of the U.S. "war on drugs" has been, is, and forever will be, a total and abject failure. This is not a war on drugs, this is a war on people— our own people—our children, our parents, ourselves.

After three decades of fueling the war with over half a trillion tax dollars and increasingly punitive policies, illicit drugs are easier to get, cheaper, and more potent than they were 30 years ago.[1] While our court systems are choked with ever-increasing drug prosecutions, our quadrupled prison population has made building prisons this nation's fastest growing industry, with two million incarcerated—more per capita than any country in the world. Meanwhile, drug barons continue to grow richer than ever before, and our citizens continue dying in our streets.

Prohibition does not work, and most of us know that. But as Dan Baum pointed out in *Smoke and Mirrors: The War On Drugs And The Politics Of Failure*, the war metaphor worked well for Richard Nixon when he initiated the idea of a "war on drugs" in 1968 so he could run for President on a "tough on crime" stand. The metaphor has continued to work well for politicians for over three decades, because

> nearly everyone has found a reason to enlist: parents appalled by their teen's behavior, police starved for revenue, conservative politicians pandering to their constituents' moral dudgeon, liberal politicians needing a chance to look "tough," presidents looking for distractions from scandal, whites—and blacks—striving to "explain" the ghetto, editors filling page one, spies and colonels needing an enemy to replace communist[s]...[2]

The fact that it is a failed policy seldom seems to enter the discussion. The attitude about drugs in the U.S. has been shaped by countless politicians raising the specter of a country lost to a zombie population of drug addicts ready to kill to get their fix. Those politicians make no delineation between soft drugs such as marijuana and hard drugs such as heroin or cocaine. They link marijuana with heroin, as a "gateway drug,"[3] which is about as sensible as linking heroin with milk as a gateway drug; after all, nearly 100% of heroin users first drank milk.

Enforcing Narcotics Laws

I've always been interested in reducing harm to others. Harm reduction is a term that sprang from the drug policy reform movement, and it was a while before I adopted its language. In 1964, when I felt I could no longer sit passively and watch one more television newscast of police beating men, women, and children for nothing more than demanding their civil rights, it occurred to me that changing police policy from the inside might be easier than changing it from the outside. I quit a perfectly good job as an ironworker and took a 50% cut in pay to join the New Jersey State Police. My purpose was to try to reduce the harms of what I perceived as nationwide, institutionalized, racist policy within police departments.

Six years later, I joined the state police narcotic bureau because I wanted to reduce the harm caused by what I believed to be a terrible scourge of drug abuse spreading across our country.

I grew up in Wichita, Kansas, in what has been called the heartland of America. We didn't have a drug problem in Wichita—or at least I didn't think so. After all, I never used drugs! My God! I had been schooled on the movies "Reefer Madness" and "Man with the Golden Arm." I wouldn't have been caught dead with a marijuana cigarette in my mouth. What I didn't realize was that I did have a long-standing drug problem. My drugs of choice were alcohol and tobacco. By the age of 14 my friends and I were getting falling-down-drunk about once a week, and I smoked two packs of cigarettes a day for over 15 years, but alcohol and tobacco were legal. "Drugs" were the illegal ones—the ones that I would never use. Actually, alcohol and tobacco are the two worst drugs anyone can use—56 times as many people in the U.S. die from smoking tobacco and drinking alcohol as are killed by the use of all the illegal drugs combined. Each year in America, thanks to the legal cigarette industry, 430,000 people die from smoking or spending time in close proximity to smokers. Thanks to the legal liquor industry, another 110,000 people die from ingesting alcohol— while around 12,000 people die as a result of using all the illegal drugs combined. And there are no deaths recorded caused by ingesting marijuana. The media love to write about the horrors of illegal drug use but seem to forget about the horrors of legal drugs such as tobacco and alcohol.[4]

When I joined the narcotic bureau, I wanted to use any means legally available to stop the use of illegal drugs in this country. Many of my colleagues, on the other hand, chose to stop the use of illegal drugs by any means necessary. It was 1970 and the "war on drugs," coined by Richard Milhouse Nixon in 1968 as a political ploy to garner votes for his run for the presidency, had just officially gotten underway. Bills for massive federal grants to police departments willing to do their part to fight Nixon's war on drugs had been pushed through Congress and were flowing to the states. The New Jersey State Police administrators knew a good thing when they saw it. Here was a chance to increase the size of their organization and thereby their power base without having to beg more money from the state. Overnight they upgraded and increased their narcotic unit of seven men to a narcotic bureau of 76 men. (At that time the state police had around 1,700 men and one woman on the force—it is still only composed of slightly over 2% women.) About a third of those 76 men were assigned to work undercover. I was one of those undercover agents.

My bosses, like those in police departments across the country, didn't know anything about fighting a war on drugs, but they did know that if they expected to keep the federal cash cow in their barnyard, they would have to exhibit statistics that reflected a drug problem of extreme proportions in their jurisdiction. As a result, much like the Vietnam War body counts, exaggeration became the norm: the sizes of seizures were greatly magnified, and drug users suddenly became drug dealers.

When an individual was arrested with illegal drugs, any unmixed cutting agents also found (quinine, mannitol, milk sugar, etc.) were included as part of the weight of the illegal drugs. This could make the seizure appear to be three, four, or more times larger than it actually was.

We also reported the monetary value of the drugs to the media as the street-level price, increasing their apparent value by as much as 66 times depending on what level dealer we had caught. In 1977, one of my targets was arrested in Houston, Texas, with 12 kilograms of cocaine that had been purchased in Colombia for $15,000 each, or $180,000 total outlay, but when the seizure hit the newspapers, the drugs became worth $12 million.[5]

Unbeknownst to my bosses or me was the fact that much of the drug war had already been based on inflated statistics, fabrications, and outright lies before we ever got involved. As Baum notes:

> Despite Nixon's assertion to the pre-election Disneyland crowd that drugs were "decimating generations of Americans," drugs were so tiny a public health problem that they were statistically insignificant: far more Americans choked to death on food or died falling down stairs as died from illegal drugs.[6]

In fact, if the diary of Nixon's Chief of Staff H. R. Haldeman is to be believed, Haldeman reported that during a meeting with Nixon in 1969, Nixon emphasized, "You have to face the fact that the whole problem is really the blacks. The key is to devise a system that recognizes this all while not appearing to." The system they devised was the war on drugs and for Nixon's purposes, he could have hardly hoped for more.[7] The war on drugs has spawned the most racist laws seen in the United States since the 1896 Supreme Court ruling of "separate but equal" in *Plessy v. Ferguson*.[8]

Destroying Lives

Institutionalized racism is reflected in our drug laws that make sentencing for possession of crack cocaine harsher than sentencing for a similar weight of powder cocaine. Crack cocaine was perceived by Congress in 1986 as a drug used in the poor inner-city neighborhoods populated mostly by people of color, while powder cocaine was the drug more likely used in middle and upper class, wealthy neighborhoods populated mostly by whites. Institutionalized racism is also reflected in the racial profiling that I believe is likely to have been practiced by every police department in the United States.

Of the 26.7 million Americans who recently used an illicit drug, 72% were white, 12% were black, 10% were Hispanic, and 6% were "other." But blacks constitute 36.8% of those arrested for drug violations and over 42% of those in federal prisons for drug violations. African-Americans also comprise almost 60% of state prisoners held for drug felonies, and

Hispanics account for 22.5%.[9] Once convicted of drug felonies in state courts, whites are less likely than African-Americans to be sent to prison; 32% of convicted white defendants receive prison sentences, compared with 46% of African-American defendants.[10]

In 1970, the New Jersey State Police started its war on drugs with street-level operations, arresting mostly drug users but claiming they were drug dealers. Each undercover detective worked by himself. He was "backed up" by one "surface investigator," a detective who coordinated undercover drug investigations with other police agencies and determined in what city the agent would work. The surface detective also supplied the informants, who were often used to introduce the undercover agents to specific, suspected drug dealers. The informants were usually people who were trying to work off drug-law-violation charges made against them at an earlier time, by other undercover agents. My experience with those informants left me with the feeling that most would lie about anything that might help them out of their predicament, as long as they thought they would not be caught in the lie. The agents always had to be aware of that possibility. If the agents did their jobs correctly, they tried in every way possible to corroborate what the informant said before reporting it as factual. If an agent became lazy or just did not care, it was easy for innocent people to suffer the consequences of investigations based on bogus, unsubstantiated statements from informants. On too many occasions, those errors have actually resulted in the deaths of innocent homeowners, when the incorrect house or apartment was raided after it had been wrongly pointed out by an informant as a drug den.[11]

The undercover agent worked an assigned town or city neighborhood until he had received illegal drugs from everyone available to him. We made criminal drug-distribution cases on an average of 80 to 90 people in each operation before moving on to the next town.

About a month after we received our last undercover distribution in any given town, the arrests were executed. At five o'clock in the morning a task force of hundreds of police armed with arrest and search warrants swept over the town, smashing down the doors of homes where our suspects resided, often with their families. All occupants were dragged from their beds and forced face down on the floor, where all adults were handcuffed for the safety of the police who conducted a search of the premises.

While searching the houses, many police applied their own brand of "street justice" to those people they considered "deviants and scum"— trashing the house and breaking belongings. If, during these arrests, a search of the house revealed any illegal drugs, all money in the house was also seized as drug profits (this could include the kids' piggy banks). As a standard ploy, we threatened to arrest uninvolved relatives who also lived in the house—a wife, a sister, or a mother—if our suspect refused to give up his connections. On occasions when all the occupants of a location were placed under arrest, we went merrily on our way, leaving smashed doors open and homes vulnerable to be picked clean by burglars (another extra little punishment for those who dared to use illegal drugs).[12]

We conducted a new operation every two or three months. The accused did not have to sell the drugs to the agent—a simple "distribution" was enough. This meant that if an individual handed an undercover agent a single tablet of LSD ("hit of acid"), amphetamine capsule ("diet pill"), or a partially smoked marijuana cigarette ("roach"), they were charged with "illegal distribution of a controlled dangerous substance" and at that time received the same punishment as if they had sold the agent heroin or cocaine—up to seven years in prison in some jurisdictions.

At first, the undercover agents were given only $100 to $200 for drug purchases, sums of money that had to last several days. As a result, everyone we charged was either a user or the smallest of dealers, who in the words of a county judge ruling on some of their cases, "were simply accommodating friends with small amounts of drugs." We could not afford to buy from any of the larger dealers at that time. In fact, of all the people from whom I bought drugs during my first three years on the street, I can remember only one person who was involved in selling multiple grams of heroin but was not himself a drug user.

Most of the drug users we decided to label as "dealers" were young people who on a given day happened to have transportation to get to the city where they could buy the drugs. Before they left, they took up a collection among their drug-using friends in order to be able to buy in some bulk and therefore get lower prices. The bulk I am referring to amounted to a half-bundle[13] of heroin, cocaine, or methamphetamine, or an ounce or two of marijuana. As soon as they returned with the drugs, they handed them out to their friends who had ordered them. Usually they were lucky if they made enough money to pay for their transportation to the city. Occasionally someone sold a little extra, but usually just enough to support their habits. However, in our press releases to the media these people all received the same designation: "drug dealer."

As with the other local and state police agencies with limited "buy money," our undercover operations were relegated to the lower echelons of traffickers. The only exceptions were when informants introduced us for one-time buy-busts, where we did not have to pay for one delivery in order to set up a larger delivery from a higher-ranking dealer.

During my first three years working undercover, my vision of what the drug war was about changed drastically because of what I saw and experienced while working the street. I learned firsthand of the family-destroying consequences of sending drug users (often mothers and fathers) to jail. I can't think of a better policy for creating the next generation of drug addicts than to remove parents from children. I also realized that when police arrested a robber or rapist they made the community safer for everyone, but when I arrested a drug pusher, I simply created a job opening for someone in a long line of people willing to take his place. I finally came to understand that the small amount of good I might have been accomplishing for the government could never outweigh the harm I was causing countless people.

The Ends Justify the Means?

Since what I was doing was obviously not working, I tried to figure out what the goal of our drug policy should actually be. I realized at that point I didn't want to stop all use of illegal drugs in some crazed kind of "zero-tolerance" obsession—an impossible task at any rate. Besides, I could plainly see that not all drug use is debilitating or destructive, and there are those who can use drugs recreationally while still becoming active and productive citizens. I'm sure the reader can easily think of a few. Some that quickly come to mind include United States Presidents William Clinton and George W. Bush, former Vice President Albert Gore, former Speaker of the House Newt Gingrich, and many others. Only about 15% of the users of addictive drugs actually become addicted, but no one should want to fall into that 15%.

So I came to a few conclusions in 1973: (1) I wanted most to reduce harm; (2) The largest portion of the harms I was observing seemed to be caused by the prohibition of drugs rather than the pharmacology of drugs; (3) I liked some of the people I was working on better than some of the people I was working for; (4) I didn't wish to imprison people for preferring to ingest a substance I would not choose to put in my body; (5) I wanted to reduce addiction to drugs, not completely stop the use of drugs; and (6) The only way to lessen the rate of addiction would be to legalize drugs.

Well then, one might ask, why did I continue to soldier on as a drug warrior for another 11 years? There are many reasons, and few have much to do with courage. By that time we had moved from arresting street users to arresting higher-level drug dealers, and I was always looking for the big case that would show my worth as an undercover agent and investigator. I was involved in something that was stimulating and exciting, something I had seen only in movies. I was pitting my mind against some very smart people, and the thrill of beating them at their own game was intoxicating. I was experiencing a great deal of freedom to work as I pleased, when I pleased. I was looked on by my peers as something of a hero, a person most of them would aspire to become. I had also seen many other officers cutting every Constitutional corner they could get away with to arrest people while simultaneously furthering their careers. I rationalized that at least if it was I who was doing the job, my suspects would be arrested for something they really did and the court case would rise or fall on true testimony. Actually, I was living very much on the edge, and enjoying the hell out of it. You could even say I was addicted to the dangers—a pure adrenaline junkie.

During those years in the state police narcotic bureau, I learned that the term "war on drugs" is the wrong metaphor to use for policing in a democratic society. Believing the metaphor to be appropriate, law-enforcement agencies across our country have trained their officers as soldiers—to go to war. The trouble is, a soldier must have an enemy—for the war on drugs, the enemy has become the American people.

The use of a war metaphor indicates to police that they can pull out all the stops because this is a no-holds-barred, unrestrained conflict. However, the "stops" we choose to pull out in this war constitute our Fourth Amendment rights, "the right of the people to be secure in their persons, houses, papers, and effects against unreasonable searches and seizures." The "holds" no longer barred are the "zero tolerance" attitudes that generate three-strikes-you're-out laws, the laws that sentence third-time felons to life in prison without the possibility of parole. And what are their heinous crimes? In some cases, the crimes amount to the strong-arm robbery of two slices of pizza or conspiring to smuggle one marijuana cigarette into a jail. As Richard Miller so rightly pointed out in *Drug Warriors and their Prey*, "[A]ctions that are otherwise intolerable can become popular when portrayed as emergency war measures."[14]

As we all know, when you fight a war you must have spies, and so much more so in the war on drugs. The use and sale of illegal drugs are in effect victimless crimes; both the dealer and the user get something they want from the transaction. In the war on drugs the police undercover operatives are the spies. A spy necessarily must covertly enter into the middle of a drug transaction if it is to be discovered and arrests are to be made.

In the longest war this country has fought, spying was my job. For 14 years of the more than three decades America has been fighting the drug war, I held that position. When I worked undercover, I imagined I was a chameleon. As children, my friends and I had bought those little lizards at the circus. When we put them on our shirts, their skin changed to the color of the material—protectively blending in with their external environment for safety. Each time I met a new person the police wanted me to target, I became that chameleon. Changing everything but the color of my skin, I quickly blended in with their environment and became exactly what they expected or wanted—easily gaining their trust. As an undercover agent my job was to *do whatever was necessary* to become people's best friend—their closest confidant—so I could betray them and send them to jail. And my job was to repeat that scenario with each new target: friendship—then betrayal—over and over again with hundreds and hundreds of individual human beings.

The main problem I experienced as an undercover agent was that I was never able to detach myself emotionally from the people whose lives I was affecting so dramatically, the vast majority of whom were nonviolent offenders and their relatives and friends. When I posed as their confidant, even for a relatively short time, I was witness to their humanity as well as their faults. Instigating each person's ultimate arrest and imprisonment cost me something also. I am not a religious man, but locked somewhere in my mind from my earliest childhood memories is the Golden Rule, as my mother taught it to me: "Do unto others as you would have others do unto you." Facing my quarries in court, testifying that all I had shared with them was lies and manipulation designed to enhance my ability to betray their trust, could in no way be interpreted as living by that rule. Why I chose to abandon my deepest belief is still something of a mystery to me, but I know it had something to do with mistakenly agreeing, "the ends justify the means"—the golden rule as taught by many drug warriors.

I would guess I took part in over a thousand arrests during the time I worked in narcotics. I don't know how many kids' lives I have ruined, but I'm sure the count is huge. I was responsible for putting away young people in their formative years whose only "crime" was testing their newfound freedoms, "dipping and dabbing," as they used to call it, in the illegal drugs so easily accessible in our culture.

Who are these people we are at war with, and how many of them are out there? The U.S. Department of Health and Human Services reports that over 87 million Americans above the age of 12 have used an illicit drug at least once.[15] Nearly all these drug users are living productive lives and contributing to our society. But what if I, or an undercover spy like me, had by chance crossed the path of each of those individuals—then what would d? Each would have been arrested and imprisoned, and the lts in our country would have been pressed into service to ......r prison guards. A ludicrous idea? Not necessarily. In the drug warriors' vision of a drug-free America, Miller suggests there would be "millions in prison or slave labor, and only enthusiastic supporters of government policy allowed to hold jobs, attend school, have children, drive cars, own property."[16]

And what happens to nonviolent drug violators when they are finally released from prison? Many are removed from school or productive jobs to be sent to prison, but once there they all learn the finer points of successful criminal activity. What happens when they apply for a job after years in prison? How many will want to hire them? Thanks to the punitive Higher Education Act of 1998, the ones who can't find work also cannot get government grants or loans to attend school to better their situation, nor can they draw welfare assistance. In many states, they even lose the right to vote. One needs to remember, you can get over an addiction but you can never get over a conviction. A drug violation conviction will track individuals by computer for the rest of their lives, no matter where they move. The only place these outcasts are likely to find a welcome and a job is back in the drug culture. So our policies result in driving people into the very lifestyle we say we are trying to save them from.

When I finally resolved to cease my calling as of one of America's drug warriors, it was June 6, 1982. That was the day I realized the federal government and I were working at the war on drugs from opposing viewpoints, and the other view was not likely to change. The contradictions of my work as a drug warrior just got to be too much for me to live with.

A Drug Policy That Works

So what should we do about this? Is there a workable alternative? I think there is. The drug policies of the U.S. have failed dismally in their dual task of preventing drug addiction and protecting citizens from the ravages of violent crime.

Every study I have seen in the past 10 years indicates that over 80% of crime in the United States is drug related (directly—possession, sale and use of drugs; or indirectly—prostitution, breaking and entering, larcenies, muggings and robberies to obtain money for the purchase of illegal drugs, or murders to ensure power arrangements within or among drug trafficking organizations).

The only way to make any real headway in correcting these terrible problems is to initiate a four-point program that I have been contemplating since 1973.

The first step is to legalize all drugs. If it is true that over 80% of all crime in the United States is drug related, then by simply passing a law to legalize drugs, we can effectively do away with most of our crimes. Therefore, the work loads of our police, courts, judges, prosecutors, public defenders, prison systems, and corrections personnel will be considerably lightened. Police will then have time to focus on preventing and solving violent crimes and neutralizing terrorist activities. Our overburdened courts will finally have resources to commit to civil law, where cases languish for years before being heard. Our prisons will no longer have to release violent criminals, who in many cases are not covered by mandatory minimum sentences, to make room for nonviolent drug law violators who are covered.

To reduce the harms created by the war on drugs, we must not only legalize drugs, we must also remove the profit motive from the equation. If drugs were legal, and they were produced and supplied by the government, then distributed free (in small quantities for personal use) to any adult who wanted them, organized criminals and world terrorists would be monetarily crippled for many years to come.

Dan Gardner pointed out in his September 14, 2001, article "Terrorists Get Cash From Drug Trade" that "[i]n 1994, Interpol's chief drugs officer, Iqbal Hussain Rizvi, admitted that 'drugs have taken over as the chief means of financing terrorism'."[17] Jason Burke reported in "Heroin in the Holy War," December 6, 1998, that Osama bin Laden "sees heroin as a powerful new weapon in his war against the West, capable of wreaking social havoc while generating huge profits…"[18]

There is currently so much money to be made in the drug business simply because drugs are illegal—$400 billion annually is spent on illegal drugs throughout the world. It is the most artificially inflated product that exists on the face of the earth, and it creates enormous profits for the drug lords and the terrorists. Heroin, ounce for ounce, is worth many times as much as gold.

The second step is to have the federal government produce drugs and control their quality.

There would be several benefits to having the federal government openly import drugs into our country. The first would be that the government would no longer have to hide the fact that for over 50 years it has facilitated the roles of certain individuals in the importation of illegal drugs into this country. With the profit motive gone, that policy would no longer be necessary or useful.

Illegal drugs are for the most part nothing but weeds. They can be grown nearly anywhere for little or nothing, and processing those weeds to extract the drugs is a simple, inexpensive practice. Today, if addicted drug users can't support their habits by any other means, they turn to theft. A "fence," the person who buys the stolen goods, usually pays the thief about 10% of what the articles are worth. That means an addict with a $300-dollar-a-day habit must steal $3,000 worth of our possessions every day. Legalization would put an end to the hugely inflated prices of drugs caused by prohibition and thereby lower the extremely high rate we have to pay to insure our homes and our vehicles from theft.

It would also put an end to most drug overdoses. If drugs were produced and supplied by the government, then users would know the exact potency of the drug they intended to ingest. Users don't overdose because they knowingly take more drugs than their bodies can handle. They overdose because some street dealer didn't mix the 50% pure product he was supplied carefully enough, and he is therefore selling users a product they think is 5% pure when it is actually 40% pure. When addicted persons injects this concoction, known as a "hot shot" and eight times as potent as thought to be, that is the end. They don't get a second chance. Actually, people who overdose with heroin die rather slowly and, if taken to a hospital, they can usually be saved. These deaths can be traced directly to drug prohibition. The reason they are not taken to hospitals is the justifiable belief by the people taking the victim to an emergency room that they will be arrested.

The third step is to have the government distribute free maintenance doses of any drugs to any adults who choose to continue to use them.

Making drugs free would completely remove any profit motive connected with the use of what had been illegal drugs. The government could supply a heroin addict with a $500-a-day habit for less than a dollar per day. No one would be forced to steal or prostitute him- or herself to buy drugs. The day step three is initiated will also be the last day a dealer or a terrorist will make a penny's profit from drugs. Nor will we have to worry about business corporations making addictive drugs even more addictive to insure sales or trying to lure our children into drug use, as we saw the big-six tobacco industry do with nicotine (the most addictive drug known) with the "Joe Camel" cartoon ads. If maintenance drugs are given free to adults, there will be no advertisements extolling the virtues of drugs, as we now see with cigarettes and liquor, because no one will make any profit from addicting one more person.

Quite the opposite will be true; the only money to be made off drugs will be by reducing the rate of addiction.

As in the bad old days of alcohol prohibition, today most violent crimes are related to the prohibition of drugs rather than to the use of drugs designated illegal. To protect billions of dollars of profits, the drug cartels murder with impunity. And what happens in your city when a local dealer's territory is infringed on? Does he go to court and say, "I've been wronged—I had a contract for that location?" No, today there are no regulators of the market in which he sells drugs to which he can turn for help. Instead, he picks up his gun and shoots it out with the interloper—or perhaps misses and strikes an innocent child. Most drive-by shootings are due to territorial infringements of drug gangs. These killings need not occur if there is no longer a profit motive in the sale of drugs.

Think of the money that would be saved if these three steps were put in place. The federal government spends around $19 billion dollars every year on the interdiction of drugs, and the state governments more than match that figure in order to arrest more than 1.6 million drug users and dealers. Add to that the cost of prosecuting the violators and imprisoning those found guilty—in some cases for the rest of their lives. Then there is the cost of parole or probation for those who served their time in prison. Add it all up and it amounts to over $70 billion each year that could be saved by simply signing a bill saying drug prohibition has ended.

That brings us to step four: Reallocating those saved billions of dollars to programs for treating the addictions of our ill citizens and proactively working to convince others not to use drugs.

We should treat drug addictions as medical and social problems—not as criminal problems. Instead of arresting our young people for using drugs—giving them a police record so no one wants to hire them, sending them to prison where they learn to be smart criminals, and in the long run giving them a great long list of reasons for continuing to use drugs to numb the pain of their existence—we could try another tactic.

In 1969, the National Commission on the Causes and Prevention of Violence wrote:

> To be young, poor, male; to be undereducated and without means of escape from an oppressive urban environment; to want what society claims is available (but mostly to others); to see around oneself illegitimate and often violent methods being used to achieve material success; and to observe others using these means with impunity—all this is to be burdened with an enormous set of influences that pull many toward crime and delinquency. To be

also black, Puerto Rican or Mexican-American and subject to discrimination adds considerably to the pull.[19]

It has been my experience that most people use drugs as an escape from their world because they have no hope for the future. Give them hope and we will end their addictions to drugs.[20]

Suppose we took all the money saved by this suggested policy and used it to (1) give hope to the poor and the disenfranchised, (2) educate the illiterate, (3) create jobs for the unemployed, (4) end racism and discrimination in our legal system, and (5) provide every person in our country with guaranteed health care. I believe then we would soon find that our drug problems, as well as many other problems, would at least be manageable, if not a thing of the past.

Notes

1. The one exception to this rule has been the price of marijuana, which has increased by over 2,600%. Police interdiction of marijuana at the U.S. borders early on both artificially inflated the price and caused many suppliers and users of marijuana to switch to harder drugs that were easier to smuggle and therefore cheaper to obtain.

2. Dan Baum, *Smoke and Mirrors: The War on Drugs and the Politics of Failure*, New York: Little, Brown and Company, 1996, page xi.

3. In March, 1999, the Institute of Medicine (IOM) issued a report on various aspects of marijuana, including the so-called "gateway theory" (the theory that using marijuana leads people to use harder drugs like cocaine and heroin). The IOM stated, "There is no conclusive evidence that the drug effects of marijuana are causally linked to the subsequent abuse of other illicit drugs." Janet E. Joy, Stanley J. Watson, Jr., and John A Benson, Jr., Division of Neuroscience and Behavioral Research, Institute of Medicine, *Marijuana and Medicine: Assessing the Science Base,* Washington, D.C.: National Academy Press, 1999.

4. The 1999 *National Household Survey of Drug Abuse* provides an estimate of the age of first use of drugs. According to the *Household Survey*, the mean age of first use of marijuana in the U.S. in 1997 was 17.2 years. The mean age of first use of alcohol in that year, on the other hand, was 16.1 years, and the mean age of first use of cigarettes was 15.4 years old. Substance Abuse and Mental Health Services Administration (SAMHSA), U.S. Department of Health and Human Services, *Summary of Findings from the 1999 National Household Survey on Drug Abuse*, Rockville, MD, August, 2000, pages G–49, G–60, and G–61.

5. We knew midlevel dealers in the U.S. were paying wholesale prices of approximately $45,000 per kilogram for nearly pure cocaine, but if the drugs had been sold at street level prices, one gram of standard quality (7%) cocaine for $100, the price for the same kilogram of drugs would be $1,600,000, returning over 35 times that dealer's initial investment. Each time a pure drug is "cut" by adding an equal amount of dilutant material, the resultant quality of the drug is half what it was: 1 kilo of 100% cocaine cut with 1 kilo of dilutants equals 2 kilos of 50% cocaine, 2 kilos of 50% cocaine cut with 2 kilos of dilutants equals 4 kilos of 25% cocaine, etc. By the time you arrive at 7% cocaine you are up to 16 kilos of the product. Then you multiply $100 times 16,000 grams and you have arrived at the price of the drug seized—$1,600,000. However, if the same drug was sold at 50% quality to street dealers, a couple of ounces at a time, at about $1,500 per ounce, as usually happened, the same drug returned a profit of 1.5 times the dealer's initial investment—still a high margin but not as misleading.

6. Baum, page 21.

7. Baum, page 13.

8. In 1896, the Supreme Court of the United States heard Plessy's case and found him guilty of sitting in the whites-only car of a train traveling through Louisiana. Speaking for a 7-person majority, Justice Henry Brown wrote: "That [the Separate Car Act] does not conflict with the Thirteenth Amendment, which abolished slavery...is too clear for argument... A statute which implies merely a legal distinction between the white and colored races—a distinction which is founded in the color of the two races, and which must always exist so long as white men are distinguished from the other race by color—has no tendency to destroy the legal equality of the two races... The object of the [Fourteenth A]mendment was undoubtedly to enforce the absolute equality of the two races before the law, but in the nature of things it could not have been intended to abolish distinctions based upon color, or to enforce social, as distinguished from political equality, or a commingling of the two races upon terms unsatisfactory to either." Justice Henry Billings Brown, "Majority opinion in *Plessy v. Ferguson*," *Desegregation and the Supreme Court*, edited by Benjamin Munn Ziegler, Boston: D.C. Heath and Company, 1958, pages 50–51.

9. SAMHSA, *National Household Survey on Drug Abuse: Summary Report 1998*, Rockville, MD, 1999. U.S. Department of Justice (U.S. DOJ), Bureau of Justice Statistics, *Prisoners and Jail Inmates at Midyear 1999*, Washington D.C., April, 2000, page 13. U.S. DOJ, Bureau of Justice Statistics, *Sourcebook of Criminal Justice Statistics 1998*, Washington D.C., August, 1999, page 343, Table 4.10; page 435, Table 5.48; and page 505, Table 6.52. Allen J. Beck, Ph D, and Christopher J. Mumola, U.S. DOJ, Bureau of Justice Statistics, *Prisoners in 1998*, Washington D.C., August, 1999, page 10, Table 16.

10. David J. Levin, Patrick A. Langan and Jodi M. Brown, U.S. DOJ, Bureau of Justice Statistics, *State Court Sentencing of Convicted Felons, 1996*, Washington D.C., February, 2000, page 8.

11. Richard Miller, *Drug Warriors and Their Prey: From Police Power to Police State*, Westport, CT: Praeger Publishers, 1996, pages 38–49.

12. Later, with the advent of the asset forfeiture laws, police were not only given the right to take all money as proceeds of illegal activities but could seize vehicles—cars, trucks, campers, house trailers, boats, airplanes—even houses and land. It mattered not whether the property owners were convicted of the crime (in many cases they were not even charged with a crime). In order to get their property back they still had to prove that the property was not used in the commission of a crime, was not the product of the crime, nor was it obtained with the fruits of a crime. This "guilty until proven innocent" form of justice is correctly referred to by Leonard W. Levy, in his book by the same name, as *A License to Steal*, University of North Carolina Press, 1995.

13. A bundle refers to 30 individual glassine packets, each supposedly containing enough powder for a single dose of the given drug.

14. Miller, page 36.

15. SAMHSA, *Summary of Findings from the 1999 National Household Survey on Drug Abuse*, Rockville, MD, August, 2000, page G–5.

16. Miller, page 191.

17. Dan Gardner, "Terrorists Get Cash From Drug Trade: Trafficking Prime Source Of Funds For Many Groups," *The Ottawa Citizen*, Ontario, Canada, September 14, 2001.

18. Jason Burke, "Heroin In The Holy War," *Indian Express*, Sunday, December 6, 1998, www.expressindia.com/ie/daily/19981206/34050684.html.

19. Arnold S. Trebach, "Can Prohibition Be Enforced in Washington?" *The Truth Seeker*, September/October, 1989, page 22.

20. "While it is difficult to pinpoint why a particular individual abuses drugs, many addiction experts target a low level of self-esteem as a critical factor. In recent history, intellectuals...have noted that the crushing impact of poverty leads to alienation and low self-esteem. Consequently, when a whole

community faces this condition, in an atmosphere that promotes identity through material consumption, social deterioration becomes inevitable. Alienation shatters the spirit and destroys the ability to love oneself and others. The escalation of violence and the devaluation of life is rooted in the isolation and nihilism symptomatic of our consumer society." Clarence Lusane, *Pipe Dream Blues: Racism & the War on Drugs*, Boston: South End Press, 1991, page 26.

Section II:

PUBLIC OFFICIALS SPEAK OUT

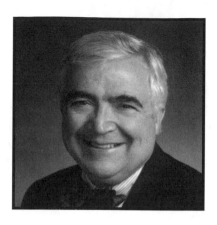

5. Policy is Not a Synonym for Justice

BY JOHN L. KANE

John L. Kane has served as U.S. district judge in Colorado since 1978, becoming a senior district judge in 1988. He has also taught at the University of Colorado, the University of Denver, Trinity College, and Metropolitan State College. His awards include a Lifetime Judicial Achievement Award in 1987 from the National Association of Criminal Defense Attorneys.

One of the casualties of the war on drugs we don't hear enough about is justice. We live in an environment of government, the institutions of which focus on administration rather than fundamental principles. The limits of government are frequently set by courts as they interpret law and refer to intuitive ideas that find approximate expression in the slippery phrases of due process, police power, liberty, public purpose, and accountability.

For over 200 years our legal system has been based on these ideas. It has sought to preserve and protect individuals while still maintaining order, but on occasion the system slips out of balance. The heart and purpose of the system are cut out when those limits on government are subordinated to the pursuit of policy goals. We hedge our bets on the ability of our society to live with freedom.

In 1972, pot-smoking demonstrators against the Vietnam War mocked all authority, ridiculed President Nixon, and challenged the very assumption of his office. His response has resulted in a threatened society subjected to draconian remedies. The war on drugs, through stringent, puritanical measures, attempts to set the public right. Not only is justice not done, it is threatened and mocked.

Our national drug policy hasn't changed significantly with changes in administration. It emphasizes interdiction, police action, and imprisonment, with a deferential nod to treatment and education. The policy persists in spite of all evidence, even the government's own, demonstrating that it is foolish and unworkable.

A Continuation of Failed Policies

On the campaign trail in 2000, President George W. Bush spoke about the need to treat drug users and decrease the demand for drugs instead of vainly attempting to attack the supply side. His administrators, however, belied his words. The public statements of John P. Walters, Bush's drug czar, and the pronouncements of Attorney General John Ashcroft pledging to escalate the war on drugs suggested nothing more than a continuation of failed policies that have produced nothing but pure folly.

Walters, by the way, asserted that, in his experience, the "biggest single contributor" to drug-related crime is not trafficker violence, but violence by people using drugs. By contrast, in 1996, the Institute of Medicine reported the most prevalent form of cocaine and heroin-related violence is the result of illicit drug selling and distribution. The report notes further that criminal activity increases significantly during times of narcotic dependence, although most are nonviolent property crimes.

Marijuana use decreases aggression and threatening behavior. The crimes by some drug users are committed in order to pay for drugs in the highly inflated black market. In other words, the crimes are caused by prohibition-induced high prices, not by the pharmacological effects of drug ingestion.

Despite the more than $18 billion spent each year by the federal government in drug enforcement programs, less than $1 out of every $100 is spent on research and evaluation. On March 29, 2001, the National Research Council (of the National Academy of Sciences and the National Academy of Engineering) advised that the nation's ability to evaluate whether the drug policies even work is no better now than it was 20 years ago. Not only has the federal government failed to respond to this report of one of the nation's most prestigious, non-political organizations, it doesn't even recognize that the report was published.

Between 1981 and 2002, federal expenditures on prohibition and supply reduction activities jumped more than tenfold. No other government activity had similar or even comparable increases. Yet there is no basis, none at all, to support this policy. Charles F. Manski, Professor of Economics at Northwestern University, and chair of the committee that wrote the National Research Council Report, said, "Neither the necessary data systems nor the research infrastructure to gauge the usefulness of drug-control enforcement policies currently exists. It is unconscionable for this country to continue to carry out a public policy of this magnitude and cost without any way of knowing whether, and to what extent, it is having the desired result. Our committee strongly recommends that a substantial, new, and robust research effort be undertaken to examine the various aspects of drug control, so that decision-making on these issues can be better supported by more factual and realistic evidence."

According to the committee report, there isn't enough reliable data to know whether any program makes any difference nor even how drug markets operate, nor how users begin to use drugs, nor how they decide to increase use, nor what factors cause them to quit. The government hasn't the faintest idea whether incarceration acts as a deterrent and ignores some evidence that suggests drug use is increased by imprisonment. Since that report was issued, no new "robust research effort" has been undertaken.

Recent non-governmental studies have shown that drug abusers who are subject to involuntary treatment have a significantly higher rate of recidivism than those who have no treatment at all! Moreover, there is no reliable data on overall consumption rates or available supply. Without this information, it is not possible for the government to determine the economic vitality of illegal drug markets.

"Who would believe," the Nobel Laureate Milton Friedman says, "that a democratic government would pursue for eight decades a failed policy that produced tens of millions of victims and trillions of dollars of illicit profits for drug dealers; cost taxpayers hundreds of billions of dollars; increased crime and destroyed inner cities; fostered wide-spread corruption and violations of human rights—and all with no success in achieving the stated and unattainable objective of a drug-free America."

Without hard, well-researched information, it is not even possible to articulate a new or improved policy. All that is left is the frequently expressed inanity that changing our drug policy would "send the wrong message to our children." In this darkest of comedies, the government, even as we speak, hasn't the slightest notion what message our children are presently receiving. Perhaps this is so because our national drug control budget spends 12% on youth drug use, 22% on treatment and 66% on law enforcement.

"Sending a Message"

The federal government does know a few things, however. Since 1972, its own surveys show that there has been a rise in adolescent drug use. Since 1975, the federal government has been asking high school seniors how easy it is for them to obtain marijuana. The research shows that adolescents' access to marijuana has remained virtually unchanged since the war on drugs was declared. In 1975, 87% of youths said it was "very easy" or "fairly easy" to obtain marijuana. Twenty-three years, millions of arrests and billions of dollars later, 89.6% of adolescents said it was "easily" obtained.

Recent data suggests the greatest increase in heroin use is among eighth graders. Not long ago two third-grade boys were arrested as adults for bringing cocaine to school and trying to sell it. Just what message is the present policy of prohibition and criminalization sending to our children? And what would be wrong with changing it?

I realize that anecdotal information is of limited value, but a recent experience merits a brief comment. A friend of mine was in his mid-60s and undergoing chemotherapy. The treatment made him very sick. When visited by his son, daughter-in-law and 11-year-old grandson, he jokingly said he wished the state would get off its butt and provide chemo patients with some pot. He said he didn't have the faintest idea where he could buy it even if he could get out of bed. The next day his grandson rode his bicycle over to visit and handed my friend three joints of marijuana. The boy said, "Don't worry, Grandpa. I don't use it myself, but if you need any more, just let me know." Are our children sending us the wrong message?

Perhaps we should send a message to our children about the causes of death in the United States. We would have to tell them that tobacco is legal and the leading substance-related cause of death at 430,700 per year; that alcohol is legal and 110,600 die from its use each year; that adverse reactions to legal prescription drugs cause 32,000 fatalities a year; that 30,500 commit suicide; 18,000 are homicide victims; and that 7,600 people die each year from taking anti-inflammatory drugs such as aspirin. Of course, we don't want to send them the wrong message that the total number of deaths caused by marijuana is *zero*.

Perhaps the message we should be sending our children is that the inmate population of the Federal Bureau of Prisons exceeds 170,000—the highest number in history. When Richard Nixon left office in 1974, there were fewer than 24,000 federal prisoners. When Ronald Reagan left office in 1989 there were nearly 50,000, and the 100,000 mark was reached in 1997. Fifty-eight percent of the total federal prison population is made up of drug offenders, most of whom are low-level or middle-level offenders. Drug kingpins are seldom found in prison populations.

Most of these prisoners are minorities. Indeed, we should tell our children that more African-Americans were imprisoned during the Clinton administration than in all the rest of United States history, but that might be sending our children the wrong message; they might somehow get the idea that drug-law enforcement is racist. In the state and federal penal systems, America imprisons 100,000 more persons for drug offenses than the entire European Union imprisons for all offenses. The European Union has 100 million more citizens than the United States does. Today, there are two million people behind bars in the United States.

It is probably not a good idea to tell our children the truth; that would clearly be sending them the wrong message. How, for example, could they deal with the fact that in 1914, when drugs were available on grocery store shelves and without prescription at the local pharmacy, 1.3% of the population was addicted? In 1979, just before the so-called "war on drugs" crackdown, the addiction rate was still 1.3%. Today, while billions of dollars are spent to reduce drug use, the addiction rate is still 1.3%.

Land of the Imprisoned

In discussing drug issues, it is essential to recognize the differences between addiction, abuse, and use. As I just mentioned, the addiction rate is constant. Drug abuse and use, however, fluctuate dramatically. Nobody has the slightest idea what causes these fluctuations, and our criminal justice system makes no distinction among them.

Local, state, and federal governments now spend over nine billion dollars per year to imprison 458,000 drug offenders. The stated national drug policy is to imprison all those who possess, sell, or use illegal drugs. In order to fulfill this policy, the various local, state, and federal governments would have to investigate, arrest, jail, convict, and sentence the 14 million Americans who smoked marijuana last month, the 1.2 million who ingested cocaine during the same period, and the nearly six million who ingested it during the past year. Moreover, the government doesn't even know how many men, women, and children took heroin and nonprescribed amphetamines during the same time. Included in these figures, to enforce this policy, government would have to imprison the 50% of high school graduating seniors who admit to having taken some controlled substance during the past three years.

What would be the cost of our current policy if it was succeeding rather than failing? Incarcerating all cocaine users would cost $74 billion, but only after constructing 3.5 million more prison beds at an initial cost of $175 billion. It would cost $365 billion to jail everyone who smoked marijuana last year—five times the total national, state, and local spending for all police, courts, and prisons combined. To contain this crowd behind walls, we would need a cadre of guards and other prison employees larger than all of our military forces combined. These projections are not entirely academic: the nation is completing the construction, on average, of a new prison every week.

More costly than money, however, is the price we now pay for this failed policy in terms of the decline in public safety, the breakdown of our criminal justice system, the erosion of our civil liberties, and the pervasive public disrespect of the law. Good citizens, who are otherwise law-abiding, ignore or evade drug laws. With literally tens of millions of people using illegal drugs or related to those who do, an ever-increasing part of the population has become cynical about all laws and our legal system and political process in particular.

Much like in the days of that other prohibition, from 1920 to 1933, when citizens, politicians, children, and gangsters met on common ground in speakeasies and paddy wagons and when judges and prosecutors sought the flimsiest of reasons to dismiss cases against those who were influential, ordinary people today transact purchases with criminals in the black market. When half of the graduating class of high school seniors have violated the drug laws, can we really be willing to regard them all as criminals?

I have yet to hear, whether as a judge or just another ordinary guy in the community, a parent who finds marijuana in his son's belongings and says, "My son, the felon." What I have heard time and time again is, "We need help—where can we get it?"

Each year since 1989, more people have been sent to prison for drug offenses than for violent crimes. At the same time, only one in five burglaries is reported, and only one in 20 reported burglaries ends in arrest. Yet detectives continue to be reassigned from burglary details to investigation of street sales of drugs. The cost for this particular aspect of our national folly is absorbed in significantly increased insurance premiums.

Using data supplied by the White House Office of National Drug Control Policy, we learn that during this war on drugs the price of heroin has dropped, not increased, while its production has risen greatly. The illegal market price of cocaine in 1981 was $275.12 per pure gram, and by 1996 it had dropped to $94.52. Because a kilogram of raw opium sells for $90 in Pakistan but is worth $290,000 when it is imported into the United States as pure heroin, law enforcement seizures have little, if any, impact on operations or profitability.

As Anthony Lewis observed in a *New York Times* column shortly before he retired, the entire interdiction effort is utterly futile. "The effort to stop cocaine exports from Peru," he writes, "has cut the flow from there substantially. But that reduction has been more than made up by a huge increase in coca cultivation and production in Colombia. As Plan Colombia, the military anti-drug program, gets underway there, production is reportedly beginning to shift to Ecuador." Lewis lists the costs to other nations of our current drug policies: the rise of drug gangs, the poisoning of peasants from crop eradication, the corruption of governments and increased deaths by violence. "Yet," he notes, "the amount of cocaine and heroin entering the United States is as great as ever."

Time to Return to American Values

Police agencies still need to protect the public by holding those who cause accidents or commit crimes while under the influence of drugs and alcohol fully accountable for their acts, but we must get the police out of the business of financing their own operations through the seizure and forfeiture of private property. The costs of law enforcement should be funded from the public fisc by legislators so that we can determine how much the implementation of government policies is costing. In other and harsher words, we need to terminate the symbiotic business relationship that law enforcement has with the illegal drug industry. Each scratches the other's back.

Indeed, the two groups that would suffer most from an elimination of the black market in drugs would be, in nearly equal measure, organized crime and law enforcement. Those who would benefit the most would be the people, especially children, who have never before tried drugs, because there would be no economic incentive to turn them into customers. Those who are already addicted or abusing drugs, or who will no matter what law obtains, can be treated rather than imprisoned at a cost of one-seventh the amount needed to imprison them.

One of the longest and most cherished traditions of this nation is that the military should be subservient to the civilian government, and that military might shall not be engaged in domestic matters. It is the American version of the Rubicon. For as long as we have been free, we have disavowed the existence of a national police force. The Posse Comitatus Act of 1878 made it illegal for the military to act as police on U.S. territory or waters. As part of the drug war, the Act was amended by Congress in 1981 to allow limited military involvement in policing. In 1991, the Act was further amended to allow the military to train civilian police.

While historically we have insisted that law enforcement is the business of local police agencies, federal grants and financing of multi-level government task forces, coupled with military assistance and the use of military intelligence in domestic matters, now seriously jeopardize local control of police action. The federal government is presently deeply involved in local drug law enforcement. This policy must change for no reason less important than that we return to the faith in freedom and liberty of our Founding Fathers.

There is an understandable temptation for state officials to shape their policies and programs to conform to federal grant requirements. What the Constitution prohibits as an exercise of delegated power, the federal government does indirectly in numerous areas of endeavor, including the drug war, by placing conditions on federal grants. In many instances, state governments have abdicated responsibility and lawful control in the grab for federal funds.

Alexis de Tocqueville called our states and communities the "laboratories of democracy," where experiments in self-government could take place and the success of one could be substituted for the failure of another. Our federally directed drug control policy has closed these laboratories. The consequence is that as a free people we continue to pursue but one path—the path of folly.

To deal successfully with drug abuse, this nation must abandon its failed policies and rhetoric of misinformation. We must permit the several states to resume their role as laboratories of democracy in which policies and programs suitable to their individual needs and conditions can be implemented. It is essential, not merely for the promulgation of a rational drug policy, but also for the restoration of a viable state of freedom.

Federal drug law should be severely cut back. The importing of unauthorized drugs should continue to be a federal crime. Manufacturing drugs for distribution in interstate commerce should be regulated for reasons of public health, but the several states should decide what activities are criminal, such as selling or inducing minors to take drugs, and which drugs, if any, should be prohibited. In sum, the policy should be to end the black market, end the free-booting financing of law enforcement by forfeiture, and treat those drug and alcohol abusers who want to be treated.

While I do not for a moment wish to be understood as diminishing or deprecating the importance of those poor souls who are filling our prisons because of drug use, I want to make note of the "other victims" of the so-called war on drugs. They are those people and businesses who can't get into court to have their cases heard. They are the victims of traditional crimes such as burglary, rape, and robbery who can't get justice because the police are tied up with drug cases. They are the merchants going bankrupt because the police no longer have time to investigate or prosecute bad check cases. They are the battered spouses whose mates are not sent to jail because there's room there only for pot smokers. They are the physicians and other medical care providers who cannot treat their patients according to conscience and the discipline of their profession. They are the sick and dying who endure unnecessary pain. They are the children whose parents are taken from them. They are the police who have given up honorable and challenging work investigating and detecting crime because they have become addicted to and dependent upon an informant-based system. They are the families forced to select one member to plead guilty lest the entire family be charged. They are the prosecutors and defense attorneys who have turned the temples of justice into plea-bargaining bazaars. They are, most painful to me, the judges who let this happen and don't say a word.

Each of us, in more than one way, is a victim of this infamous war. It is, as Michael Douglas said in the movie *Traffic*, a war on our own families.

At the present time, our national drug policy is inconsistent with the nature of justice, abusive of the nature of authority, and ignorant of the compelling force of forgiveness. Our drug laws, indeed, are more mocked than feared. We endure a policy that will never achieve its stated purpose, but sends a very clear message that people are not to be trusted with the freedom to choose.

6. A View of the Drug War from Capitol Hill

BY RON PAUL

Ron Paul has represented Texas' 14th Congressional District since 1996, and he previously served in Congress from 1976 to 1984. After earning his medical degree from Duke University School of Medicine, Paul served as a flight surgeon in the U.S. Air Force during the 1960s. He is the author of several books, including Challenge to Liberty; The Case for Gold; *and* A Republic, If You Can Keep It.

Most readers of the essays in this book already understand that the federal drug war is a miserable failure. Any honest examination of drug prohibition reveals that it does virtually nothing to reduce drug use, but instead creates a number of criminal and social problems that are far worse than drug use itself. What kinds of problems? Criminal gang violence, foreign military intervention, overcrowded prisons, threats to civil liberties, and a staggering waste of both tax dollars and law enforcement resources, just to name a few. Many of these problems could be reduced or eliminated through sensible federal drug policies, and the promotion of such policies is precisely the task before us. Those brave Americans who oppose the drug war must be prepared for an uphill battle, however, because the drug warriors have the full power of the federal government at their disposal.

Philosophically, the argument against drug prohibition is quite simple. We can start with the premise that freedom is preferable to slavery. The most basic freedom is freedom over one's physical body. Every free human being enjoys "ownership" of his person, so to speak. Therefore, the fundamental question in the drug debate is this: do you own your body or not? If you believe in freedom, the answer is unequivocally *yes*. If you support drug prohibition, however, the uncomfortable answer is no: the state owns your body and will tell you what you can and cannot put into it.

Although these philosophical questions rarely surface in the drug debate, they are critically important. When we fail to adopt a consistent guiding philosophy, we allow emotions rather than principles to frame the debate. The rule of law cannot survive on emotions or the *ad hoc* whims of the latest gang in Congress, devoid of any guiding philosophy. The drug issue, like all issues, should be approached with basic principles in mind. In America, the overriding principle should be that human freedom is our greatest priority.

The Hysterical Congress

The practical failures of the drug war have been thoroughly chronicled, and I won't attempt to duplicate those efforts here.

My goal instead is to provide readers with a view of the federal drug war from the perspective of a medical doctor on Capitol Hill. I represent the 14th district of Texas in the U.S. House of Representatives, having been elected as a Republican in 1996 and reelected three times since. Before then I was an obstetrician for 30 years, except for the late 1970s and early 1980s when I represented a neighboring congressional district. Serving in Congress gives me a front-row seat for the lawmaking process that created and perpetuates the drug war. This process, I hasten to add, is completely nonpartisan, a testament to the abandonment of privacy and civil liberties as vital issues for either political party. When it comes to drug prohibition, as with so many other issues, there really is just one party in America today: the federal state. Both sides enthusiastically support complete federal preemption of state drug laws, and both sides enthusiastically fund a dizzying array of federal agencies and programs ostensibly designed to rid the nation of the scourge of drugs. There is remarkably little open opposition to federal drug policy in Congress.

During my first tenure in Washington, my focus was primarily on economic and monetary issues. I believed in many of the same things conservatives used to believe in: limited government, low taxes, fiscal restraint, and noninterventionism. Although I was less interested in social issues, I certainly believed that government should stay out of the private lives of adults unless they were actively harming someone else. It was obvious that government intervention in social matters produced the same unintended consequences, distortions, and inefficiencies as government intervention in economic matters. The false split between so-called economic and social issues was very much a creation of the socialist legislatures and activist courts of the 20th century. No such distinctions were made by our Founders, nor found in the Constitution. So simply by strictly adhering to the Constitution, my congressional votes naturally followed a libertarian pattern. This put me very much at odds with proponents of the nanny state from both parties.

During the early 1980s, the neo-prohibitionists in the Reagan administration launched a full-scale campaign that blossomed into today's official "War on Drugs." Suddenly, drugs were the biggest issue facing the nation. Virtually every social ill—poverty, crime, the destruction of families, urban blight, etc.—was instantly linked to illicit drug use. Of course, some of these problems were indeed exacerbated by drug abuse, but the sudden and highly orchestrated elevation of drugs to the number-one issue facing the nation was absurd. We were subjected to the childish and shrill "Just Say No" public relations blitz, designed to convince us that inanimate drugs were dangerously poised to cause the downfall of our nation. Yet the severity of the drug problem, if government propagandists were to be believed, was overwhelming proof that drug prohibition was a dismal failure.

If certain drugs had been banned by the federal government since the 1930s, why on earth were Americans still taking them? This rather obvious question went unasked amid the fanfare surrounding the new campaign; the only solution offered was escalation of the same failed prohibition policies. If the federal government simply poured more money, energy, and manpower into the drug war, we were told, drug abuse could be eradicated. Never mind that prohibition had never and could never work; never mind that far and away the biggest problem was criminal violence stemming from the artificial profit created by drug prohibition itself. This was war, and damn the casualties.

As much as the doctor in me hated drug abuse, I knew that the war on drugs was a dangerous and costly new form of government hysteria. Like most government programs, it would do nothing to address the stated problem—drug use—but it would make all of us poorer and less free. Although congressional support for the new war was widespread, I voted against funding it and urged my colleagues to do the same.

The Critics Emerge

Ironically, the new drug war began in a decade when conservative, limited-government thinking was otherwise ascendant. The Reagan Revolution had correctly identified the failure of 1960s Great Society programs to solve social ills. President Reagan famously told the nation that government was the problem, not the solution. Reagan conservatives argued that individual initiative and personal responsibility, rather than a government check, were the keys to a better life for Americans. Yet the war on drugs turned the idea of personal responsibility upside down, placing the blame for personal moral failures on drugs rather than the individuals abusing them. Drugs became a national boogeyman, while individuals were reduced to helpless victims. In this sense the war on drugs mirrored the gun-control movement's push to ban firearms, as both attempted to blame inanimate objects for the misdeeds of individuals.

By the time I left Congress in 1984 and returned to my medical practice, the federal drug war was in full force. My opposition to drug prohibition became well known when I ran for President in 1988 as the Libertarian Party nominee. My decision to seek and accept the Libertarian nomination was based in part on my desire to speak out against the drug war, which I viewed as disastrous for our civil liberties. The issue was a natural for the Libertarian Party and anyone who held libertarian beliefs, as it perfectly framed the ultimate political principle: people should be left alone by the state unless and until they use force or fraud against another. Harm to oneself, however defined, is not a legitimate justification for the state to intervene. In my travels across the country as a candidate in 1988, it was obvious that more and more Americans were starting to understand and embrace this principle. I shook hands and spoke with literally thousands of ordinary citizens who were questioning the drug war and wondering why our government was pursuing such a destructive drug policy. That experience gave me hope that the American people were ready for a serious, rational discussion of the wisdom of the drug war.

Also, although the 1980s were clearly a feverish time for the prohibitionists, some opposition began to surface toward the end of the decade. Several notable national figures had come out in favor of at least some degree of drug decriminalization, including conservative icon William F. Buckley, Jr.; Nobel Laureate economist Milton Friedman; former Reagan Secretary of State George Shultz; and Baltimore Mayor Kurt Schmoke. Organizations like the Cato Institute and the Reason Foundation began to publish papers and hold conferences that were critical of the drug war. The first cracks in the government's drug hysteria were beginning to appear, and a new movement opposing federal drug prohibition was growing.

The Illegal and Destructive War

In 1996 I decided to attempt a return to Congress, running as a Republican. I knew my libertarian position on drugs would be fair game, especially in a socially conservative, rural district. Predictably, the Republican Party was less than thrilled when I announced my candidacy. The Democrat holding the seat was persuaded to switch parties and run against me in the primary. He did bring up my stance on the drug war, but I managed to edge him in a three-way race. My opponent in the general election also tried to use the drug issue against me. He attempted to paint me as a radical who wanted to "legalize dope." His campaign considered my opposition to the drug war such a vulnerability that they highlighted it in television spots and stump speeches. But ultimately this approach backfired, because voters knew me as a medical doctor who had delivered thousands of babies in the area. They knew me as a family man, a father of five with more than a dozen grandchildren, who abhorred drug use. I was anything but a wild-eyed radical, so people accepted that my opposition to the drug war was sincere—even if they disagreed with me. Since then, none of my opponents have made much of the drug issue. The lesson learned is that we must personalize the drug debate, exhibit good moral character ourselves, and work hard to show that sober, rational people oppose drug prohibition.

Since returning to Congress, my position as a federal legislator has often been distorted. I'm frequently accused of wanting to "legalize drugs." This is not accurate. My position is that Congress must strictly follow the Constitution, which grants the federal government only limited powers. The enumerated powers clause of Article I clearly grants Congress no authority whatsoever to regulate drugs. Therefore I am against federal drug laws, including a theoretical law legalizing drugs nationwide. Constitutionally, which means legally, drugs are simply none of the federal government's business. In other words, the federal drug war is illegal.

Under the Ninth and Tenth Amendments, all powers not expressly given to Congress are reserved to the states. This means the regulation of drugs, as with virtually all criminal and regulatory matters, is wholly up to the individual states. State legislatures can do a much better job than Congress can in determining appropriate local standards for dealing with drugs. One can imagine a conservative state like Utah choosing to enact harsh drug laws, while a freewheeling state like Nevada might choose to completely legalize all drugs. This is precisely what the Founders envisioned, a loose confederation of sovereign, independent, even competing states. The people of the various states could either influence their own legislatures—far easier than influencing Congress—or vote with their feet and move to a state that more closely reflects their values. This is called freedom, but the centralizers of both parties in Washington cannot imagine a society not dominated by the federal government.

We must understand that the federal drug war is essentially a jobs program. Imagine how many federal agents, bureaucrats, police officers, prosecutors, defense attorneys, drug counselors, and prison builders make a living simply because drugs are illegal! This is not to say these are bad people or opportunistic people; on the contrary, most believe in what they do and perform their jobs admirably. Yet it would be foolish to ignore the unmistakable element of self-interest that underlies the drug war industry. Government programs naturally expand; government employees and contractors naturally seek to justify their existence. A lot of people would be unemployed if the nation's drug problems disappeared tomorrow.

This is the reality we all have to fight against if we hope to move the drug debate forward. The federal government exists to grow, and the drug apparatus is no different. To argue effectively against the drug war, one must fight for smaller government across the board. We cannot pick and choose the areas where government will be large and invasive or small and benign, because government is neither wise nor virtuous. Big government simply is not capable of restraint in any sphere of human activity for long.

Ultimately, the fight against drug prohibition must be fought on practical grounds, because the American people are far more interested in practical benefits than philosophical arguments. We are a uniquely results-oriented society. Our job is to convince the American people that ending the drug war would help clean up the streets; reduce gang violence; lower taxes; restore civil liberties; free up our courts, jails, and law enforcement resources; and generally make America a better and safer place.

We must argue that prohibition does nothing to reduce the great demand for drugs in this society, and that only a culture of personal responsibility can deter individuals from destroying their lives with drugs. We must argue that the drug war produces black markets that impose huge economic and social costs on all of us. We must argue that sending troops into Colombia and Afghanistan and Mexico does nothing to stem the flow of drugs into America, but does entangle us in dangerous and intractable civil strife in those nations. We must tell the American people that various federal agencies waste tens of billions of dollars on the drug war each year. Finally, we must explain to the American people that the drug war destroys the lives of countless nonviolent offenders, any of whom could be our family members, friends, neighbors, and co-workers.

7. Forging a New Consensus in the War on Drugs

BY KURT SCHMOKE

Kurt Schmoke served as mayor of Baltimore from 1987 to 1999, and he is currently dean of Howard University School of Law. He gratuated from Yale University in 1971 and from Harvard Law School in 1976. Schmoke joined President Carter's staff, then worked as Assistant U.S. Attorney and State's Attorney in Baltimore. The following article is based on a speech originally published by Temple Political and Civil Rights Law Review, *Vol. 10:351, Spring 2001.*

Marc Mauer, Eric Sterling, and Judge Robert Sweet have all been very active in trying to help us as a country to try to live out the central tenets of our philosophy of equal justice under the law. I've heard them speak and they have heard me speak on a number of occasions, and I do believe we are all trying our very best to make improvements in the country. I am going to give a basic view on what I'm hoping will occur: with the turn of the new century there will be new thinking on the war on drugs. But I'm also going to talk a little bit about the need to reach out across the ideological lines and achieve common ground with people you don't necessarily think will agree with you and try to move this agenda forward.

When I was mayor of Baltimore, I tried my best to focus not only on the issues of service delivery at the local level, but to get myself involved in discussions of national policies that impacted the quality of life in the city.

Clearly there was no policy that had more impact than the way in which the national government was conducting the war on drugs. I got involved in March of 1988 to take advantage of a speaking opportunity with a group of police chiefs and mayors at a conference in Washington. I simply said we should consider the issues of decriminalization of drugs, looking at the problems we had with alcohol prohibition. I said, "At least let us debate." And at that point, that day, that was all I had to say about the issue. Let's talk about it. Let's think about it. Well, as you know, Washington, D.C. is about 40 miles from Baltimore. By the time I got back to my office in Baltimore from that speech in Washington, the Associated Press had run a story, "Mayor Calls for Legalizing Drugs." This was my label for a good five or six years.

But here is why I take you back to 1988, after I fought through the issue about labeling and having people just assume what they thought I was going to say whenever I spoke. I tried, particularly with skeptical audiences, to get people thinking in a different way, again trying to reach common ground. And I would ask skeptical audiences—usually parents and some policy makers—three questions. I'd start off by asking, "Do you believe that we have won the war on drugs?" Second, "Do you think that doing more of the same for the next ten years will win the war on drugs?" Now, by asking that, people would sit back and generally the overwhelming majority would say, "No, I don't think we've won." "I'm not sure we're even winning." "And certainly doing just the same thing over the next ten years is not going to win it." So then I would ask, "Would you consider with me for a few moments some alternatives?" That usually got people thinking. But as we went through the rest of the 1980s and 1990s and people started seeing the crime rates go down, incarceration (they didn't really think too much about that impact) was going way up. But crime rates were going down. It was harder to get people to think about the alternatives to the way we were conducting the war on drugs.

So I came up with a different approach. At a recent conference, I was with Eric Sterling and I tried this with skeptical audiences, generally parents. I said, "Look, think about yourselves with two children. First your son. You get a call and you find out your son makes an admission. Your son is a drug user—a serious, long-term drug user. What do you do as a parent? Do you call the police and have them arrest your child? Do you call health professionals and have them put your child in some kind of counseling, treatment? Do you attempt to get that person off drugs through health care professionals? Do you view your son as a criminal, or as a potential patient who is going to be able to get off drugs?" Or, as I said to one group,

"Do you think of your son as a potential presidential candidate who may still have a good life if we don't impose criminal sanctions?" Well, that's your son.

Now your daughter. Imagine your daughter is a recent high school graduate who goes off to college. She's doing okay in school, but not super, and then you learn she has decided to go out with this guy whom you don't particularly like. She claims he is an upperclassman. You are skeptical, but she is definitely in love with this man. One day the police come by and tell you that this guy is now under arrest and your daughter is going to be charged. They tell you this guy has been running a multi-state crime ring, a drug ring, and that your daughter assisted him by putting her name on an apartment and an automobile. She didn't benefit from it; she didn't get money; she didn't sell drugs. That is all she did, and we are charging her as a co-conspirator in a drug conspiracy. How do you react? Well, of course, you are very concerned about it. You want her to do everything possible, so she comes to you for advice and says, "What do you think I should do?" And you tell her, "Tell the truth, and if we can't get out of it any other way, you'll enter a plea, you'll get some leniency. You testify and then go about your life." She takes your advice. She does everything you say and, because you didn't factor in mandatory minimum sentencing laws, your daughter ends up with a twenty-four-and-a-half year prison sentence.

Now, many of the people in the audience, when I talk to them about this, think this is an outrageous result. But those of you who follow this realize I was just describing the plight of a young woman named Kemba Smith. And Kemba not only had those things occur to her, but Kemba was five months pregnant before sentencing. They ended up taking her out of her jail cell, bringing her to a hospital, shackling her to a bed, and letting her see her child for one month and then she was off to prison. And she was there for six years. One thing President Bill Clinton did before leaving office is commute that sentence. But it is simply another outrageous example of the overkill of the war on drugs.

Human Rights Watch said the following: "There are…five times more white drug users than black, relative to population; black men are admitted to state prison on drug charges at a rate that is 13.4 times greater than that of white men." When you look through that report and you consider all the other factors that are going on in terms of the disparity in sentencing, what you see is very much that the drug war, as currently carried out, is really contrary to our values—especially our commitment to equal justice under the law. And you might agree with Congressman Barney Frank, who notes that the war on drugs is not intentionally racist in its development, but it has become an enforcer of racism. Or as Ira Glasser of the ACLU has said, drug laws have become the new Jim Crow.

Approaches to the Drug Problem

So how do we get out of this? The bottom line is that we need new thinking for this new century. We need to reconsider the objectives and the strategies. And the first thing we have to remind people is that when they talk about the drug problem, the drug problem is actually three interrelated problems. It is the problem of addiction. It is the problem of crime. It is the problem of AIDS. Addiction, crime, AIDS. Now two of those matters are quite clearly health issues. One is primarily a criminal justice matter but arguably a public health problem, too. What I'm suggesting is yes, indeed, in this century there needs to be a war on drugs, but that war on drugs should be primarily a public health war, rather than a criminal justice war.

In order to figure out where we go, we have to review a little bit of history. Too many people, when I'm talking to them about the war on drugs, start with Richard Nixon. And they say, "Well we've been fighting a war on drugs for 30 years." Not so, not so. They should go back a little bit more. Much further back. I start with the Harrison Act, but one could arguably go back even further. But particularly the Harrison Act of 1914 was a law passed dealing specifically with illegal drugs in this country. But if you read that law, read all the commentary, the Harrison Act was a regulatory law. It was not supposed to be prohibition. It was not the Volstead Act. Later interpretations of the Harrison Act by the Supreme Court have changed it to a Volstead Act-type prohibition law. But in fact it was to be a regulatory matter. It was to put this problem primarily in the hands of the health professionals. It was not to put it into the hands of the criminal justice system. And in fact, it permitted things like clinics, an extensive system of clinics around the country. It actually allowed health professionals, under certain circumstances, to distribute drugs that are now classified as illegal, if the doctors thought it would be helpful in terms of finally getting somebody off of the drug—that is, stepping them down from their usage. All of those things which they can't do now, which are illegal, the Harrison Act on its face would have permitted. But as time went on, it became more and more prohibition, and the policies became harsher and harsher.

I look back at the rationale for a lot of our drug policies, and it seems one of the common factors in the rationale is that it was driven more by politics than by health policy. Let me give you a quick example: needle exchange. Baltimore is a city with a population of about 600,000 to 700,000 people, and Baltimore has a long history, going back to World War II, of heroin use. We have a large population of heroin users, and when I became mayor in 1987, crack was coming into the city. So, we had a large number of drug users. In fact, we got to the point that our health commissioner felt about one in eight adults in our city had a serious drug abuse problem. We particularly had a problem with heroin and with intravenous drug users sharing dirty needles with one another and then passing bodily fluids, and having sex with innocent partners who would then pass along HIV to babies. We said, "We have to do something to intervene here." And what did we want to do? We wanted to have a sterile syringe exchange program.

Well, when I announced I was going to do that, a number of my friends at the national level, particularly in the Congressional Black Caucus, said this once again showed Kurt Schmoke is one of the most dangerous men in America. That was a bit of an exaggeration, I thought, but that was the strong and initial reaction to needle exchange. I could give all kinds of rationales for it, but the bottom line was that, after doing all kinds of other public health messages, advertising, interventions, street walking, all this sort of stuff, the IV drug-using community wasn't getting it. They were still sharing dirty needles, and AIDS was a big, big problem.

We spoke to some recovering addicts and they said, "You are going to have to get out there in the street and make sure that drug addicts have clean needles. That is your responsibility now." So, I made a deal with them. I said, "All right, if I do this, if I go out on the line, will you run the program?" I asked recovering addicts to run the program, along with some nurses. We didn't try to fight the neighborhood by putting it in a building. Then we would have battles. We would have been in court. So we did trailers. We had two vans that were outfitted by our health department, and we had the recovering addicts in there; we registered the needles. We knew what was going on, and of course the national government said no to this. They emphasized they had a national policy that said any health care institution receiving federal funds would lose its funds if it operated a needle exchange program. But we have a clever health commissioner who said, "They didn't say that a hospital or university couldn't study it." That was fine. So Johns Hopkins School of Public Health studied our program, and our health department operated it. It was the largest government-run needle exchange program in the United States.

In order to do it, though, I had to get a waiver of the state paraphernalia law, because, except for diabetics who are able to get needles through prescriptions, anybody else with needles was considered to be selling drug paraphernalia. So I went trundling off to the legislature. Remember now,

Baltimore has about 20-some votes out of about a 144-person legislature. I went to the legislature and said, "I'd like to give out clean needles in Baltimore, with your permission." I didn't get it. The second year I brought with me the chief of police from Amsterdam, the Hopkins professors, and our health commissioner to explain the health aspects of this and why we didn't think it was going to increase drug use in Baltimore. Second year, no deal. Third year, this time we had been out in the neighborhoods, and the Interdenominational Ministerial Alliance had been persuaded because the ministers were tired of burying people due to AIDS. So we went down this time with the police, with the ministers, and with our health commissioner, and we got a bill passed to allow us to do needle exchange for a three-year period. We won that by one vote.

We did our three-year needle exchange program with the vans. Hopkins did the study. We had another outside group rigorously review their effort. And the numbers showed that we were reducing the spread of AIDS by about 40% in this IV-drug-using community. The numbers were powerful, just overwhelming in terms of the positive impact of the needle exchange program on health in this community. So when we went back to the legislature after this three-year period to get an extension for the needle exchange program, this time only one person voted against us—a dramatic change in that three-year period.

One of the things I have become a real believer in is the power of applied research. That is important; there are some folks who will really listen if the right message comes down with the right data, explaining what is needed. There were people who were strongly opposed to this, who said it sent the wrong message, that it wasn't going to work, and yet they became persuaded that this was right. But after our experience a number of other cities that are doing needle exchange through private, non-profit groups went to Congress and showed them the data, and Congress wouldn't budge the federal restrictions. We went to Health and Human Services, and Health and Human Services wrote a wonderful report saying, "Needle exchange in the United States has been shown safe and effective in reducing the incidence of the spread of AIDS without an increase in drug use in the communities in which it's been involved. But we still don't think this is the appropriate time to lift the restriction." Politics intrudes.

Common Ground

We don't need any new money; we just need to change the allocation of criminal justice money to public health money. Let's tilt the balance more towards public health and invest in effective treatment programs. Some treatment doesn't work; I understand that. But every time some Congressman tells me, "Treatment doesn't get people off drugs, because I know someone who was in a 30-day treatment program, and it didn't work," the first thing I ask him is, "Congressman, have you ever smoked cigarettes? When we consider long-term cigarette smokers who try to stop smoking, there are a few people who can put it out and just stop smoking. There are thousands of people who start, then stop—it takes a while. Some things work for some people. The patch works for some people. Nicorette® works for other people. Give me a break here." I try to explain it on the level they will understand. The bottom line is that there are effective drug treatment programs.

Eliminate mandatory minimum sentences. They are an outrage. At one point Congress considered mandatory minimums for methamphetimine, but they excluded ecstasy. Why? Obviously, we know whom ecstasy is going to hit. If we started putting mandatory minimum sentences on ecstasy and the prisons started loading up with suburban Jane and John Doe's children, you might see a major change in drug policy. I don't want to go in that direction. I just want to say, "Let's eliminate mandatory minimum sentences. They are not consistent with our values."

I do believe we should permit easier record expungment for youth offenders. When we had the Youth Corrections Act and the Young Adult Offenders Law, back before the drug warriors got on their high horses, at least there was an opportunity for young people who got involved in drugs, for whom it was a one-time thing, to get their lives straightened out by expunging the record after a certain period of time. Then they could go to an employer and answer the question, "Have you ever been convicted of a crime?" and say "no" and not have to lie.

We must eliminate racial profiling. That is, I believe, an important effort that needs to occur. We also must impose alternatives to incarceration for nonviolent offenders. Those things I think could be done in a race-neutral basis to make this war on drugs a bit more just.

Finally, I still believe, as I did in 1988—though I know how difficult this will be—that we are not going to win this war on drugs until we implement strategies that take the profit out of distributing drugs at the street level. At least in my city, murder and most other crimes are not driven by people injecting a substance and going crazy. The murders are related to the war over profits, the war over distribution rights, the war over territory. A policy that takes the profit out of distributing drugs at the street level is most important.

We need to begin taking some of the emotion out of this issue and seek common ground. Going back to my needle exchange example, when people first heard I wanted to do needle exchange or sterile syringe exchange, their minds closed. They came up with all these horrible dreams; they felt I was this horrible human being, instead of just listening to me. And I think we have to listen across party lines. We cannot label people. Just because somebody comes in and identifies himself or herself as a conservative Republican or a Libertarian, don't just automatically assume where they are going to be on this issue. Let's try to listen. Let's try to seek common ground. Let's get beyond political labels and simply recognize, as I have, that the war on drugs, as far as I'm concerned, is our domestic Vietnam. It lacks rationale. It lacks a sound basis in policy. And it is time for a different direction. This has gone on far, far too long.

Section III:

HARMS OF THE DRUG WAR

8. A Businessperson's Guide to the Drug Problem

BY ERIC E. STERLING

Eric E. Sterling is President of the Criminal Justice Policy Foundation (www.cjpf.org) in Silver Spring, Maryland. He was Counsel to the U.S. House of Representatives Committee on the Judiciary from 1979 until 1989. He was a principal aide in developing the Comprehensive Crime Control Act of 1984, the Anti-Drug Abuse Acts of 1986 and 1988, and other laws.

Most persons engaged in business routinely reanalyze the factors that affect their business—economic trends, employment conditions, credit rates, tax policy, trade, competition, current customers, potential customers, etc. Every factor that raises costs or depresses revenues should be identified and minimized. But such analyses have almost never considered the nation's drug problems as factors affecting costs or revenues. Those who are paid to analyze the business climate—locally, regionally, nationally, and internationally—almost never look at the significant economic effects of drug prohibition policy.

The hypothesis of this chapter is that drug prohibition hurts the business climate, profits, and investor returns. Drug prohibition both raises costs and reduces revenues. While intoxication from drug use increases the risks of accidents and lowers productivity, more significant influences on the business climate flow from the uncontrolled behaviors in the illegal drug market and the effects of enforcement.

Nine Ways the War on Drugs Hurts Businesses

First, the consequences of drug enforcement and convictions reduce the purchasing power of at least five million American consumers. Second, the crime, violence, and disorder from drug prohibition make hundreds of urban commercial districts undesirable for retail and other commercial development. Third, the crime, violence, and disorder from drug prohibition make hundreds of urban residential districts undesirable for housing and housing development.

Fourth, the direct costs of drug enforcement, now exceeding $50 billion in federal, state, and local spending each year, are a terrible opportunity cost—as taxation that restricts investment and profits. This is taxation withdrawn from the productive economy, a wasted public expenditure that does little to improve public safety and the economic climate.

There are substantial indirect costs from enforcement that accrue to the business community and hurt profits. These include, for example, fifth, the costs of compliance with onerous and ineffective money laundering regulations; sixth, the inflation of insurance premiums to pay for underwriting losses attributable to drug-prohibition crime; seventh, the significant costs of added security; and eighth, the slowing of international trade to search for contraband and as a result of growing reporting requirements in financial matters and shipments of industrial chemicals.

Ninth, still other costs are the lost productivity from drug enforcement. Among the factors reducing productivity due to drug prohibition is incarceration. Between 1992 and 1998, the productivity loss due to incarceration grew by 9.1%, according to the White House report on the economic costs of drug abuse issued in September, 2001.

Drug Use in the Workplace is a Cost

Of course, when employees are under the influence of certain drugs in the workplace, this is a real danger to other workers and to quality control. Illegal drug use in the workplace is a subset of the larger problem that includes alcohol use and the impairment from legal drugs—including prescription pain relievers and over-the-counter cold and allergy medications—that lead to motor vehicle crashes and other accidents. (The use of caffeine is not problematic in the workplace. The use of nicotine— i.e., tobacco—is increasingly problematic as a health insurance premium cost and as a litigation risk if smoking is permitted in the workplace. Taking cigarette breaks may reduce productivity. But no one is concerned about the psychic effects of nicotine on behavior or productivity.)

When employees become addicted to drugs or alcohol, they often incur expensive treatments that result in increased health insurance premiums and frequently result in lost work. Such workers may also cause accidents that may be expensive and that may lead to lawsuits. (On the other hand, certain drug use may stimulate the creativity useful to industries that rely on innovation such as software design, computer engineering, and the many components of the entertainment industry. Many such firms do not drug test employees or prospective hires.) If our current drug policy is not reducing the costs associated with drug use, then the drug policy is hurting business, not helping it.

Is prohibition the most effective way to reduce drug use in the workplace? No. Unwanted drug use in the workplace is more effectively controlled by incorporating appropriate rules in employment contracts and employee handbooks, by effective management, and by employee assistance programs when problems develop. Stigmatizing drug use as illegal interferes with the identification and acknowledgment of unwanted and problematic drug use. This stigma significantly interferes with treating problematic drug use, as an April, 2003, report from Join Together and the American Bar Association demonstrated.[1]

Off-duty drug use usually is not problematic. Using new technologies to test for actual impairment has been applauded by the business and government agencies that adopted such technologies, according to a report by the National Workrights Institute.[2]

Drug prohibition is less of a public health policy than a moral crusade. As a crusade, it is justified not by its effectiveness, but by its aspirations. Yet the costs of prohibition are too high and its failures too expensive for the crusade to be carried on any longer. America's business leaders must apply the rational analysis that has led to our economic greatness—and end one of America's great economic blunders.

The Economics of Drug Prohibition

In March, 1980, Peter Bensinger, the head of the U.S. Drug Enforcement Administration, testified before the Subcommittee on Criminal Justice of the U.S. House of Representatives about the DEA's strategy and success. I was the counsel to the subcommittee who set up the hearing and questioned the witness. Bensinger testified that the fundamental goal of drug enforcement is to reduce supply and to drive up the retail price of illegal drugs. The objective is to make illegal drug use more expensive so that casual users will reduce their consumption and addicts will enter treatment and demand will be reduced. The proof of the DEA's success is measured by the increasing price of drugs in the marketplace, he testified. However, addict demand for narcotics is relatively inelastic, seriously undermining this strategy's effectiveness for those who use the bulk of the supply of heroin and cocaine. For casual users, there is evidence that when drug prices go up, use goes down.

But this rationale for drug enforcement policy doesn't make economic sense. While increasing arrests and seizing drugs may drive up the price and may reduce the quantity demanded in the short term, it has another inevitable economic effect—it draws more entrepreneurs into the business. Wherever there is increased profitability, it will draw new economic actors seeking to maximize their return on their labor or investments. This will then drive down prices. This is an unintended but simply inevitable economic result of drug enforcement.

The strategy to reduce supply by arresting participants in the distribution actually has a positive, strengthening effect on the illegal drug market. Illegal markets are inefficient in providing information to actors. There is no Dow Jones, Bloomberg, *Forbes*, *Business Week* or CNBC providing market trend and price data. There are no phonebooks, Web sites, or advertising campaigns to assist or recruit customers. Contrary to conventional businesses, disseminating information about one's products, business location, hours of operation, etc. risks shutting the enterprise down by attracting law enforcement as well as buyers. Typical competition over price, quality, and service is greatly hindered.

Drug enforcement weeds out the less effective, less ingenious participants and encourages the more ruthless and the more cunning. The illegal drug market has actually thrived over the past 20 years and become more efficient.

The data regularly reported by the Drug Enforcement Administration shows that for 20 years it has failed to drive up the prices of the narcotic drugs. The traffickers have become so efficient, the price for a pure gram of cocaine delivered at retail has gone from $433 in 1982 down to $184 in 1999. The price of a pure gram of heroin at retail has gone from $3,285 in 1982 down to $1,929 in 1999.

And the traffickers are delivering a better product at retail. Cocaine average retail purity has increased from 36% in 1982 to 64% in 1999. Heroin average retail purity has increased from 5% in 1982 to 27% in 1999.[3] And yet more than 300,000 drug sellers are arrested every year! There has been no dramatic decline in consumption of heroin. (Cocaine consumption data is more ambiguous than the heroin data.) Doesn't this price and performance data sound like some of our most successful businesses such as computers, cell phones, DVDs, VCRs, etc.?

Reflect upon how profitable the illegal narcotic drug business is. The prices of cocaine and heroin are measured at retail in the hundreds or thousands of dollars per pure gram. An ounce of gold selling at $330 per troy ounce means that gold is selling at $10 per pure gram. Cannabis sells in the range of $4 to $19 per gram, depending on quality.

Typically, as goods move down the supply chain from manufacturer to retailer they become more expensive. But the inflation in price in illegal drugs is measured not by a few percent but in multiples. An importer of cocaine or heroin can sell the drug for three to seven times what he paid for the drug outside the United States. A retailer can sell cocaine or heroin for two, three, or four times what he paid at wholesale.

Entering the business, especially as a retailer, involves very small capital investments. A few hundred or a few thousand dollars worth of initial inventory is all that is needed. Profits accumulate rapidly. There is no capital investment in a physical plant or equipment, other than a scale and perhaps a cell phone. There is no initial need to hire or train employees.

Thus hundreds of thousands of drug sellers, primarily retailers, can be arrested annually with little impact upon the overall market for illegal drugs.

Supply Enforcement Ineffectiveness

The other side of the supply enforcement effort focuses on stopping manufacturing. A key effort is to stamp out the supply of the raw materials, the plants—opium, coca, and cannabis. But the greater the success of the plant eradication efforts, the higher the price the harvests command in the market. Again, the inevitable consequence of law enforcement strategy is to make illicit drug cultivation more economically attractive, not less attractive. The prices for crude opium and coca leaf in bulk fluctuate widely. But even at their lows, they are still profoundly more valuable to the growers than any alternative legal crops.

One reason why coca and opium are grown in the most remote regions of Asia and South America is that the farmers are very far from any market for legal crops. Crops such as coffee, bananas, coconuts, flowers, etc. are either bulky or perishable. Effective marketing requires good roads, ports, or airfields. Coca, opium, and cannabis are grown in mountainous or jungle regions without adequate roads or rivers suitable for rapid, large-scale shipment of bulk produce. Coca leaf and opium gum are quickly and easily refined using widely available industrial chemicals. Coca paste and morphine base, the compact semi-purified plant extracts that are the raw materials refined into cocaine and heroin, are relatively easy to ship, and enormously more valuable.

In August, 1983, I toured drug-producing regions of Peru and Colombia with the Select Committee on Narcotics Abuse and Control of the U.S. House of Representatives. We had to fly hundreds of miles from the national capitals over mountain ranges that were unbridgeable obstacles for the shipment of bulky, legal agricultural products. As I stood next to a senior member of Congress while observing government-paid laborers chop down coca bushes in Peru, he turned to me and said, "Now I understand the meaning of the phrase, 'pissing into the wind'." The futility of this effort was obvious—but politically inexpressible. And even though eradication has grown enormously—now conducted by fleets of pesticide-spraying aircraft—the price of coca still draws tens of thousands of growers, and the supply of cocaine remains plentiful.

Coca cultivation is now taxed by rival guerilla armies and paramilitary forces that destabilize Colombia, destroy pipelines and power transmission lines, assassinate public officials, and kidnap businesspersons. Prohibition makes this cultivation very profitable.

It must be understood that the absolute quantities of illegal drugs that are produced and shipped are infinitesimal in terms of global trade. U.S. consumption of drugs in 2000 was about 260 metric tons of cocaine, 13 metric tons of heroin and 1,047 metric tons of cannabis.[4] All of that cocaine, for example, could be shipped in a couple dozen tractor trailers. For comparison, 1,624,000,000 metric tons of sugar were imported into the U.S. in 2001, according to the Washington Report on the Hemisphere published by the Council on Hemispheric Affairs. The U.S. price for sugar was about $0.21 per pound (454 g) in early 2002.

If the drug problem is a costly one for American business, one of the goals of the anti-drug strategy ought to be reducing the cost to the economy. However, the latest report from the White House shows the overall economic cost of drug abuse rose 5.9% between 1992 and 1998. At the same time, Federal anti-drug spending grew from $11.9 billion in FY 1992 to $16.1 billion in FY 1998, a 35% increase. Evidently this has been a growing investment of public resources with a decreasing return.

Prohibition is Driving Away Your Customers

Each year since 1990, a minimum of a quarter million persons have received a felony conviction for a drug offense. I estimate that since 1980, at least five million persons have been sentenced for a drug felony (though this number fails to account for repeat offenders). Between one-third and one-half of these sentences are for simple possession.

These five million persons with drug felony convictions have greatly reduced access to lawful employment. Their earnings are profoundly reduced. Ex-felons don't get a pre-approved application for a credit card with a 0% introductory APR in their mailbox on a weekly basis.

Without a Visa card, Mastercard, or Discover card, the desire of these millions of potential customers to purchase many goods and services is effectively blocked. This large number of felons has reduced the customer base for most businesses.

Millions of potential subcribers can't sign up for AOL or the Internet because they can't automatically bill their credit card. Millions of drug felons can't order Christmas presents by phone from catalogs. They can't order CDs or music equipment from Amazon.com. They can't order tickets to take their kids to basketball games or the circus by calling Ticketmaster or Ticketron.

Drug felons cannot qualify for mortgages to buy homes for their families. Thus, millions of potential home buyers are excluded from the marketplace. Millions of new washing machines, refrigerators, stoves, sofas, bedroom suites, and so forth are not purchased. Paint, wallpaper, and carpet are not purchased.

Without access to credit, drug felons can't buy new cars. Also at the retail level, the sale of music is depressed. Yet the overwhelming majority of those convicted of drug offenses are young, prospective consumers of music CDs. The opportunities to travel by air, stay in hotels, or go on a vacation are all much more limited because the former felon has no credit card.

It is not a cliché that the American economy is driven by consumer demand: it is an economic truth. In times of economic slump, the consequences of the war on drugs sap the economy like an intestinal parasite.

Many of these ex-felons, rehabilitated after serving the sentences and now many years away from their crimes, still can't get jobs. Many of the former drug traffickers worked hard, long hours and were successful as entrepreneurs. William M. Adler[5] and Phillipe Bourgois[6] have described how successful managers of drug distribution operations demonstrate the ability to solve all of the management problems of large retail organizations. But in most instances, they can't get hired for the simplest managerial positions.

Millions of workers, disheartened by their former felonies, simply don't try to enter the legal workplace. Yet from an employer's perspective, if they were seeking jobs, they would help keep the price of labor down. From a social perspective, they would be attractive partners for marriage and could support their families. The need for public assistance for their families would go down dramatically. They would be paying taxes instead of receiving income from the government.

Competitors You Don't Want to Have

From 1984 to 1986 I conducted congressional investigations and hearings into the laundering of money by criminal organizations. I was the attorney on the staff of the Subcommittee on Crime of the U.S. House of Representatives principally responsible for developing the Money Laundering Control Act of 1986 (P.L. 99-570) that created the federal crimes of money laundering (18 U.S.C. 1956 and 1957).

Money laundering is a necessary business challenge for any large-scale drug operation. Large-scale drug trafficking is the only major vice that relies upon cash. Prostitutes and pornographers take credit cards. Gambling casinos and race tracks take credit cards. Only the sale of dope remains on a cash-only basis.

It is a pathetic irony that if one uses or possesses large numbers of Federal Reserve Notes that say, "This note is legal tender for all debts, public and private," one becomes suspected of being a criminal. In routine police stops, if the officers find more than a small amount of cash, the officers seize it to forfeit it on the presumption that the cash is the proceeds of drug trafficking. The burden of proof is on the citizen to prove he has acquired his cash lawfully. It is a sad fact that when it comes to large transactions, usually only criminals use legal tender.

The successful drug dealer cannot have a very full enjoyment of the fruits of his crimes if he has only cash. He can't buy a car, an overseas vacation, real estate, and so forth with large sums of small bills. How can a drug dealer enjoy his profits? How can a drug dealer protect his profits?

This is the problem solved by money laundering. Numerous strategies can be employed. One approach is to open a business that typically generates large volumes of cash—a candy store, an ice cream store, a small restaurant, etc. The business does not need to be successful. Indeed, how many times have you seen a crummy little business, a lousy restaurant, for example, and wondered, "How can they stay in business?" Such businesses have a legitimate reason to make cash deposits every day. Included with the meager receipts from a few legitimate sales are sums of cash from illegal operations. After paying appropriate taxes, the "profits" of the crime have been laundered and can be used like real money.

Of course, a successful restaurant can launder money, too. Conversely, many cash businesses don't record all of their receipts in order to avoid paying sales and income taxes. But the revenues of these "mom and pop" operations pale in comparison to even modest drug-selling operations.

Other money-laundering schemes involve informal money exchanges, currency exchanges, or the use of precious stones or precious metals. The essence of money laundering is the concealment of the criminal origin of the funds or the concealment of the identity of the owner of the funds.

For decades, numerous countries have adopted rules designed to protect the privacy of bank customers to attract deposits. The anonymous, numbered "Swiss bank account" is the most famous example. Many other countries and jurisdictions, such as the Cayman Islands, Palau, Vanuatu, Luxembourg, and the Channel Islands, have numerous banks set up exclusively for overseas customers. While acceding to pressure from U.S. law enforcement agencies to cooperate in criminal investigations, many of them have adopted laws designed to frustrate investigators by requiring various legal processes and documents to be completed before financial records will be released.

In most capitalist nations, almost any individual can create any number of corporations, which in turn can open any number of bank accounts, in any number of other nations. Funds can now be transferred electronically from account to account, from corporation to corporation, from country to country. A great many transactions can be completed very quickly. Thus, a well-structured money-laundering scheme can take many years to unravel. In that time, the owners of the funds have numerous opportunities to further hide their tracks. A drug dealer laundering his money can comfortably gamble that at some point along a well-constructed, well-concealed money-laundering chain, the investigating agent is likely to be reassigned to a higher-priority case.

However, every bank and bank customer incur ever-growing expenses to comply with the record keeping and other regulations designed to facilitate money-laundering investigations. A decade ago the American Bankers Association estimated informally that the compliance costs for banks exceeded $300 million annually. Since then the demands for compliance training and expensive software have grown enormously.

The demand for money laundering creates powerful incentives for criminals to branch out into legitimate business. Many legitimate businesses need a line of credit. A business designed to launder money doesn't need a line of credit; it actually has more capital than it can handle. A legitimate business needs to make a profit to remain viable. A money-laundering business does not need to make a profit. Indeed, the operating losses are simply a cost of the extremely profitable principal business, drug selling. Thus, any legitimate business in a field attractive to money launderers has to fight competitors who don't care if they lose money because such losses are merely a cost of keeping their major revenue generators viable.

Who Owns Your Assets? The Impact of Forfeiture

Among the government tools for fighting money laundering and drug trafficking are the civil asset forfeiture laws. Since the first Revenue Act of 1789, property used to evade the tax laws, such as smuggling vessels, has been seized by the Treasury Department. Property used to smuggle drugs, and the proceeds of drug smuggling and trafficking, have been seizable for decades. But in the 1980s Congress put pressure on the government to use forfeiture more frequently as a tool to "take the profits out" of the illegal drug trade. A major incentive they provided was to allow law enforcement agencies to keep the assets they seize instead of turning the proceeds of forfeiture sales over to the general receipts of the Treasury.

Keeping the assets means law enforcement agencies profit if they let the drug traffickers sell the drugs before they stage a raid. Simply seizing drugs does not contribute to the drug agency's budget.

To obtain forfeiture of financial assets is sometimes a more important objective of money-laundering investigations than prosecuting the criminal. But this has generated a number of problems for innocent property owners. Historically the burden of proof for the government is low. To succeed, all that must be established is probable cause that the property is derived from drug trafficking.

The government often argues, for example, that cash is forfeitable if there is any evidence of the residue of cocaine on the currency. That residue, they claim, is evidence that the money was used in a drug transaction. However, powder cocaine is often snorted through rolled-up dollar bills. The rollers on high speed currency-counting machines in banks and businesses become contaminated with cocaine residue and spread it to other currency. In fact, much of American currency has been contaminated with very slight but detectable amounts of cocaine. In the 1980s, the *Miami Herald* reported that currency borrowed from prominent citizens, including State's Attorney Janet Reno, tested positive for cocaine. Yet after a sum of cash is seized and it tests positive for cocaine, the burden of proving that the currency was obtained lawfully shifts to the citizen. When it comes to asset forfeiture, there is no presumption of innocence or proof beyond a reasonable doubt.

Who are Your Partners?

One of the virtues of the American economy has been that since the earliest settlement, it has been a place for foreign investors to invest. Since the 17th century, and especially in the 19th and 20th centuries, money has flowed into the United States to develop real estate, to build factories and railroads, to buy securities, and so forth.

Criminals with funds that have been laundered seek the same kind of security and dependable rates of return that other investors have found in the United States. Today, developers seeking capital are always at risk that ostensibly legitimate investors are actually using laundered funds. One consequence of money laundering and the forfeiture laws is that any investor with partners is always at risk that the government will forfeit a partner's share of the property and become a new partner, inquiring into all of the advantageous elements of the investment.

Buy Property, Lease Property, or Squat

The business of drug trafficking adversely affects the real estate market in other ways. When drugs are used or sold out of a fixed location—an apartment or a business—the owners of the property, if they fail to take sufficient steps to stop the use or sales, are subject to prosecution under state "nuisance" laws. In 1993, the law firm of Cadwalader, Wickersham and Taft published a guide to using such laws titled "A Civil War: A Community Legal Guide to Fighting Street Drug Markets." A federal law, the so-called "crack house act," (21 U.S.C. 856), is also being used against property owners. This law carries a penalty of 20 years imprisonment and a $500,000 fine, and corporate property owners can be fined two million dollars per count. On April 30, 2003, President Bush signed the Illicit Drug Anti-Proliferation Act (P.L. 108-21), which now allows a civil fine of $250,000 per incident. And such properties can be forfeited. Actions taken by the property owner or managers to deter drug use or sales, ironically and unjustly, have been held to be evidence that the property owner was aware the illegal drug use or sales were taking place.

If dilapidated property happens to be occupied by persons using or selling drugs, such laws are a deterrent to buying the property in order to rehabilitate the property.

Because of such high penalties, drug sellers don't buy real estate in which to sell drugs. And property owners work as hard as they can to push drug sellers outside onto the street. As a consequence, many neighborhoods are plagued with outdoor illegal drug markets. These drug markets are inevitably places of violence.

Business Problems for the Drug Dealer: Security

Imagine you are a cutting-edge, out-of-the box retailer: imagine you are a drug dealer. Whether you have located your retail operation indoors or on the street, you share a problem with most of your legitimate cousins: providing security for your employees, your customers, your inventory, and your receipts. Shoplifting isn't much of a problem, as your wares are not on display for customers to examine before purchase. You have techniques to send a very strong message to your employees that employee pilferage won't be tolerated.

Your big security problem is the professional robber. Think of the places someone can rob for money. The obvious targets are businesses with very high volumes of cash—banks, liquor stores, drug stores, food stores, fast food outlets, convenience stores. For many of these high-volume retail outlets, a high proportion of the receipts are non-negotiable credit-card slips and, to a lesser extent, checks. Those with the most cash usually have security systems of safes, video cameras, alarms of varying sophistication, and professional security guards, even off-duty police officers. But your receipts, as the illegal drug seller,are exclusively cash.

You also have a unique inventory. Every other inventory that might be stolen will be sold for a substantial discount. Stolen computers, televisions, jewelry, clothing, automobiles, farm equipment, medical supplies, steaks, or disposable diapers are sold or fenced for much less than their retail price. Uniquely, however, stolen cocaine or stolen heroin can be sold for the same price you were asking. No one asks the drug sellers any questions about where the heroin or cocaine came from.

Illegal drugs are compact, extremely valuable, and an ideal product for the robber to run away with, unlike, say, television sets. Thus your illegal drug market is always being cased by professional robbers.

Unlike conventional retailers, the illegal drug seller cannot employ security firms such as Wackenhut, Brinks, or Wells Fargo, nor legitimate off-duty police officers. You can't go to the Yellow Pages to find a security firm. You must deploy your own security force to protect employees, receipts, inventory, and customers. How would you as a drug dealer recruit security employees? What are the qualifications you would like to see from job applicants for providing security to your illegal drug market?

The ideal candidates to provide security at street markets have widely known reputations for committing extreme acts of violence. Imagine the job interview: You: "Who have you shot?" Job candidate: "John Doe." You: "I never heard of that shooting." Or "How do I know you shot him? If you shoot so and so [your rival or disloyal former employee], you've got the job."

The security guard always has his weapons. The violence he has inflicted always faces retaliation. The danger of accidental or non-job related violence is always very high as well.

If the robber is successful, he does not have to worry that the victims will call the police. He escapes with cash and drugs many times more valuable than gold, that are easily sold.

America's $50 billion per year retail drug business is the nation's greatest employer of killers and psychopaths. Drug prohibition assures that they are fully employed, well-armed, and standing on street corners throughout the nation.

Dispute Resolution

The illegal drug business faces the inevitable disputes of any business. A supplier fails to deliver goods as promised. A customer fails to pay for goods he has accepted. But unlike the other businesses in your community, you have no recourse to the courts to enforce your contracts. You can't sue for breach of contract or to enforce a warranty of merchantability under the Uniform Commercial Code. The courts won't award you a judgment to obtain payment for goods you have sold.

Or imagine that a senior employee decides to leave your organization to go into business for himself, taking valued suppliers and customers. One can't go to court to enforce a covenant not to compete. Imagine an employee has been embezzling receipts or inventory. You can't call the police or district attorney and file a complaint for embezzlement or theft.

All of these conflicts are resolved exclusively through the application of violence. These problems can be prevented only by threatening violence. With the presence of illegal drug markets in a neighborhood, violence is all but inevitable, utterly depressing the attractiveness of the neighborhood for housing, business, and employment.

And, of course, homes and businesses in such neighborhoods must pay higher insurance premiums, totaling hundreds of millions of dollars each year.

All of this violence, and all of this increased cost of doing business, is exclusively the result of the fact that the sale of these drugs is illegal.

A Barrier to Treatment

Drug prohibition actually undermines the impetus to get drug treatment. The stigma of the illegality of drug use is a major barrier to effective treatment that doesn't exist for alcoholics. For example, former Congressman Bill Emerson (MO) announced a number of years ago that he was taking a leave of absence to enter an alcohol treatment program. He was re-elected several times and elevated to Vice-chairman of the House Agriculture Committee.

At about the same time, it was widely known and rumored in Washington, D.C. that Mayor Marion Barry was using cocaine. Because he was the honorary chairperson of every anti-drug program in the city, he and his advisers could never admit that he had an illegal drug problem. Law enforcement efforts to find corruption in his administration never reached him, but he was trapped by the FBI using an ex-girlfriend to lure him to a hotel room to have sex and smoke crack cocaine. Only then did his cocaine problem lead to drug treatment. The stigma of illegality blocked admission of his problem and delayed his treatment.

Controlled Substances: Our Great Oxymoron

In an effort to fight the growing illegal drug problem, in 1970 a Uniform Controlled Substances Act was proposed by the National Conference of Commissioners on Uniform State Laws. It has been adopted by almost every state. In 1970 Congress enacted the Controlled Substances Act. Yet these drugs are the most out-of-control substances in the American economy. Calling them "controlled substances" is an oxymoron.

The American government has demonstrated a genius for regulation. While libertarians will gag at that characterization, they will completely concur that nearly every aspect of the American economy is subject to some form of regulation—except the illegal drug business. While libertarians will dissent that much of this regulation is necessary or wise, they will concur that prohibition makes the peaceful mechanisms of market control and non-government regulation impossible.

The illegal drug seller—even one inclined to nonviolence—must resort to arms because the state, with its monopoly on the lawful use of force, will not intercede to protect him. When every other participant in the market relies upon implicit and explicit threats of violence, it is disastrous not to do so as well.

Part of what drives many businesspersons to the Libertarian Party is their desire to make as many of their business practices as possible be considered legal. One goal of a sane and just society ought to be to bring as much as its commerce under the protective umbrella of the law as possible.

When defenders of the prohibitionist *status quo* claim to be considering the merits of drug legalization, they commonly ask if crack cocaine should be sold in the supermarket next to the sugar or the cigarettes. They frame legalization in this way to imply that potentially addicting drugs will be sold everywhere, with the complete absence of any controls. Yet today, crack cocaine is readily purchased outside or behind supermarkets in every state, without any control, and with little effective restraint.

Some proponents of drug legalization argue that the state should be given the monopoly in selling drugs, or that the liquor stores run by some states should become the somewhat antiseptic outlets for cannabis, cocaine, heroin, and other drugs. But the regulatory options are not simply between these two poles. Drug policy scholars Rob MacCoun and Peter Reuter have identified seven types of regulatory models for drugs in their outstanding book, *Drug War Heresies.*[7]

Libertarians recognize there is a vast range of private regulatory control mechanisms available as well. Drug sellers could organize in professional guilds, with professional standards. They could offer warranties of the purity of their products and obtain insurance to make such warranties meaningful to customers who may be injured by adulterated or mislabeled products. Injured users could seek redress in the courts for any of the product liability protections the public is entitled to.

The Bottom Line

American business is being hurt by drug prohibition. Vast pools of customers are cut off from the tools of the marketplace—credit cards, catalog shopping, Internet shopping, telephone ordering—by drug convictions. Society has outlawed the drug business, forcing it out of the nonviolent dispute mechanisms that reduce conflict and violence in the society. Yet a vast, prohibited drug trade remains, burdening communities with the very high costs of the violence that prohibition makes necessary and inevitable. A vast taxpayer-supported industry operates futilely to enforce the drug laws but is structurally incapable of doing so. This industry is counterproductive and justifies itself with a parade of horribles that are largely a consequence of its work.

Of course, throughout the American economy and throughout our history, there are numerous instances in which industries or individual businesses have taken advantage of the government's power to regulate to give themselves advantages over their competitors. Many industries directly profit from drug prohibition even though the nation's economy, as a whole, does not.

The challenge for all businesspersons interested in public policy is to determine whether their business climate is being damaged as the collateral damage of the war on drugs. If they find such damage, they have an obligation to the owners, and to their community, to mobilize to end this drag on profits, on economic growth, and on society, with the same zeal they mobilize to change tax policy or other regulations perceived to be costly and unnecessary.

Notes

1. Join Together, *Ending Discrimination Against People with Alcohol and Drug Problems*, April, 2003, www.jointogether.org/discrimination.

2. National Workrights Institute, *Impairment Testing—Does it Work?* www.workrights.org/issue_drugtest/dt_impairment_testing.html.

3. White House, *National Drug Control Strategy*, February, 2002, page 81.

4. *Ibid.*, page 85.

5. William M. Adler, *Land of Opportunity: One family's quest for the American dream in the age of crack*, Atlantic Monthly Press, 1995.

6. Phillipe Bourgois, *In Search of Respect: Selling Crack in El Barrio*, Cambridge University Press, 1996.

7. Rob MacCoun and Peter Reuter, *Drug War Heresies*, Cambridge University Press, 2001.

9. A Foreign Policy Disaster

BY MIKE KRAUSE AND DAVE KOPEL

*Mike Krause is a senior fellow with the Independence Institute (www.i2i.org).
While serving in the U.S. Coast Guard from 1987–1991, he was a boat
coxswain for drug interdiction operations during joint agency drug patrols
in the Caribbean Sea. Dave Kopel (www.davekopel.org), research director of
the Independence Institute, formerly served as assistant attorney general
of Colorado. He is the author of many books, including* No More Wacos:
What's Wrong with Federal Law Enforcement and How to Fix It.

In 1986, President Ronald Reagan declared illegal drug trafficking
across America's borders to be a "national security threat." In 1989,
President George H.W. Bush issued National Security Directive 18, calling
for $250 million in aid to fight the Andean drug trade, followed quickly by
another $65 million for Colombia alone, in the form of military, law
enforcement and intelligence assistance. He dispatched U.S. Special Forces
soldiers to train the Colombian military and police in counter-narcotics.[1]

At the time, Colombia was the source of 80% of the cocaine coming
into the U.S., and Peru was the main coca-producing nation. A gram of
cocaine retailed for about $100 and was readily available to almost anybody
who cared to use it. Meanwhile, Colombia was being ripped apart by
violence and corruption fueled by narco-dollars.

In 2002, U.S. Army General James Hill, the new commander of the
U.S. Southern Command and the man in charge of military operations in
Latin America, called illegal drug trafficking across America's borders a

"weapon of mass destruction."[2] U.S. aid to fight the Andean drug trade, with the lion's share to Colombia, has surpassed $2 billion and President George W. Bush promised yet more. The U.S. has trained three battalions of the Colombian army—about 2,800 men—and supplied equipment including UH-60 Black Hawk and UH-1N helicopters, fixed-wing aircraft, and gun boats.

Today, Colombia is still the main source of cocaine coming into the U.S., plus about 10% of the heroin, and Peru is the second largest coca producer (behind Colombia). Cocaine is still readily available in the United States, and a gram still retails for about $100, making it one of the few commodities that is cheaper today in real dollars than it was a decade ago. And Colombia is still being ripped apart by violence and corruption fueled by narco-dollars.

The ongoing destruction linked to the drug trade comes not from the nature of drug trafficking itself, but rather from the drug war, which in Colombia and Peru long ago stopped being mere metaphor.

The last decade of the U.S.-led drug war in the Andes has thwarted free-market capitalism, destroyed the livelihood of subsistence farmers, enriched narco-terrorists and criminal thugs, strengthened the role of the military, weakened civilian rule, propped up government corruption, and hindered Andean anti-insurgency efforts.

Colombia: The Drug War Enriches Terrorists

In the early 1990s, the U.S. government embarked on a "Kingpin Strategy" of dismantling the Colombian drug cartels, which controlled production and distribution of the roughly six billion dollar a year Andean cocaine trade.[3] Drug warrior theory was that taking down the cartel leaders—the Medellin and Cali cartels in particular—would also destroy the trafficking infrastructure and end the cocaine business in Colombia. The Kingpin Strategy was thwarted, however, by the black market economics of prohibition.

By the mid-1990s, most of the Medellin and Cali leaders were either dead or in prison. Yet just as the 1931 imprisonment of Al Capone did not shut down the illegal liquor business in America, the destruction of particular drug cartels in Colombia simply created a void that was quickly filled by other drug cartels. The transition to new cartels proved to be quite harmful to American interests.

In 1964, a Marxist guerilla organization calling itself the "Revolutionary Armed Forces of Colombia" (FARC) began a campaign to overthrow the government. The group financed itself with kidnapping and extortion. Operating on the fringe of the drug trade, FARC also acquired income by protecting (or leaving alone) cartel coca fields and processing plants.[4] With the cartels dismantled, the FARC began directly taxing traffickers and coca growers for protection from government anti-narcotics forces; then FARC moved into both the production and distribution of narcotics and the control of local coca base markets.

In other words, the net financial result of the "Kingpin Strategy" was to change who made the profits from the illegal drug trade. Formerly, the revenues had gone into the hands of apolitical organized crime syndicates. Now, the revenues flowed to communist terrorists.

Before the United States government militarized the "drug war" in the Andes, a majority of coca was cultivated in neighboring Bolivia and Peru, then processed in and shipped from Colombia. At the same time guerillas were taking over the drug trade in Colombia, the success of the U.S. "Airbridge Denial" program—the shooting down of suspected drug flights delivering coca paste for processing—prompted traffickers to simply move their growing operations into Colombia. The result was a 150% increase in Colombian cultivation. Already the largest producer of cocaine, Colombia became the largest coca-growing country as well.[5]

It was a great boon for the terrorists. As one State Department official explained it, "All of the sudden, their coffers were running over."[6]

The new terrorist wealth resulted in an unprecedented wave of guerilla violence. FARC displaced government authority in large parts of Colombia. In 1999, Colombia's President Pastrana simply abandoned a chunk of southern Colombia twice the size of New Jersey to the FARC. The U.S. escalated financial and military aid to $1.3 billion in 2000, and sent more CIA and Special Forces "trainers" and civilian "contractors" into Colombia to assist in further eradication and interdiction efforts. This was called "Plan Colombia," but a better title would be "Plan Vietnam: Cultivating an unwinnable jungle war in South America."

The United Self-Defense Forces of Colombia (AUC) was a private Colombian army, or autodefensa, formed to kill the FARC and supported by moneyed interests (including the cartels) and the Colombian military (and thus, tacitly, by the U.S. government through its military assistance to Colombia). After the destruction of the Medellin and Cali cartels, the AUC too jumped into the drug trade, transforming from anti-communist death squads to an umbrella group for drug trafficking and narco-terror. The AUC have been officially—though many believe not unofficially—outlawed by the Colombian government; in 2002, AUC leader Carlos Castano was indicted by the U.S. for smuggling some 17 tons of cocaine into the U.S. and Europe since 1997.[7] And in November, 2002, AUC terrorists were arrested in an FBI sting trying to trade cocaine and cash for guns and bombs.[8]

Estimates for how much money the Colombian narco-terrorists garner from the drug trade range between $100 and $500 million per year. Whatever the precise amount, the FARC and AUC, both accurately listed as terrorist organizations by the U.S. Department of State, have profited handsomely from drug prohibition.

Before the drug war, Colombia faced an insurgency run by rag-tag guerillas; now the nation suffers from a full blown civil war, and the Colombian military is fighting not just the remarkably well-funded FARC but also the military's ex-allies, the AUC.

Enriching one's deadly enemies is a terrible military strategy. But that is precisely what the U.S. drug war has accomplished in Colombia.

Peru: The Shining Path Needs the Drug War to Prosper

Beginning in 1980, Peru—having just emerged from over a decade of military rule—was forced to wage a bloody and brutal war against the Shining Path (Sendero Luminoso), an army of Maoist guerillas fighting to turn Peru into a totalitarian socialist state. Some thirty thousand Peruvians were killed by one side or the other. Like the FARC and AUC, Shining Path were narco-terrorists, funding their murder through the fruits of prohibition. As Rand Beers, Assistant Secretary of State for International Narcotics and Law Enforcement, told a Senate committee in 2002, the Shining Path's ability to "cut a brutal swath" through Peru had been "largely funded by levies it imposed on cocaine trafficking."[9]

The war culminated in the 1990s, during the early days of the presidency of Alberto Fujimori, when thousands of Shining Path were captured and the insurgency was crushed.

The destruction of Shining Path was accompanied by the destruction of Peru's fledgling constitutional democracy. In 1992, Fujimori launched a coup, dissolved the courts and Congress, and instituted military tribunals. The results, as described by U.S. State Department human rights reports, were what one would expect in a country with a tradition of corrupt and brutal government: "The military and police continue to be responsible for numerous extra-judicial killings, arbitrary detentions, torture, rape and disappearances... Besides beatings, common methods of torture include electric shock, water torture and asphyxiation..." Of the over 3,900 Peruvians convicted in the secret courts, more than 600 have since been released by a review.[10] Similarly, swaths of Colombia have recently been turned into "theaters of operations," with constitutional protections removed and martial law in place.[11]

Another prong of Fujimori's war on Shining Path was to call off U.S.-backed coca-eradication programs. The Shining Path was thus deprived of income from drug-trade protection rackets and deprived of peasant support. As Ian Vasquez, director of the Cato Institute's Project on Global Economic Liberty, describes it, "At the time Fujimori claimed, 'Peruvian-American anti-drug policy has failed' and from 1990–1995 there simply wasn't any eradication going on in Peru."[12] Fujimori, it seems, took a lesson from the past.

Melanie Tammen, writing for the Cato Institute, details how Peruvian counter-insurgency efforts in the 1980s were undermined by U.S. driven counter-narcotics efforts:

> In 1984 President Belaunde Terry declared the Upper Huallaga Valley an emergency zone and dispatched the military with the mission not to fight drugs but to fight Shining Path. The top military commander forbade anti-narcotics operations in the area, arguing that they disrupted counterinsurgency efforts. With no reason to oppose security personnel and no need for guerilla protection, coca growers withdrew their support and even revealed the identities of Shining Path members. The guerillas retreated and the coca industry in the valley boomed. From 1985 to 1989 the new government of President Alan Garcia cooperated closely with U.S. DEA officials to carry out succesive eradication and interdiction campaigns, and Shining Path gained control of as much as 90 percent of the Huallaga Valley.[13]

This prompted President Garcia to stop listening to U.S. drug police and start listening to his terrorist fighting General, Alberto Arciniega. Coca farmers were again left unhindered and a coca growers cooperative was promoted. As Tammen continues, this opened the door for succesive strikes against Shining Path:

> Arciniega conducted at least 320 offensives against Shining Path guerillas in 1989, killing 700 guerillas (more than half the number killed nationwide that year), and greatly improved security in the towns of the Upper Huallaga Valley. But U.S. officials, concerned that Arciniega had done nothing to fight coca cultivation, pressed the Peruvian government for his transfer.

In recent years, Peru has again acceded to U.S. demands to prioritize coca eradication. In 2002 alone, Congress provided $156 million in drug war aid to Peru. At the same time, Shining Path was beginning a comeback. As Beers continued at the 2002 Senate hearing, "In 2001 the Shining Path had a slight resurgence in areas like the Huallaga and Apurimac Valleys, where cocaine is cultivated and processed, indicating that the remnants of the group are probably financing operations with drug profits from security and taxation services."

The Shining Path is being joined in the Peruvian valleys by FARC guerillas from Colombia. The FARC and Shining Path bear gifts of poppy seeds, money, and protection to recruit Peruvian farmers into their drug-running racket.[14]

A February 8, 2002, Stratfor intelligence brief reported that, thanks to an expanding alliance with Colombian drug traffickers and the FARC, "Shining Path is trying to re-build its numbers and weaponry by working in the heroin trade. Peru is poised to become one of the world's heroin producers." A State Department official explained in 2001, FARC terrorists "are making so much money they could probably double the size of their armed forces."[15]

Further expansion of U.S. anti-narcotics efforts in Peru may drive traffickers and growers under the wings of the reborn Shining Path and FARC, allowing the terrorist groups to develop into a major threat again in Peru. A vicious cycle requiring more and more U.S. involvement appears very possible.

Terrorists in the United States cannot overthrow our government, but they are far stronger in South America. The drug war in the United States attempts to protect American consumers from the consequence of their own bad choices, but the effect of the effort to protect North American fools is to put fragile South American governments in danger of being destroyed by terrorists.

Starve a Farmer, Feed a Trafficker

In September of 2002, some six weeks after taking office, new Colombian President Alvaro Uribe made his priorities clear: "We will not stop. We will spray and spray. We will intercept. We will seize. We will do all the best every day and every night to destroy narcotics in Colombia."[16]

In 1996–1997, the Clinton Administration had decertified Colombia as a "cooperating" nation in the drug war. To stave off trade sanctions against lawful industries and a loss of U.S. foreign aid, Colombia began U.S. backed coca-eradication efforts, including slashing and burning on the ground and aerial herbicide spraying of coca fields. It has thus far been a smashing success...at destroying the livelihoods of subsistence farmers. As one State Department official put it, "If the spraying is successful it kills their (the growers') income."[17]

A core weakness of the eradication policies is the pricing structure of drugs. The production cost of cocaine is around 3% of the U.S. retail price, with smuggling to U.S. borders adding another 10%. So, eradication and interdiction comprise a relatively small part of the cost of doing business for drug traffickers.[18]

That the Colombian or Peruvian farmers receive no more than 3% of the street value of cocaine in the U.S. means that drug importers have a lot of flexibility to increase what they pay to farmers. If pressure from the police or military causes trouble for too many growers, then traffickers can double or triple the prices paid to farmers, or simply move their operations, as they did from Bolivia and Peru into Colombia, with only minor or no price increases required at the U.S. retail market.

Another aspect of the eradication effort is to fund alternative crop development. For example, from 1995–2001, the U.S. Agency for International Development provided $107 million worth of assistance to Peru.[19] In 2001, Robert Brown, from the Office of National Drug Control Strategy, testified before Congress on the "success" of Peruvian interdiction strategies: "By the summer of 1996, the U.S. Embassy in Lima was reporting widespread hunger in the coca growing regions. Coca farmers began abandoning their illicit crops, clamored for U.S. alternative development assistance and welcomed the presence of Peruvian governmental institutions necessary to deliver aid."[20]

Yet while Peruvian coca farmers went hungry, the traffickers, who had moved their operations elsewhere, continued to eat well. And while coca growers abandoning their illicit crops may make for compelling congressional hearings, Brown's optimistic testimony flies in the face of simple market forces.

Americans have provided alternative crop subsidies in Peru for coffee, a crop whose production costs on many Peruvian farms exceed its market value. In 2002 the regional cost of growing coffee was about $1.50 per kilogram, while the world price was just half a dollar.[21] In contrast, the 2002 price farmers got for coca leaves was at an all time high of $3.50 per kilo, compared to just 40 cents per kilo in 1995, when there was no eradication going on in Peru.[22]

The U.S. also tried alternative crop subsidies in Colombia until it was discovered that much of Colombia's growing regions, especially the coca-rich

Putamayo region, while ideal for growing coca, are not very suitable for other, legal, commercial crops. The program was essentially abandoned. The spraying, of course, continued.[23]

Half the population of Colombia and Peru lives in poverty.[24] Not the American "below the poverty level" lifestyle of color television and so much food that obesity is a serious problem, but rather third world poverty, with starvation and abject desperation.

The hard reality is that farmers in Peru and Colombia are being starved out by a militarized anti-narcotics strategy. They cannot see why they should be prevented from growing an export crop that feeds their families.

In Peru, coca consumption dates back to the days of the Inca, with coca consumed by chewing its leaves. The effect is not all that different from caffeine consumption. (In Bolivia, the cultivation of 12,000 hectares of coca is actually allowed under the law for traditional use.) In the United States, though, the illegality of coca encourages sellers to sell the product in much more concentrated (and therefore much more concealable) forms: powder and crack cocaine. The psychoactive effects and dangers are much greater. Similarly, American prohibition of alcohol caused a consumption shift away from beer (large volume, low "kick") to gin (low volume, high "kick").

It is unrealistic to expect that Andean farmers trying to feed their families are going to care much about how American drug laws change the way that coca is consumed in North America. The farmers are ideal targets for terrorists, who offer to protect and buy the coca crop. Now, terrorists are convincing the farmers to plant poppy seeds, too.

The "starve an Andean peasant to save an American cokehead" strategy has been largely unsuccessful. According to the U.S. State Department, from 1995–2000, coca cultivation in Peru was reduced from over 100,000 hectares to around 34,000 hectares. The Peruvian Center for Social Studies disputes the claim and reports about 70,000 hectares under cultivation in 2001. Peru's new drug czar, Ricardo Vega Llona, suggests that the previous estimates of acres under production may have been far too low. In any case, it is undisputed that coca production is thriving, partly because producers have learned to plant more crops per acre.

In Colombia, according to the U.S State Department, between 1993 and 2000, about 100,000 hectares of coca were eradicated. Yet during that same period, coca cultivation more than tripled, from 793 hectares in 1993 to over 183,000 hectares in 2000.[25]

According to *The Washington Post*, in the last quarter of 2002 some 115,000 acres of Colombia's Putamayo province alone were sprayed with herbicide, killing not just coca, but the few legal crops that are grown there.

The result has been the displacement of scores of Colombian farm families, offered only the hollow promise of an international welfare program funded by American taxpayers.

At the same time, the number of Colombian provinces being used for coca cultivation has reportedly doubled over the previous three years.[26]

Prohibition makes narcotics amazingly profitable, which in turn allows narco-traffickers to move their operations with relative ease in response to eradication and interdiction efforts.

Drugs, Thugs, Money, and Murder

During the reign of Peruvian President/dictator Alberto Fujimori, spy chief Vladimiro Montesinos was the *de facto* head of the Peruvian National Intelligence Service (SIN). He was also a long time drug war ally of the U.S. and head of his own anti-narcotics division (DIN), to which the CIA reportedly gave funding.[27]

In 2002, Montesinos found himself in a Lima jail cell, charged with over 80 crimes, including money laundering, organizing death squads, protecting drug traffickers, and illegal arms trafficking (selling 10,000 AK-47s to the Colombian FARC terrorists). So far over $200 million (including over $50 million in U.S. banks) of Montesinos' illicit fortune has been tracked down and seized.[28]

More than 70 high-ranking military and intelligence officials have been arrested in association with the scandal. Among them is retired General Nicolas Hermoza, Chief of the Peruvian Armed Forces Joint Command through most of the 1990s, who was arrested in 2001 for gun running and protecting drug traffickers, and who confessed that the millions in his Swiss bank account were from "illicit activities."[29]

Hermoza was America's partner in "Airbridge Denial"—the program to shoot down planes suspected to be carrying drugs. Apparently the General was making sure that his favored traffickers got through unhindered. Not so fortunate was an airplane full of American missionaries, some of whom were killed in a shoot-down in 2001. Bad publicity from shooting down a plane full of innocent Americans led to a temporary suspension of the program, which was subsequently resumed.

In January of 2002, at the request of the new Peruvian president, the U.S. released a decade's worth of diplomatic cables on the relationship between the U.S. and Montesinos.[30] As a 1999 cable noted: "Like it or not, he is the go to guy, short of the president himself, on any key issue, particularly any counter-narcotics issue."

As the declassified documents show, Washington was aware as far back as ten years ago that our "go to" guy might be working both sides of the street as a narco-trafficker. A 1991 embassy cable acknowledged that Fujimori's "senior advisor on national security matters (Montesinos) is however linked to past narcotics corruption."

U.S. officials have justified the ongoing relationship with the known murderer, drug smuggler, and terrorist gun-runner on the grounds that although "Montesinos carries a significant amount of negative baggage with him," he is a "valued ally in the drug fight…"

But of course, he was only valuable insomuch as American officials made the drug war in Peru a priority over human rights and counter-terrorism.

As Mark Bowden explains in his book *Killing Pablo*, from 1989–1993 the U.S. "underwrote a secret war in Colombia." In Medellin, Colombia's second largest city, with a justice system thoroughly corrupted by narco-dollars, the cartels killed at will. Bystanders, journalists, judges, prosecutors, police and their families—even a front-running presidential candidate—were all victims. In one 15-day period, 30 members of a special anti-narcotics unit were murdered, with the help of the Medellin police. In November of 1989, an Avianca jetliner was blown out of the sky by cartel sicarios (paid gunmen)—150 dead in a failed attempt on a politician's life.

During much of that time, Pablo Escobar, one of the most wanted men in the world—made into a billionaire and nearly a law unto himself by prohibition —hid in plain view. Intelligence provided by the U.S. to one part of the Colombian government would simply be passed on to Escobar by another.[31]

Today, the U.S is underwriting an open war in Colombia. In Medellin, in the latter half of 2002, thousands of government troops were running pitched gun battles in the streets, trying to take back an entire section of the city controlled by guerillas.[32]

Meanwhile, anti-narco dollars have joined narco-dollars as a corrupting force. An investigation was opened into an embezzlement scheme by scores of Colombian anti-drug police who had stolen millions in U.S. drug-war aid.[33] The war on drugs continues to cut a brutal swath of violence and corruption through Latin America, not just in Andean source countries, but all the way through Central America and into Mexico.

It has been more than a decade since the unprecedented U.S. invasion of Panama to arrest ex-president Manuel Noriega on drug-smuggling charges. Today Panama, a land bridge from Colombia into the rest of Central America, remains, according to the State Department's 2001 narcotics control report, a "major drug transit country," with corruption as "the major impediment to law enforcement."

In 2002, in Guatemala, a narcotics trans-shipment country, the U.S. Drug Enforcement Administration stopped all major joint counter-drug investigations because, as the *Miami Herald* reported, "narcotics gangs now permeate the (Guatemalan) agencies."[34] Corruption is so rampant, Guatemala's Department of Anti-Narcotics Operations (DOAN) was simply dissolved and all of the Justice Department's drug prosecutors fired. As one U.S. official said at the time, "Large amounts of cocaine are being trans-shipped through Guatemala with almost complete impunity."[35]

Also in the latter half of 2002, in Mexico, where the military is heavily involved in the drug war, two full generals were convicted in military court for aiding in the smuggling of cocaine and marijuana through Mexico,[36] and the entire 65th Infantry Battalion was disbanded because it had been "infiltrated by drug traffickers."[37] At the same time, the Gulf cartel, whose influence rivals the old Colombian cartels, is cutting a path of corruption and murder through some ten Mexican states in a drug trafficking pipeline that reaches all the way into Michigan and New York.[38]

And the Drugs Keep Coming

In March of 2001, the U.S. Coast Guard, in the largest maritime drug bust ever, seized 26,000 pounds of cocaine from a Belize-flagged ship, the *Svesda Maru*. An optimistic drug warrior would see this as a victory in the war on drugs. Actually, what the Svesda Maru bust suggests is that more drugs are getting through than ever before.

Over the past five years, the Coast Guard has been involved (often in joint agency operations) in the seizure of over 490,000 pounds of cocaine with a value of some $17 billion.[39] Add in hundreds, even thousands of other seizures over the same number of years by the FBI, Customs, DEA, and state and local police agencies and the numbers become numbing. Yet today in America, cocaine (like heroin) is cheaper and purer than it was 15 years ago.

In 1995, according to U.S. State Department narcotics reports, Colombia and Peru jointly produced about 690 metric tons of cocaine. In 2000, according to those same reports, they produced a combined 730 metric tons. The United Nations disagrees, putting Colombian production alone at between 800–900 tons.[40]

Whatever the case, one thing is clear. After a decade's worth of interdiction, spraying and subsidizing, there is actually more of the stuff on the world market than ever before.

In November of 2000, at the Ibereoamerican Summit of Chiefs of State in Panama City, Uruguay's President, Jorge Battle, asked the question, "Do you think that as long as that substance (cocaine) has such fantastic market power there could be any mechanism created to prevent its trafficking?"

Battle continued: "If that little powder were worth only 10 cents, there would be no organization dedicated to raising a billion dollars to finance armies in Colombia."

Speaking at President Vincente Fox's inauguration in Mexico City, Battle observed, "The day it is legalized in the U.S., it will lose value, and if loses value there will be no profit."

The FARC, AUC, and Shining Path have murdered tens of thousands of innocent people in Colombia and Peru. They have made life into living hell for many peasants and other people. They provoked the destruction of a young democracy in Peru and are doing the same to an older one in Colombia. Only because of the drug war have these terrorist groups been able to accumulate the money and power to inflict such widespread harm.

If a magic spell somehow eliminated every last molecule of coca from Colombia and Peru, Americans bent on chemically-induced self-destruction would still have many other substances available, including alcohol. Eliminate coca from Peru and Colombia, and the reduction in substance abuse in the United States would not be great.

On the other hand, the conquest of Peru by the Shining Path or Colombia by the FARC would be the worst possible disaster for the people of those nations, who would be subjected to the most vicious extremes of communist oppression. For decades, American foreign policy has correctly recognized that the establishment of a communist regime anywhere on the Latin American continent would be a disaster for the United States.

Similarly, the rise of the AUC threatens Colombia's already faltering constitutional democracy, and a takeover by para-military terrorists would subject Colombians to the brutal rule of an extreme right-wing junta and a new human-rights conflagration.

Revelations in late 2002 that the South American terrorists are cooperating with Al Qaeda and other Islamic terrorists make it all the more important to destroy the power of the South American terrorists. The way to destroy their power is to take away their money, and this can be accomplished only by ending the drug war.

The drug war in Colombia and Peru has done little to protect the health of American drug users or, for that matter, the national security of the United States. But it has caused immense harm to the innocent people of Peru and Colombia who do not use drugs. The drug war in Colombia and Peru causes the unintended—but quite visible—consequence of enriching and empowering both communist and right-wing terrorists, and even their Islamic terrorist allies.

America has a self-interest in a pragmatic foreign policy that does not indirectly assist the enemies of America, and Americans have a humanitarian interest in a good-neighbor foreign policy that does not inflict starvation, human-rights abuses, death, and the destruction of civil government on the people of Peru and Colombia. For both pragmatic and moral reasons, it is time to change the failed drug war policies in Latin America.

Notes

1. Mark Bowden, *Killing Pablo*, Atlantic Monthly Press, 2001, pages 43, 64, and 65.

2. "U.S. to speed intelligence assistance to Colombia," *Miami Herald*, October 5, 2002.

3. Professor Russell Crandell, *Plan Colombia: Should we Escalate the War on Drugs?* Cato Institute Policy Forum, March 13, 2001.

4. Bowden.

5. Ian Vasquez, *Plan Colombia: Should we Escalate the War on Drugs?* Cato Institute Policy Forum, March 13, 2001.

6. James Mack, State Department Bureau of International Narcotics and Law Enforcement Affairs, *Plan Colombia: Should we Escalate the War on Drugs?* Cato Institute Policy Forum, March 13, 2001.

7. "Colombian warlord's pledge to surrender described as ploy," *Miami Herald*, September 24, 2002.

8. "Seven held in attempts to buy weapons," *Miami Herald*, November 7, 2002.

9. Rand Beers, State Department Bureau of International Narcotics and Law Enforcement Affairs, Testimony, *Narco-Terror: The world-wide connection between drugs and terrorism*, U.S. Senate Judiciary Committee, March 13, 2002.

10. Associated Press, *Military tribunals helped Peru beat terrorism but at a cost*, December 25, 2001.

11. Associated Press, *Colombia expands military powers*, August 16, 2001.

12. Vasquez.

13. Melanie Tammen, "The drug war vs. land reform in Peru," *Cato Institute Policy Analysis* #156, July 10, 1991.

14. "Terrorism down South," *Washington Times*, December 30, 2001.

15. Mack.

16. "Uribe vows to go after rightist militias," *Miami Herald*, September 25, 2002.

17. "Colombia spraying plan may be rethought," *St. Petersburg Times*, August 17, 2001.

18. "The International War on Drugs," *Cato Handbook for Congress*, Cato Institute, 2001.

19. Agency for International Development, U.S Embassy, Lima, Peru, "Reduced illicit coca production in target areas of Peru," (no date for report).

20. Robert Brown, Acting Deputy Director, Office of National Drug Control Policy, Testimony, House Sub-Committee on Criminal Justice, Drug Policy and Human Resources, May 1, 2001.

21. "Coffee slump fuels Peru's coca bonanza," *BBC News*, September 18, 2002.

22. "Spectres stir in Peru," *The Economist*, February 14, 2002.

23. Associated Press Latin America, *Official: Eradication hurts Colombia*, October 10, 2001.

24. Economic Commission for Latin America and the Caribbean, *Social Panorama of Latin America 2001–2002*, November 7, 2002.

25. www.state.gov/g/inl/rls/nrcrpt/2001/rpt/8477.htm.

26. "Colombia's air assault on coca leaves crop, farmers in its dust," *Washington Post*, November 13, 2002.

27. Angel Paez, Center for Public Integrity, *CIA gave at least $10 million to Peru's ex-spymaster Montesinos*, December 7, 2001.

28. International Consortium of Investigative Journalists, Center for Public Integrity, *U.S. shrugged off corruption, abuse in service of the drug war*, December 7, 2001.

29. "Peru preoccupied with scandals, presidential race," *USA Today*, June, 2001.

30. "U.S. documents: Montesinos 'no choirboy'," *CNN.com*, January, 2002.

31. Bowden.

32. "Street battles expand in Medellin," *Miami Herald*, October 18, 2002.

33. Drug Reform Coordination Network, "Drug War Corruption in Colombia and Mexico," *The Week Online with DRCNet*, Issue 259, October 18, 2002, www.stopthedrugwar.org/chronicle/259/drugwarcorruption.shtml.

34. "Corruption in Guatemala worsening, Panel told," *Miami Herald*, October 11, 2002.

35. "Anti-corruption drive targets prosecutors," *Miami Herald*, October 18, 2002.

36. "Fox: Mexico to target drug use, not just Cartels," *Miami Herald*, November 5, 2002.

37. Drug Reform Coordination Network.

38. "Mexican town beset by drug-related murders," *Miami Herald*, October 18, 2002.

39. "Drugs 2001," *U.S. Coast Guard News and Events*, May 16, 2001.

40. Ted Galen Carpenter, *Plan Colombia, Washington's latest drug war failure*, Cato Institute, July 27, 2002.

10. The Social Costs of a Moral Agenda

BY FATEMA GUNJA

Fatema Gunja is the director of the Drug Policy Forum of Massachusetts, a statewide nonprofit organization working to reduce the harms associated with illegal drug use and our current drug laws. She previously served as the communications coordinator of the ACLU Drug Policy Litigation Project.

"My administration's efforts rest on an unwavering commitment to stop drug use. Acceptance of drug use is simply not an option for this administration... I believe the only humane and compassionate response to drug use is a moral refusal to accept it."—President George W. Bush, May, 2001[1]

The Price of a Simplistic Moral Agenda

Ever since the "War on Drugs" was first declared, politicians have advocated the criminalization of drugs using the rhetoric of morality. They have justified the harsh criminal penalties and collateral consequences of the drug laws by stigmatizing all drug users as moral deviants. Yet government surveys show that more than 94 million Americans ages 12 and over, representing 42% of the United States population, have used an illicit drug at least once in their lifetimes.[2] If even one quarter of these people were arrested and imprisoned for their behavior, the national landscape would be dramatically different. While we are not now and will not likely ever be at a point where such mass incarceration would be logistically possible, the language of prohibition demands exactly such a course. The nature of the debate, limited by its moral framework and strict adherence to a criminal justice response, prevents policy makers from contemplating any other path such as addressing drug policy from a public health perspective.

This refusal to consider other options reflects the discourse of righteousness that has characterized drug prohibition for decades. Guided blindly by a fierce sense of morality, drug prohibition has become a way of life, a calling that must be answered at all costs. For those who argue passionately in favor of the *status quo*, the debate is simple and the urgency is real: drugs are evil, and they cause serious harm and pose a significant threat to our communities and democracy. By this same logic, drug users are viewed as weak and flawed individuals who must be punished by the government for committing immoral acts. Punishment, instead of treatment, becomes the dominant paradigm, fueling a moral agenda that trumps science, economics, and common sense. Abstinence and zero tolerance policies become the only legislative options and the only context in which it becomes acceptable to talk about drugs.

In the post 9/11 world, this view of morality has taken on a new meaning, one that has become embedded in the language of patriotism and national security. In an atmosphere of increasing fear dominated by threats from rogue nations such as Iraq and North Korea, the government has incorporated the language of terror into everyday discourse. The war on drugs is no exception. From television ads airing during the Superbowl to full-page ads in *The New York Times*, the government's campaign on the drug war has found a new niche, one that rests on manipulating existing fear and anxiety over national security matters to advance the drug war agenda. Asa Hutchinson, former administrator of the Drug Enforcement Administration (DEA), has repeatedly advanced this theme by asserting that "most Americans now understand that drug money went at least in part to protect the terrorists that attacked American lives. Unless this drugs-terrorism linkage is broken, history is bound to repeat itself."[3] Drugs have become the scapegoat in explaining terrorism; by linking drug prohibition with patriotism, drug warriors have once again simplified the issues to ones of right versus wrong, American versus un-American.

This simplistic view of morality, originally intended to create a safer and healthier society, has instead maximized harm to our most vulnerable communities.[4] Meanwhile, prohibitionists, trapped in a moral quagmire of their own making, insist on escalating the *status quo*. Blocked by tunnel vision, their simplistic analysis of the drug war allows them to ignore its ugly realities or dismiss them as collateral consequences, sad but unavoidable and all in the name of a higher cause. But unlike the collateral damage faced in a military war, beginning and ending with military action, the caustic effects of drug policies are never-ending and are borne in the United States by a civilian population. The human costs of the drug war are so incredible that they are quickly rewriting chapters in our history of addressing race relations, social welfare, and public health. Eventually, as a country, we will have to face this reality. But until that day comes, individuals and communities continue to pay the price of a moral agenda fueled by rhetoric and conviction.

Race Relations

For many Americans today, our history of slavery and Jim Crow is a tragic memory of our past. For many young Americans who never lived through the civil rights movement, this history is firmly behind us and disconnected from the present. As a country, we have supposedly learned invaluable lessons for the future. This veneer of racial harmony is comforting and plausible enough that few realize that the next chapters of racial injustice and disempowerment are currently being written. Ironically, while there could hardly be a more immoral time in our past than the years of slavery and Jim Crow, the morality driving the drug war is again replicating the institutions and repressions of the plantation, with incredible levels of public support.

The criminal sanctions of drug laws have fallen disproportionately on minority communities, leading to the mass incarceration of blacks and Latinos. Although 72% of all drug users are white, and African-Americans and Latinos represent only 15% and 10% respectively[5] of all drug users, blacks comprise 74% of those imprisoned for drug possession. One in three black men between the ages of 20 and 29 is currently either on probation, on parole, or in prison. Latinos represent almost half of those charged with a federal drug offense. And though youth of all races use and sell drugs at similar rates, minority youth represent 60% to 75% of drug arrests.[6] In fact, black youth are incarcerated at 25 times the rate of white youth, and Latino youth at 13 times the rate of their white counterparts.[7]

Law enforcement practices fuel racial inequalities in the criminal justice system. Over the years, the DEA has helped train police to profile highway travelers for potential drug couriers.[8] This profile is based on an association between people of color and crime, creating a phenomenon known as "driving while black or brown." In Maryland, for instance, although only 21% of drivers along a stretch of Interstate 95 are minorities including blacks, Latinos, Asians, and others, 80% of those who are pulled over and searched are people of color.[9] In California, between 80% and 90% of all motorists arrested by law enforcement officials since 1991 have been members of minority groups.[10] Open-air drug busts in inner-city communities, body searches at customs checkpoints, and drug "sweeps" within minority communities further create disparities in the criminal justice system. Overzealous local prosecution and minimal discretion given to judges in the sentencing process exacerbate the situation.

Texas, for instance, has seen many racial exploits related to the war on drugs. In 1999, 10% of the African-American population in Tulia, a small town of 5,000 in the Texas Panhandle, was falsely arrested on drug charges. In 2003, a judge threw out the drug convictions of 38 Tulia defendants because they were based solely on patently unreliable testimony from an undercover agent accused of racial prejudice.

In Hearne, 15% of the town's young black men were arrested in a 2000 drug sweep based solely on the word of an informant who had agreed to implicate targeted individuals. The American Civil Liberties Union (ACLU) filed a lawsuit arguing that these race-based sweeps and unwarranted detentions of innocent citizens violate the Constitution's protections against discrimination on the basis of race, unreasonable search and seizure, and the deprivation of liberty without due process of law.

And in Dallas, dozens of Mexicans and Mexican-Americans were arrested in 2001 for possession and distribution of cocaine on the word of two undercover cops and a paid informant. Subsequent lab tests revealed that the "drug" in question was really powdered wallboard gypsum, a substance found in sheetrock.[11]

A very clear incentive exists for police departments to engage in racial profiling. Civil asset forfeiture laws allow police to seize and sell property without proving the guilt of the owner, and the police keep a portion of the assets for themselves. In fact, police departments are now dependent on forfeiture revenues in order to match funds for federal grants and regular operational costs, including the salaries of the very police officers who are responsible for the seizures.[12] By targeting minority communities whose voices and political power are marginalized,[13] law enforcement agencies can abuse the power of forfeiture without many Americans ever learning of the practice.

Social Welfare

These inequalities are not just limited to people of color; rather, the war on drugs has turned into a war on minority communities *and* a war on the poor. Across the political spectrum, politicians seem ever more determined to create new laws that single out drug users and continually punish them for often-unrelated incidents. The punitive stance of these laws stems from the basic premise behind drug prohibition that links drug use with morality: those who use drugs commit immoral acts and, therefore, should not be granted the same privileges afforded to those who choose to abstain. The end result is the passage of laws that disregard the realities of social and economic conditions and embrace a rhetoric that is as politically powerful as it is socially destructive.

In 1996, Congress passed the Welfare Reform Act that dismantled a 60-year old welfare system. Introduced and ratified in just two minutes with bipartisan support, Section 115 of the Act made felony drug offenders, including nonviolent drug offenders, ineligible for welfare benefits and food stamps. No other crime, including murder or rape, results in the loss of such benefits. As Senator Phil Gramm (R-TX), sponsor of the felony drug provision, declared, "If we are serious about our drug laws, we ought not to give people welfare benefits who are violating our Nation's drug laws."[14] Reports show that over 92,000 women, half of them women of color, are currently affected by the ban, and over 135,000 children are at risk of coming in contact with child welfare services and the criminal justice system.[15]

The Welfare Reform Act also allows states to impose drug testing as a condition for receiving welfare benefits, despite the fact that welfare recipients are no more likely to use drugs than are members of the general public.[16] Michigan became the first and only state to implement mandatory random drug testing as a condition for receiving welfare benefits. Refusal to be tested resulted in denial or termination of Family Independence Agency (FIA) income support and the possible termination of medical insurance, food stamps, and support for pregnant women or nursing mothers. FIA participants who submitted to drug testing also risked losing vital assistance if they "failed to comply" with a substance abuse treatment plan.[17] The courts recently struck down this policy, recognizing the law's inherent stigma and discrimination against the poor.[18]

Similar federal legislation on public housing,[19] higher education,[20] adoption, and foster care[21] follow the welfare model, denying drug offenders the most basic needs for survival. In theory, these laws are justified mostly on punitive or deterrent grounds. In reality, their effects delay successful reintegration of ex-drug offenders into society, leading many back to prison. The destructive impact on their families and communities is reflected in high rates of poverty, instability, and crime. Instead of implementing rational economic and social policies, lawmakers continue targeting the poor with punitive drug laws and succeed only in trapping them in a vicious cycle of poverty and helplessness, with little chance of escape.

Public Health

Finally, while concern for the health and well-being of our nation has purportedly been one of the driving forces behind drug prohibition, federal drug policies actually undermine public health initiatives, helping to expedite health epidemics such as HIV/AIDS and promising to deny relief to those suffering from chronic pain.

In 1998, a total of 16,926 people died of drug-induced causes in the United States, both legal and illegal.[22] By year-end 1999, there were a total of 733,374 reported cases of AIDS in the U.S., and 35% of these were linked to injection drug use.[23]

Most advanced democracies have implemented harm reduction policies, including needle exchange programs to prevent the spread of AIDS and other blood-transmitted diseases. As the U.S. Surgeon General, Dr. David Satcher, found, "after reviewing all of the research to date, the senior scientists of the Department [of Health and Human Services] and I have unan-imously agreed that there is conclusive scientific evidence that syringe exchange programs, as part of a comprehensive HIV prevention strategy, are an effective public health intervention that reduces the transmission of HIV and does not encourage the use of illegal drugs."[24]

Federal drug policies, however, block funding for clean needles, make it illegal in most states for injection drug users to possess syringes,[25] and arrest anyone attempting to provide clean injection equipment using private funds.[26] Even in states such as Connecticut and Massachusetts that have recognized the importance of needle exchange and have passed health initiatives permitting these programs, law enforcement continues to harass participants.[27] Given the gravity of the HIV/AIDS epidemic in the United States and the effectiveness of needle exchange in stemming this tide, refusal by the federal government to even consider syringe exchange undercuts the very premise of the drug war as an effort to save lives.

Federal drug policies also target the lives of chronically ill patients. Since 1996, 10 states have recognized that marijuana can reduce nausea and eye pressure; increase appetite; and control muscle spasms, seizures and chronic pain for those suffering from serious, and often terminal, illnesses. These states, with a clear mandate from the public, have passed medical marijuana laws permitting the use of marijuana for patients suffering from diseases such as HIV/AIDS, cancer, and glaucoma. Since California sanctioned medical marijuana in 1996, providing protection from state prosecution to patients who choose to use marijuana recommended by their doctors, federal officials have swiftly responded by pledging to punish individuals involved with medical marijuana. These threats have targeted doctors and patients, undermining the unique nature of doctor-patient relationships that rely on free speech and causing undue hardship for patients already suffering from terminal illnesses and chronic pain.[28]

In recent years, the DEA has raided a number of medical marijuana suppliers in California; this includes the 2002 raid of a marijuana farm in Santa Cruz, California, which resulted in the arrest of the owners who grow marijuana for a medical users' club, despite tremendous support from the local community, government, and law enforcement.[29] The prosecution and conviction of Ed Rosenthal in Oakland led to national coverage of several jurors protesting the fact that the judge refused to allow the jury to hear that Rosenthal had been growing marijuana for medical purposes. The jurors apologized for the conviction, generating significant controversy about the federal prosecutorial tactics. In March, 2003, another medical marijuana provider, Scott Imler, entered a guilty plea for fear of being convicted in the same manner as Rosenthal.[30]

Conclusion

This is the grim nature of the war on drugs. It started out as a moral premise, a feel-good policy that quickly blossomed into an awesome ground war, complete with American casualties. Instead of blindly continuing down this path of destruction, as a nation we need to reassess where we are and where we want to be.

If our ultimate goal is to reduce harm and create a society that values racial and social equality, the time has come to reexamine our current drug policy and explore alternative options. If, however, our aim is to preach morality even if the consequences themselves are immoral, then we need not do a thing.

Notes

1. Remarks by the president in "Announcement of the Director of the Office of Drug Control Policy," 2001, www.whitehouse.gov/news/releases/2001/05/20010510-1.html.

2. U.S. Department of Health and Human Services, Substance Abuse and Mental Health Services Administration (SAMHSA), *2001 National Household Survey on Drug Abuse: Volume 1, Summary of National Findings*. Rockville, MD: Office of Applied Studies, August, 2002, page 109, Table H.1, and page 110, Table H.2.

3. Asa Hutchinson, Speech, Conservative Political Action Conference, Arlington, VA, *News from DEA*, 2002, www.usdoj.gov/dea/speeches/s020102p.html.

4. While overall spending on the drug war has increased exponentially from $65 million during the Nixon administration to $18 billion during the Clinton administration, and while the number of prisoners serving time for drug offenses has increased tenfold since 1980, drugs are more readily available today than at any time in our past. Teenagers and adults alike continue to use drugs, and violent drug-related crime continues to endanger and define life in our cities. Hearings on Federal Drug Enforcement before the Senate Committee on Investigations, U.S. Congress, 1975 and 1976. Office of National Drug Control Policy, *National Drug Control Budget, Executive Summary, Fiscal Year 2002*, page 2, Table 1, www.csdp.org/research/budget_fy2002.pdf. Margot Roosevelt, "The War Against the War on Drugs," *Time*, May 7, 2001, www.cnn.com/ALLPOLITICS/time/2001/05/07/against.html.

5. SAMHSA, *National Household Survey on Drug Abuse: Summary Report 1998*, Rockville, MD, 1999, page 13.

6. Kevin J. Strom, U.S. Department of Justice (U.S.DOJ), Bureau of Justice Statistics, *Profile of State Prisoners Under Age 18, 1985–1997*, Washington, D.C., February, 2000, page 6.

7. "¿Donde Esta La Justicia?" *Executive Summary: Building Blocks for Youth*, July, 2002, www.buildingblocksforyouth.org/latino_rpt/exec_eng.html.

8. California Legislature's Task Force on Government Oversight, *Executive Summary: Operation Pipeline*, September, 1999, www.aclunc.org/discrimination/webb-report.html.

9. David Harris, *Driving While Black: Racial Profiling on our Nation's Highways: An ACLU Special Report*, American Civil Liberties Union, June, 1999.

10. *Ibid.*

11. Drug Reform Coordination Network, "Backlash Emerges as Texas Drug Task Forces Run Amok," *The Week Online with DRCnet*, Issue 223, February 8, 2002, www.stopthedrugwar.org/chronicle/223/texasbacklash.shtml.

12. Eric Blumenson and Eva Nilsen, "Policing for Profit: The Drug War's Hidden Economic Agenda," *Chicago Law Review*, Winter 1998.

13. Almost all states deny convicted felons the right to vote while incarcerated, but in 13 states, ex-felons remain disenfranchised for the rest of their lives. Felony disenfranchisement laws, first enacted as part of Jim Crow, continue to have a disproportionate impact on African-Americans: 13% of black men, totaling 1.4 million people, are denied the right to vote. If the current pattern in incarceration levels continues, 40% of the black male population in some states will be unable to vote.

14. Patricia Allard, "Life Sentences: Denying Welfare Benefits To Women Convicted Of Drug Offenses," *Policy Report*, The Sentencing Project, February, 2002, www.sentencingproject.org/news/lifesentences.pdf.

15. *Ibid.*

16. National Institutes of Health, *NIAAA Researchers Estimate Alcohol and Drug Use, Abuse, and Dependence Among Welfare Recipients*, 1996, www.nih.gov/news/pr/oct96/niaaa-23.htm.

17. Michigan Legislature, "Social Welfare Act," *Michigan Compiled Laws*, 1999.

18. American Civil Liberties Union, *ACLU Hails Appeals Court Decision Striking Down Michigan's Welfare Drug Testing Law*, 2003, www.aclu.org/DrugPolicy/DrugPolicy.cfm?ID=12317&c=79.

19. In 1996, the Department of Housing and Urban Development (HUD) enacted a new "One Strike and You're Out" policy as a way of addressing the issue of crime in public housing complexes. The guidelines require that if the tenant, another member of the household, a guest, or any other person

connected with the tenant is involved with drugs, the entire household can be evicted. In 2002, the Supreme Court upheld this policy in *HUD v. Rucker*.

20. In 1998, Congress passed an amendment to the Higher Education Act of 1965 that denies federal financial aid only to individuals with a drug conviction. Over 90,000 students have so far been denied aid under this amendment. To learn more, visit www.raiseyourvoice.com.

21. In 1997, Congress passed the Adoption and Safe Families Act which includes a lifetime ban on adoption and foster care for those convicted of child-related crimes (child abuse, rape, neglect, etc.) and a five year ban for those convicted of physical assault, battery, or drug-related crimes.

22. Centers for Disease Control (CDC) notes, "The category 'drug-induced causes' includes not only deaths from dependent and nondependent use of drugs (legal and illegal use), but also poisoning from medically prescribed and other drugs. It excludes accidents, homicides and other causes indirectly related to drug use. Also excluded are newborn deaths due to mother's drug use." CDC also notes the total number of deaths in the U.S. in 1998 was 2,337,256 (Sheila L. Murphy, "Deaths: Final Data for 1998," *National Vital Statistics Reports*, Volume 48, Number 11, July, 2000, pages 1 and 10, www.cdc.gov/nchs/data/nvs48_11.pdf).

23. CDC, *HIV/AIDS Surveillance Report*, Volume 11, Number 2, December, 1999, page 14, Table 5, www.cdc.gov/hiv/stats/hasr1102/table5.htm. The percentage given is based on the number of AIDS cases for which the method of exposure is known.

24. U.S. Surgeon General Dr. David Satcher, *Evidence-Based Findings on the Efficacy of Syringe Exchange Programs: An Analysis from the Assistant Secretary for Health and Surgeon General of the Scientific Research Completed Since April 1998*, Department of Health and Human Services, 2000.

25. State-established needle exchange programs currently operate in California, Colorado, Connecticut, Illinois, Maryland, Massachusetts, Minnesota, New York, Ohio, Pennsylvania, Rhode Island, Washington, and Wisconsin. Each of these 13 states has passed laws exempting program participants from criminal liability for carrying hypodermic syringes. According to AIDS Action, a leading advocacy group, there are currently 140 needle exchange programs operating in 39 states, the District of Columbia and the territories (including the 13 states where the programs are legal).

26. E.g., *State v. McCague*, 714 A.2d 937, 944 (NJ Superior Court Appellate Division, 1998) (finding members of nonprofit organization operating needle exchange program guilty of giving hypodermic needle to another, even if members acted with purpose of halting spread of AIDS virus). Ricky N. Bluthenthal, Alex H. Kral, *et al.*, "Drug paraphernalia laws and injection-related infectious disease risk among drug injectors," *Journal of Drug Issues*, Volume 29, Number 1, 1999, pages 1–16.

27. In 2001, a federal district court issued a permanent injunction prohibiting the Bridgeport, CT police department from harassing needle exchange participants of the city program in *Doe v. Bridgeport*. In 2002, the Massachusetts Supreme Court ruled in *Massachusetts v. Landry* that members of lawful needle exchange programs may possess needles obtained from the programs throughout the state, even in cities or towns that have not allowed the programs themselves to locate there. For more information, see www.aclu.org/drugpolicy.

28. In 2002, the Ninth Circuit Court of Appeals ruled that the federal government could not revoke the licenses of California doctors who recommend medical marijuana to their patients in *Conant v. Walters*. For more information, see www.aclu.org/drugpolicy.

29. In 1992, 77% of Santa Cruz voters approved a measure ending the medical prohibition of marijuana. Four years later, state voters—including 74% of those in Santa Cruz—voted in favor of Proposition 215, allowing marijuana for medicinal purposes. And then again, in 2000, the city council approved an ordinance allowing medical marijuana to be grown and used without a prescription.

30. Jacob Sullum, "Tokers and Terrorists," *Reason Online*, March 28, 2003, www.reason.com/sullum/032803.shtml.

11. A Frightening New Trend in America

BY NICOLAS EYLE

Nicolas Eyle is the founder and executive director of ReconsiDer (www.reconsider.org), a New York-based non-profit organization that promotes alternatives to our current drug policy.

When an assistant district attorney recently told me that she doesn't handle any of the county's drug cases, I was taken aback. With drug cases filling our courts, how could she not handle them? "Let me clarify that," she said, " I don't handle drug cases *per se*. I handle the homicides, assaults, robberies and child abuse cases, probably 75% of which are related to drug prohibition."

Her point was clear: The drug war doesn't reduce crime and violence. It breeds them. And the public is angry—but at the wrong people.

Shouldn't we be angry at prohibition and those who create this forbidden fruit? At those who throw so many of our children in jail? Who take away their chance for financial aid for college? Who make our children grow up in a culture of violence created largely by the illegality of the drug trade? Who saddle them with felony convictions that will remain with them for their entire lives, long after they've stopped committing their "youthful indiscretions"? Who waste billions of our tax dollars each year on a policy that increases, instead of decreases, the harms caused by drug use among our children?

None of these punitive measures helps us. Yet, recent news stories make me think that this misdirected anger is only growing stronger in America. Like young children lacking the communication and problem-solving skills necessary to resolving conflict, we lash out in anger when we think others are misbehaving.

A newspaper reported that when Ramon Eduardo Arellano-Felix, a Mexican drug lord, was arrested, law enforcement worried that the breakup of this gang would result in a large-scale war, with drug cartels fighting over who would replace Arellano-Felix in the drug smuggling business. They worried because they knew this would happen. They know that whenever a drug dealer is taken off the street, another takes his place. If police arrest a burglar, there is one less burglar and burglaries go down for a while. If they arrest a drug dealer, they simply create a job opening, and a turf battle ensues. Rival factions fight over control of the market, and often innocent people get hurt in the resulting battle. What scares me is the realization that police know that the result of their drug busts will be loss of life—and no difference in the availability of drugs on the street—yet many continue to support prohibition.

Police officers have actually told me that after a major drug bust, they wait and see if it is followed by a series of murders. If it is, they consider this proof that they have indeed arrested the top dealers in that market and the smaller fish were fighting over who was to take over the business. So, while gun battles were raging in the streets, there were back-slapping and congratulations at the precinct house. The carnage among dealers proved they were doing their job!

As for the users—they don't stop using when their source is killed. They find another source. The new source's product is often different, perhaps a bit purer, or cut with something different. With no way to judge the strength or purity of their new supply, there are frequently deaths from overdose. This, too, is predictable, and again, law enforcement knows this will probably happen.

Another recent news story indicates this trend of focusing on punishment rather than prevention has spread to other areas of law enforcement.

Newspapers reported that two upstate New York towns were changing the look of the cars they used for traffic enforcement by painting them black and removing the roof lights. Why? So they could give more tickets. The cars wouldn't be so noticeable, so police would have a better chance of catching speeders.

Why would these communities choose this approach, when the deterrent effect of a marked police car is well known? For years, police departments have parked empty police cars alongside roadways and have seen traffic slow down immediately as drivers see the vehicle. Everyone was happy with the results; traffic slowed, drivers drove more cautiously, and streets were safer.

But today, the goal isn't to slow traffic. It's to catch and punish speeders (and collect fines). A driver coming into town from the highway would slow down on his way through town if he saw a police car alongside the road. Now he speeds through town, and is chased and ticketed a mile or two down the road.

Which scenario is safer for the kids crossing the street?

Yet another news report indicated to me that punishment, not prevention, is our main goal. This story involved a teacher who saw a student drop a bag of marijuana on the floor at school. The teacher picked it up, returned it to the student, and reported the student to the principal. The result? The teacher was arrested for criminal sale of marijuana. Even though no money changed hands, the act of giving the student the marijuana technically constitutes "sale." What is the point here? To me, it's clear that the local sheriff was determined to arrest somebody, even if there was clearly no intent to commit a crime.

These stories are reinforcing my belief that law enforcement is creating dangers for the very people it's supposed to "serve and protect." Perhaps they've lost sight of these goals in their rush to punish lawbreakers. But police are charged with providing for the public safety. That should be their primary concern.

Americans imprison more of their countrymen than any other country on the planet. We have about three-quarters of the world's prisoners but only about one-fifth of the world's population. We also lock them up for extraordinarily long periods of time. No other Western country routinely hands out the 10- and 20-year sentences that are commonplace here. Mandatory minimum sentences are common. New York State's famous Rockefeller Drug Laws, for instance, call for a 15-year-to-life sentence for certain drug charges—with no parole.

The Eighth Amendment states, "Excessive bail shall not be required, nor excessive fines imposed, nor cruel and unusual punishments inflicted." It would seem obvious, based on the text of the amendment, that when fines are out of proportion to a crime, when they are "excessive," they violate the Constitution. Yet these days the Supreme Court has upheld all sorts of extraordinarily punitive sentences as constitutional. Recently the court threw out the appeals of two men sentenced under California's "three strikes and you're out" law. One of the men received 25 years without parole for stealing golf clubs, and the other 50 years for stealing children's videotapes. Two members of the majority in that decision, Scalia and Thomas, stated that they believe the Eighth Amendment prohibits "only extreme sentences that are 'grossly disproportionate' to the crime." Twenty-five years for shoplifting is apparently not considered grossly disproportionate to these judges.

Most criminologists will tell you that it is not the severity of punishment that deters crime, but the certainty of it. Yet we persist in pretending the opposite. Ask yourself, "If the fine for speeding increased from $100 to $200, would I stop speeding?" My guess is, you'd still speed. Why? Because you would be reasonably sure that you won't get caught. If, however, a system existed whereby speeders were caught 99% of the time, you'd be far more likely to obey the law, even if the fine was only $50.

Try as they might, law enforcement has never caught more than a tiny fraction of drug dealers and users.

Not content with charging law enforcement with punishing people for possession or sale of controlled substances, today American civilians can partake in this punishment frenzy. The rise of the drug-testing industry from being almost nonexistent 20 years ago to a multi-million dollar industry today is further evidence of America's passion to punish. School administrators, factory managers, and store owners can, through the increasingly common practice of drug testing, detect those who have used marijuana in the past, and punish them as well. This is accepted because it hides under the mantle of "workplace safety." Of course, whether or not someone used marijuana, say, two weeks before the drug test has nothing to do with safety (the effects of the drug have long since worn off); still, we are able to intrude into a person's personal life under the guise of workplace safety. Were we serious about safety, we would insist on some form of impairment testing that showed whether or not the worker was fit for duty before he started work, not whether or not he may have consumed an illegal drug at some time in the past. Such testing devices exist and have proven to be effective tools at detecting not only illegal drug use, but a host of other causes of workplace accidents such as lack of sleep or alcohol impairment.

Ostensibly the rationale for drug testing is to find the drug user and help him, but the reality is quite different. Testing positive for drugs, regardless of one's performance on the job or in school, typically results in some form of punishment. A schoolchild testing positive will usually be forced to cease all extracurricular activities after school (giving him more time to hang around the street with his drug-using friends). The theory is that the punishment will deter him from using drugs. Pre-employment drug screening ensures a job applicant won't be hired if the test comes back positive. Now, even the occasional, recreational user of marijuana is forced to become an unemployed, poor drug user who can't get work and may have to turn to robbery and even violent crime to survive. How this is supposed to help ensure the public's safety is not clear to me. What is clear is that this fits into the punishment trend.

Catching someone in the commission of a crime is not enough, either. Police still entrap citizens daily. Female officers dress in provocative clothes and walk the streets waiting for some unsuspecting male to proposition them so they can arrest them. Undercover officers talk people into selling them drugs so they can arrest them later. Sometimes these setups are so outrageous that they are thrown out in court, but this is the exception to the rule. A recent case involved officers not only urging someone to buy drugs for them, but even providing him with money to do so. He agreed, used the officer's money to make the buy, and was promptly arrested. In another case in New York City, when an innocent man pushed away an undercover officer who accosted him on the street and was badgering him to buy drugs, he was shot and killed. Remember, these cases involve consensual crimes. There is no complainant. Still, we find the need to go to these extraordinary lengths to catch and punish people.

Perhaps this alarming trend toward punishment at all costs is sparked by our inability to eliminate or vastly reduce drug sales and use. Perhaps this frustration causes us to strike out in anger. We seem to get some sort of satisfaction in knowing that even though the behavior has not ceased, some of the perpetrators are suffering.

But our war on drugs is destroying far more lives than the drugs themselves do. Families are destroyed as a result of parents being sent to prison for drug possession. Almost two million American children have one or both parents in prison. Parents doing prison time for drug possession do not generally make good parents. They're not there. Kids grow up in broken homes, look for easy money, get into trouble with the law. Children grow up neglected at home and roaming desolate neighborhoods, only to resort to crime to survive.

Houses are destroyed in the course of drug raids. Countless inner-city homes now sit, abandoned, because of the damage caused by narcotics officers and SWAT teams as they carried out a drug raid. These houses often drop off the tax rolls and become host to squatters and addicts until they burn down or are torn down by the city. Entire neighborhoods, even entire cities, are destroyed by this breaking up of families and houses. All this destruction—and the drugs are still there, cheaper, purer, and more available then ever. Needless to say, these neighborhoods become breeding grounds for criminals.

Perhaps we see these problems as insoluble. Perhaps, after generations of our nation's leaders telling us to do what they say and we'll win the war on drugs, we're resigned to it. "Nothing has worked," we're told. "We need to get tougher." But we have tried only this one approach—prohibition— and that, as we should have learned when we prohibited alcohol, only brings violence. Alcohol prohibition was not repealed because Americans suddenly decided they wanted to drink. It was repealed because of the dramatic increases in crime and violence so obviously tied to it. With its repeal, crime dropped steadily until the start of our current drug war, when it began rising rapidly.

To change our course will be difficult. It involves admitting we made a mistake, something that's very hard for human beings to do. It's easier to continue doing what we've always done. To point fingers at others, and say that "they" are causing the problem. That "they" cause all the crime. That "they" use drugs. And so "they" must be punished.

There is a blood-lust in America today, a desire to punish those who offend, no matter what the cost. Punishment, not safety, seems to be our goal. But do traffic police sneaking around in unmarked cars really make our streets safer? Do police scanning houses from aircraft using heat sensors to detect marijuana growers really make our neighborhoods safer?

Over 170 years ago, Sir Robert Peel, the founder of modern policing, said, "The test of police efficiency is the *absence* of crime and disorder, and *not* the visible evidence of police action in dealing with them."

Peel's lesson is lost on us today, as police departments, district attorneys and politicians brag about soaring arrest statistics and conviction rates, and foster a climate of violence.

A nice, in-the-open police force deters crime. A marked police car parked under a streetlight slows traffic. A friendly uniformed cop walking the beat ensures orderly streets. Isn't that what we really want?

12. How Drug Laws Hurt Gunowners

BY JOHN ROSS

John Ross is the author of the novel Unintended Consequences. *He has also written* Self-Defense Laws and Violent Crime Rates in the United States *and technical articles for* Precision Shooting *and* Machine Gun News. *Ross is a certified personal protection instructor and an investment broker and financial adviser in St. Louis, Missouri.*

I frequently use the term "gun culture" in my writing. The popularity of my novel *Unintended Consequences* has helped bring this term into widespread use, even by the mainstream media. For those not familiar with the term, let me define it here, in one sentence. The gun culture is comprised of those people for whom shooting skills hold great importance.

People in the gun culture do not necessarily own a lot of guns, just as accomplished musicians may not own many instruments, though of course some do. However, members of the gun culture shoot whatever guns they do own quite a bit. They are voracious consumers of ammunition because they are serious about improving and maintaining their skills, just as serious musicians practice daily, and serious readers spend hundreds (or thousands) of dollars and many hours each year on books. An estimated 100 million people in this country own at least one gun, but these are not all members of the gun culture.

Though a few police officers are members of the gun culture, these days most are not. This should not surprise anyone who thinks about it for a few moments. Police have many responsibilities, but firing a gun in the line of duty is something many never need to do during decades of service.

Police training is comprised mostly of the things officers have to do every day: investigative techniques, crime scene evidence gathering, interrogation, report writing, radar gun operation, etc. Firearms training is all too often last on the list. This works fine, for there are many officers who go work for over 20 years without ever drawing their duty weapon, although frequently the officers who are best with guns are the ones least likely to use them. It's a truism that the only gun that most officers have ever used in the line of duty is a radar gun.

It was not always so. Years ago, people with military and/or hunting experience gravitated toward law enforcement. These were the people who liked to hunt and target shoot, and were apt to develop marksmanship skills on their own for enjoyment, whether required to or not. They were members of the gun culture.

Now, such people are actively screened out of many departments (and virtually all urban ones) with psychological testing. I cannot remember the last time I met a big-city police chief who was in the gun culture, so in big departments, the tendency is more noticeable the higher up you look.

We now have entire urban police departments without a single officer in the gun culture, and the result is that no one on the force fires any handgun except when he or she has to. In many cases this is 50 rounds a year. By contrast, many dedicated sport shooters fire ten times that many rounds per week. In some cases, where range facilities have closed or where there is a friendly supervisor, officers go years without firing a single practice shot. Get a police instructor's certificate, train some officers, and get an eye-opening education on current police firearms proficiency.

This situation, where few police are members of the gun culture, has created an unfortunate mentality among police chiefs in big cities. Though the general shooting public has greater gun-handling skills than the general law enforcement community, many big-city chiefs have adopted attitudes of "we're the professionals and you can't be trusted" when it comes to private citizens and guns. This is especially true when the issue of lawfully carrying concealed weapons comes up. To this unfortunate state of events, we have to add another reality...

The Drug Culture

Despite (or because of) the expenditure of billions of taxpayer dollars, there is now a large and growing worldwide drug culture. These are people for whom using recreational drugs is a regular part of their lives. There are also people who do not use recreational drugs, but accept without rancor the fact that others do. This latter group is huge. Consider this little gem: on February 8, 1998, 26-year-old Canadian snowboarder Ross Rebagliati won the men's giant slalom in the Olympic Winter Games in Nagano, Japan, then immediately tested positive for marijuana and was stripped of his gold medal on February 10. (For those who don't know this, pot is not a drug which enhances athletic performance.) The following day, the IOC returned the medal, saying it did not have the power to take it. The Olympic Court for Arbitration of Sport (CAS) voted unanimously to reinstate Rebagliati's gold medal. The unspoken understanding here is pretty obvious: hey, he's a snowboarder, for Christ's sake, of course he smokes pot—you might as well start testing rugby teams for beer consumption! The other unspoken understanding is that no one really believes that marijuana is all that bad for your health.

This reality was driven home four years later at the 2002 Winter Olympics. In front of journalists, one competitor held out an imaginary microphone and, in a mock newscaster's voice, "interviewed" his teammate (who had just won a silver medal snowboarding): "Danny Kass, you've just won the silver medal. What's next? Are you going to go home and—smoke crack?" Kass started to answer in the enthusiastic affirmative, then gave an exaggerated double-take in recognition of his surroundings, and launched into "Noooo, noooo, drugs are bad! Bad!"

The journalists ate it up, and it was reported in one of the major weekly news magazines. So did the public, who thought it was hilarious when they read about it. It's common knowledge, assumed and expected: college students and other young people smoke pot and enjoy other recreational drugs such as ecstasy. Bodybuilders and other strength athletes do illegal anabolic steroids. Hollywood types who can afford it hire call girls. Pro athletes and other people with way too much money do cocaine. The general public *does not care* if productive members of our society (people who pay income tax) do these things. They may pretend to care, however, because there is one segment that cares about this issue a very great deal.

The Police Culture

Years ago, we called policemen "peace officers." Our mental image of

117

a peace officer in a rural area was Andy Griffith, resolving disputes with gentle reason and only rarely needing to back it up with something stronger. In a big city like New York, a peace officer was the cop who walked his beat on the sidewalks of his precinct. He knew all the neighborhood kids by name, who their parents were, and if a kid was being raised without a father.

The peace officer has now in many jurisdictions been replaced by the "law enforcement officer." There wasn't much money in being a peace officer, but there is a veritable gold mine in law enforcement. The laws most regularly being broken are speed limits and anti-drug laws. Thus, Andy Griffith may now be a deputy with a radar gun, hiding on a 200-yard section of limited-access highway that traverses a corner of his jurisdiction. The fines he collects make his department very flush indeed. Never mind that the people who live in his town are unaffected by the speeders on the interstate.

The beat cop is largely gone, too, replaced by faceless two-person teams in patrol cars who drive around all day but don't know any of the people in the neighborhood because they never stop and get out of the patrol car to talk to them. Urban departments now have extensive drug squads, and whenever a big bust happens, there is always a big pile of cash. Who's to say the cops need to turn in all of it? Or any of it, for that matter.

Make no mistake, money (and power) is the key. Automatic photo radar is here, to nail people running lights at intersections and fine them. Interesting catch: municipalities installing photo radar are reducing the time the "yellow" is on for their traffic signals from five seconds to three. Why? Because if the yellow is on for five seconds, almost everyone stops in time.

Similarly, to help justify ever-increasing budgets, more and more substances are demonized and scheduled as illegal drugs. A personal example: I sometimes have trouble getting to sleep, and I used to go to health food stores to buy a natural supplement (the body itself produces it) called gammahydroxybutyrate.* When I took this with water at bedtime, I would fall into deep REM sleep within 20 minutes and awake five hours later feeling great. Now GHB is illegal and called a "date-rape drug," because somebody allegedly raped a girl after she took it and fell asleep. News flash: there are other sleep aids out there, including the heavily advertised Ambien®. Ambien is addictive, which is why I won't use it anymore, though that hasn't stopped the people who get prescriptions from getting more than one billion dollars worth of Ambien every year. Is Ambien a "date-rape drug"? I guarantee if a guy powders two pills (they're really small) and mixes them into his date's margarita, she'll fall asleep.

Demonizing more substances, personal activities, and inanimate objects means more power, money, and authority for law enforcement, and less for you and me. What if things were not this way? How many people would choose to be policemen if their only permitted duties were to apprehend those who had committed crimes against known, specific victims who had made a complaint? What if the entire drug squad was disbanded and the officers reassigned to burglary and stolen-property recovery? What if the vice squad cops had to quit getting freebies from hookers and join robbery and homicide? What if the speed trap cops were all reassigned to auto theft? We'll probably never get to find out.

I realize I am being harsh here and that someone reading this in a small town in Wyoming may see no resemblance here to his local department. But make no mistake: being a policeman has become, for many people, a lifestyle choice. More than once I have heard a cop extol the joys of "f—ing with people" as a benefit of his employment. But the greatest benefit is something else.

Police are Exempt

How often have we seen a police car cruise by us at a speed 20 miles per hour over the posted limit? How often do we see police cars parked in no parking zones, and policemen getting free meals? How often do we read about the big undercover drug operation, where officers immerse themselves in the drug trade for months at a time, buying and using drugs to gain the trust of drug traffickers? In all these cases, the officers are exempt from the laws everyone else must obey. When the laws don't appear to apply to the police themselves, it amplifies the "us versus them" police mentality that is so damaging to good relations with the public.

But these laws that the police get to ignore pale next to the most appalling problem: out-and-out stealing from citizens, and sometimes murdering them. The asset forfeiture laws as currently being administered encourage police to steal from the people they are supposed to be helping. Entire farms have been seized because police found a few marijuana plants growing on the property (it does grow in the wild, after all).

In California, millionaire Donald Scott was shot dead by law enforcement agents in his own home in 1992. Several dozen law enforcement officers from various federal agencies stormed his 200-acre ranch. Scott, thinking he was being robbed, came to investigate with a gun in his hand and was immediately shot and killed.

The warrant permitting this invasion had been issued based upon the claim that Scott was growing marijuana. None was found, and the warrant was later ruled invalid when the real reason for the raid was discovered.

The real motive was to increase the size of a national park next to Scott's ranch, but Scott had refused to sell his property. That was when park service officers realized they could use the asset forfeiture laws to get Scott's land for free.

Stories like this one happen frequently. Most of them don't involve millionaires, so they don't make the news. According to the Washington-based Institute for Justice, the number of federal seizures of property under asset forfeiture laws increased fifteenfold between 1985 and 1991. This is one of the many great tragedies of the drug war.

The Law of Unintended Consequences

I said earlier that there was once a strong connection between shooting interests and law enforcement. Though that is no longer true in most large departments, many shooters and gunowners don't realize it. They think of the older cops they knew years ago who were shooting buddies, and still see themselves as law enforcement's strongest supporters.

They haven't yet figured out that the rules have changed. The drug war has taught the police how to steal without running afoul of internal affairs. The asset forfeiture laws abused by the drug cops in the drug war are now starting to be abused by the gun cops in the War on Gunowners.

Many gunowners, thinking they are showing support for law enforcement, take offense at the notion of people using any drug the government says is evil, and wouldn't dream of lighting up a joint or ingesting the "date-rape" drug GHB. Drugs are bad, and drug dealers are worse; lock 'em up and throw away the key, if you can't figure out a way to execute 'em.

This is a dangerous attitude to take, given the draconian antigun laws that have been sprouting up around the country. The gun that was perfectly legal to own last month has become illegal today. (Police, of course, are exempt.) The list of banned guns keeps growing, just like the list of banned substances or prohibited activities. Law enforcement's standard response to a law's failure is, *we need more of it.*

This always creates unintended consequences the exact opposite of the desired result. Our country is awash in cocaine as a direct result of the DEA's concerted efforts in the 1970s and early 1980s to stop marijuana imports. There was a big crackdown, and the DEA seized many tons of marijuana bales. This caused major importers, producers, and smugglers to rethink their businesses, and realize that cocaine was much less bulky than marijuana and the per-ounce value much greater. Thus, cocaine was easier and more profitable to import, and well worth the extra money and effort it cost to produce. This resulted in extra profit left over to buy off more cops, customs agents, and judges. Is that what the authorities had in mind? And since the switch in the big players' focus to cocaine gave the DEA more work to do, it made marijuana importation more attractive to smaller new players in the drug game. The result: more of all illicit drugs. And then the cycle repeated itself with crack.

The drug war is like the man who says, "I've sawed this board off three times, and it's still too short." As long as we continue redoubling our efforts in the drug war, it will be used as the law-enforcement template for other prohibitions. Guns are at the top of the list. We already have entire classes of guns that are banned. It won't take much to add to the list every year. Or every month. When it gets to where people can't get any of the guns they want legally, smuggling will start. Then it will really start to get interesting.

Unlike drugs, guns don't smell any different than, say, tractor parts. So forget about using drug-sniffing dogs in the warehouses full of shipping containers. Also, unlike heroin, there are factories all over the world producing weapons with complete legality and the official blessing of their governments. So forget about having other governments even pretend to help the U.S. stop world gun production.

Last of all, the manpower used to catch people smuggling small arms (that were legal to own a short while ago) has to come from somewhere. Every law enforcement asset focused on catching the groups trying to sneak shipping containers full of carbines into the U.S. is one less asset focused on catching the guy with the nuke.

Come to think of it, that's a pretty compelling reason to end the drug war and reassign all the drug cops, isn't it?

Note

*Biologist Henri-Marie Laborit synthesized this compound in 1960 and publicly advocated its use as a safe sleep aid and anti-aging supplement until his death in 1995. He considered his work with GHB as great an accomplishment as the work he is best known for, developing the therapeutic use of Thorazine as the first drug to effectively combat schizophrenia.

13. The Drug War as the Problem

BY DOUG CASEY

Doug Casey, a best-selling financial writer, is the author of The International Man *and* Crisis Investing. *He writes a column for* World Net Daily, *serves as contributing editor for* Liberty, *and publishes* International Speculator *(www.dougcasey.com).*

On April 5, 1992, reporter Steve Kroft of CBS News' *60 Minutes* reported about forfeiture laws, dealing with two victims. Kroft introduced the segment by stating, "If someone were to tell you that, thanks to the forfeiture laws, a law enforcement officer can seize your property, your car, and your money without ever charging you with anything, without arresting you and without ever convicting you of a crime, you'd probably say, 'That's not possible—not in America.' Well, it is. Just ask Willy Jones."

Willy Jones is a black man who ran a small landscaping business outside of Nashville. Once or twice a year he went out of state to buy shrubbery. In 1991, Jones went to the Nashville airport and paid cash for a round-trip ticket to Houston. A few minutes later, two Nashville police officers stopped, questioned him and, with Jones' permission, searched him, finding $9,000 in his money belt. Jones insisted the money was for shrubbery, since he got a better deal when he paid cash. The police didn't believe him and seized the money, using the forfeiture law.

Kroft said, "Jones has never been charged with a crime, nor is there any indication he ever will be. The way the forfeiture law works, the police officers didn't have to arrest Willy Jones or, for that matter, prove he was a drug courier. In effect, all they did was arrest his money; all they needed was probable cause that the money was somehow drug-related."

Why did the cops zero in on Jones? Because the agent who sold him his ticket called them. Drug interdiction units at airports throughout the country pay airline employees for tips on people who might be carrying money or drugs. Kroft wanted to find out how easily it could happen, so he sent a reporter to buy a ticket to Houston with cash; within 15 minutes, the reporter was accosted by two officers who proceeded to interrogate him. It was clear that the reporter's cash was going the way of Willy Jones' until he identified himself as being with *60 Minutes*.

Kroft interviewed Robert Bonner of the Drug Enforcement Agency (DEA). The conversation was nothing short of an outrage, as Bonner correctly explained that probable cause was all the grounds necessary for seizure, and that Jones could get his money back if he proved it wasn't drug money by presenting his case to a federal judge or a jury. The situation is similar to that under the tax laws, where the citizen can be considered guilty until he proves his innocence.

Jones' lawyer, Bo Edwards, commented, "If the government takes your property and you get your day in court, you must prove to the government and the court that the property was not involved in a drug transaction and that you didn't intend for it to be involved in a drug transaction. The Bill of Rights applies to criminal cases: for example, the right to have a lawyer, the right to a trial by jury, and the right to require the government to prove its case beyond a reasonable doubt. None of those rights applies in a civil case where the government is bringing a civil forfeiture case against your property." In fact, where seizures involve real estate or items likely to be contested, the cases have names like *U.S. v. $150,660.00* and *U.S. v. Approximately 2,538.85 Shares.*

60 Minutes then looked at the case of Bill Munnerlyn, who ran a successful air charter business. In October 1989, he flew a man named Albert Wright from Little Rock, Arkansas, to Ontario, California, where they were met by a group of DEA agents. The agents confiscated Wright's locked baggage, containing $2.7 million in cash, suspected of being drug money. Wright and Munnerlyn were both arrested, although charges against Munnerlyn were dropped for lack of evidence. Munnerlyn thought the episode was over until the government confiscated his plane, calling the action *U.S. v. One 1969 Gates Lear Jet*, because the plane broke the law by transporting cash that may have been drug-related.

As it turned out, the government decided not to prosecute Wright, who was released. The Lear jet sat in the government's possession, deteriorating, while Munnerlyn spent $85,000 in legal fees in an attempt to get it back. In 1991, a Los Angeles jury ruled in his favor, but a judge overruled the verdict and ordered another trial, which Munnerlyn could not afford.

These two examples are especially worth noting, because *60 Minutes* is widely viewed. Hundreds of examples of this type of outrage are documented yearly. But the public's attention span is short, people forget, and they eventually become inured to any state of affairs. In any event, there appears to be widespread support for the drug laws.

Revenue Enhancement by Seizure

You may believe that these laws are so onerous, and such an affront to the concept of America itself, that they will be overturned. The opposite is more likely, because government at all levels is financially strapped and the laws are an excellent vehicle for "revenue enhancement."

On the local level, hundreds of millions of dollars are now retained by local police annually. They like the extra income, which they use to pay themselves overtime, finance college degrees, and buy exotic police toys and other items to enhance law enforcement. Local police have a high incentive to pursue forfeitures vigorously.

Further, the victims are not a coherent group, like widget manufacturers or even taxpayers in general; they are disparate, have no common bond, and often have no assets after the seizure. The public broadly approves of actions taken in the war on drugs, and many of those who do not are loathe to comment (I suspect for some of the same reasons that few spoke up at the Salem witch trials).

The intent of forfeiture laws is to discourage crime by seizing the profits it generates. But strong evidence suggests that the income forfeitures can generate will become a bigger motive for applying these laws as time goes by. The fact that a majority of seizures are fairly small confirms this; it's uneconomical for a victim to spend the legal fees required to redeem most things worth less than $10,000. It is, therefore, more economic for the government to target seizures that are not likely to be contested. Prosecutors allege that most seizures are not contested because the victims are guilty and do not want to draw further attention to themselves.

A more realistic reason is the monumental amount of time, energy, and money it takes to challenge the seizure, and the fact that many just do not know where to start because the law is unusually complex. Seizures are not contested in other cases because the prosecutors appear to intimidate the victim with the threat of criminal prosecution should that happen.

A further problem that will lead to the ruthless implementation of these laws is corruption. Laws that permit large amounts of cash to be seized in secrecy encourage corruption. It is not difficult to see how an agent might get ideas about alternative uses of the cash and goods that pass through his hands.

The police in many countries around the world expect to retire wealthy, and the police chief of Mexico City traditionally becomes a near-billionaire. It is the nature of their legal system that permits—even encourages—this abuse. There is no reason why, as laws in the United States permit financial seizure without due process, corruption will not soar here as well.

William Bennett Meets Doug Casey

One personal experience I had on the issue occurred when William Bennett, the drug czar under the first Bush administration, spoke before a small group that I attend occasionally. The group serves as a forum for the free exchange of ideas. I believe it is an immoral omission to condone wrongfulness, even if widely accepted, through silence. Bennett spent most of his time justifying his failures as Secretary of Education, but I was interested in his performance as drug czar and the civil rights and due process abuses sanctioned under his guidance. Was he simply uncaring, or unaware of the tragic consequences of his drug laws for many law-abiding Americans caught like dolphins in his tuna net?

It was as if Himmler or Eichmann, both of whom could show great personal charm, had spoken before a luncheon group in the Germany of the early 1930s, couching theories in socially acceptable terms. Groups suffer from groupthink even if the individuals comprising them are sharp. Few people want to cause embarrassment by pointing out the unpleasant implications of a certain belief system, so speakers can often get away with murder, as it were.

Of course, I couldn't help but lay into Bennett. I received no encouragement from the assembled group. But afterward several attendees privately expressed support, as well as surprise that anyone would dare challenge the ex-drug czar. I found their fear of confronting his views openly both symptomatic and disturbing. On leaving, I was accosted by a man identifying himself as a DEA agent—remember, this was a private function—who, while conceding that I was accurate on specific examples, assured me that the incidents of abuse were "not as bad" as they seemed.

A Reign of Terror

As invasive as the current legislation is now, it will almost certainly get worse because of the type of person who tends to be drawn to the DEA and its sister agencies. In every society there are a certain number of criminal or suppressive personalities. Many of them like kids and dogs, live in nice neighborhoods, and play weekend softball. They are not psychopaths who froth at the mouth; they are more or less ordinary people. However, when they encounter the wrong environment, serious flaws in their character emerge. Education or intelligence levels are irrelevant.

Most Gestapo and KGB operatives were also rather ordinary people, and most of them sincerely felt they were doing necessary and honorable work. Bill Bennett, for instance, is familiar with Hannah Arendt's writing on what the "banality of evil" can lead to, although he doesn't believe it applies to him. I hope he's right.

In any event, a certain small but significant percentage of the population will fill the same type of slots in America they would have occupied had they lived in Germany, the Soviet Union, or the deep South at the relevant time. You wouldn't know they were there unless a particular set of conditions drew them out of the woodwork. And creating such conditions is exactly what the sweeping drug laws are doing. Since the war on drugs is far from victorious, and there is now an enticing prospect for abusive revenue generation, you should anticipate more and harsher laws of a similar kind to be enacted.

The nature of American law and law enforcement has changed radically, and at an accelerating rate, since the 1950s. It's quaint, in today's context, to see Broderick Crawford on "Highway Patrol" or even Jack Webb on "Dragnet" dealing with malefactors. The idiom of the 1990s is SWAT teams, clad in midnight-blue uniforms (black still carries too many overtones from Germany to be fashionable), Kevlar® vests and helmets and Nomex® masks and gloves, breaking down a door at the crack of dawn. Almost every town of substance in the United States, as well as most federal agencies, has its own SWAT team. Even the FDA has used exactly this approach in raiding doctors' offices for alleged vitamin violations.

The Drug War as the Problem

Some Americans simplistically believe an opposition to the war on drugs amounts to an endorsement of drugs and an unwillingness to see their destructive effects on the society eliminated. I see drug use as debilitating at best, and I tend to eschew the company of those who use them. But destroying liberty isn't an even remotely acceptable method to discourage drug addiction, nor is it effective.

In any event, the drug problem is, in large measure, a creation of the government. A certain portion of the population will always have problems dealing with life and will seek solace in drugs, legal or illegal; some evidence suggests there is actually a genetic predisposition to addiction. The war on drugs will necessarily fail, if only because the more successful it is at interdicting the supply, the higher it will drive drug prices, creating larger profits. Higher profits will be a greater inducement for new individuals and organizations to get into the business. Some allege that elements of the U.S. government have an active interest in the continued existence of the drug trade.

Those who are caught in the "drugnet" are not rehabilitated by logging hard time in prison as convicted felons. Their condition is, if anything, exacerbated. The war on drugs is the major reason the United States has the highest percentage of its residents incarcerated of any country on earth, including South Africa and the former Soviet Union. High drug prices on the street not only encourage supply but force the typical user into crime to get his hands on enough money to support his habit, a significant form of "collateral damage." Just as Prohibition in the 1920s was the major force leading to the success of the U.S. Mafia, today's prohibition is almost solely responsible for the creation of new, and much more aggressive, organized crime syndicates.

There is no reason to believe the current drug war is any more effective than was the prohibition on alcohol, from 1920 to 1933. In 1926, six years after alcohol was prohibited, state insane asylums reported the number of persons "demented" due to alcohol had increased by 1,000%. In 1929, Metropolitan Life reported that deaths from alcoholism had increased 600%. Drug hysteria is growing and is now starting to impinge on users of alcohol and tobacco, America's two traditional recreational drugs. In their case illegalization is unlikely, although taxes on both will undoubtedly soar, perhaps sufficiently to create black markets in them as well. In brief, the hundreds of billions that have been spent since the war on drugs was declared have probably served only to make the "problem" worse.

It is unfortunate that some who argue for the legalization of drugs and against the forfeiture laws do so almost entirely on pragmatic grounds: the laws do not work, or they are inefficient. This begs the far more important question of whether an individual has the right to dispose of his own life and property as he pleases, as long as he doesn't violate the rights of another person—the two tenets of common law.

Where is all of this likely to lead? Few laws are ever struck from the books; the distortions and additional "criminality" they cause tend to be dealt with by yet more laws. Each of these laws, and the regulations they spawn, requires additional funds and personnel for enforcement and produces grounds for more lawyers and more suits between citizens.

Like most broad trends, there is little reason to believe this one will reverse itself, although there will certainly be short-lived reactions against it, like past vogues for "sunset" provisions, "paperwork reduction," "freedom of information," "taxpayer rights," and the like. These reactions are positive, but they inevitably lack the momentum to effect a change. As with trends in the financial markets, the laws will not change until some true crisis makes change imperative or unavoidable.

Civil loss of freedom will exert a persistent and dismal effect on the financial markets. Part of the fallout will be increasing capital flight and relocation of wealthy or talented individuals from the United States. Weak property rights in developing countries result in depressed prices of hard assets and account for their best people being abroad.

Are there any positive aspects or potential for profit? An investment banker asked Bill Bennett that question at the luncheon I mentioned earlier. He responded: "Buy prison construction bonds. We're going to be building a lot of them."

Section IV:

ANSWERING THE PROHIBITIONISTS

14. America's Unjust Drug War

BY MICHAEL HUEMER

Michael Huemer is an assistant professor of philosophy at the University of Colorado, Boulder. He is the author of Skepticism and the Veil of Perception *and the editor of* Epistemology: Contemporary Readings. *His web page is at http://home.sprynet.com/~owl1.*

Should the recreational use of drugs such as marijuana, cocaine, heroin, and LSD be prohibited by law? *Prohibitionists* answer yes. They usually argue that drug use is extremely harmful both to drug users and to society in general, and possibly even immoral, and they believe that these facts provide sufficient reasons for prohibition. *Legalizers* answer no. They usually give one or more of three arguments. First, some argue that drug use is not as harmful as prohibitionists believe, and even that it is sometimes beneficial. Second, some argue that drug prohibition "does not work," i.e., is not very successful in preventing drug use and/or has a number of very bad consequences. Lastly, some argue that drug prohibition is unjust or violates rights.

I won't attempt to discuss all these arguments here. Instead, I will focus on what seem to me the three most prominent arguments in the drug legalization debate: first, the argument that drugs should be outlawed because of the harm they cause to drug users; second, the argument that they should be outlawed because they harm people other than the user; and third, the argument that drugs should be legalized because drug prohibition violates rights. I shall focus on the moral/philosophical issues that these arguments raise, rather than medical or sociological issues. I shall show that the two arguments for prohibition fail, while the third argument, for legalization, succeeds.

I. Drugs and Harm to Users

The first major argument for prohibition holds that drugs should be prohibited because drug use is extremely harmful to the users themselves, and prohibition decreases the rate of drug abuse. This argument assumes that the proper function of government includes preventing people from harming themselves. Thus, the argument is something like this:

(1) Drug use is very harmful to users.

(2) The government should prohibit people from doing things that harm themselves.

(3) Therefore, the government should prohibit drug use.

Obviously, the second premise is essential to the argument; if I believed that drug use was very harmful, but I did *not* think that the government should prohibit people from harming themselves, then I would not take this as a reason for prohibiting drug use. Furthermore, premise (2), if taken without qualification, is extremely implausible. Consider some examples of things people do that are harmful (or entail a risk of harm) to themselves: smoking tobacco, drinking alcohol, eating too much, riding motorcycles, having unprotected or promiscuous sex, maintaining relationships with inconsiderate or abusive boyfriends and girlfriends, maxing out their credit cards, working in dead-end jobs, dropping out of college, moving to New Jersey, and being rude to their bosses. Should the government prohibit all of these things?[1] Most of us would agree that the government should not prohibit *any* of these things, let alone all of them. And this is not merely for logistical or practical reasons; rather, we think that controlling those activities is not the business of government.

Perhaps the prohibitionist will argue, not that the government should prohibit *all* activities that are harmful to oneself, but that it should prohibit activities that harm oneself in a certain way, or to a certain degree, or that also have some other characteristic. It would then be up to the prohibitionist to explain how the harm of drug use (to users) differs from the harms (to those who engage in them) of the other activities mentioned above. Let's consider three possibilities.

(1) One suggestion would be that drug use also harms people other than the user; we will discuss this harm to others in Section II below. If, as I will contend, neither the harm to drug users nor the harm to others justifies

prohibition, then there will be little plausibility in the suggestion that the combination of harms justifies prohibition. Of course, one could hold that a certain threshold level of total harm must be reached before prohibition of an activity is justified, and that the combination of the harm of drugs to users and their harm to others passes that threshold even though neither kind of harm does so by itself. But if, as I will contend, the "harm to users" and "harm to others" arguments both fail for the reason that it is not the government's business to apply criminal sanctions to prevent the kinds of harms in question, *then* the combination of the two harms will not make a convincing case for prohibition.

(2) A second suggestion is that drug use is generally *more* harmful than the other activities listed above. But there seems to be no reason to believe this. As one (admittedly limited) measure of harmfulness, consider the mortality statistics. The Office of National Drug Control Policy claims that drugs kill 18,000 Americans per year.[2] By contrast, tobacco causes an estimated 440,000 deaths per year.[3] Of course, more people use tobacco than use illegal drugs,[4] so let us divide by the number of users: tobacco kills 15 people per 1,000 users per year; drugs kill 2.6 people per 1,000 users per year.[5] Yet almost no one favors outlawing tobacco and putting smokers in prison. On a similar note, obesity may cause 420,000 deaths per year (due to increased incidence of heart disease, strokes, and so on), or 11 per 1,000 at-risk persons.[6] Health professionals have warned about the pandemic of obesity, but no one has yet called for imprisoning fat people.

There are less tangible harms of drug use—harms to one's general quality of life. These are difficult to quantify. But compare the magnitude of the harm to one's quality of life that one can bring about by, say, dropping out of high school, working in a dead-end job for several years, or marrying a jerk—these things can cause extreme and lasting detriment to one's well-being. And yet no one proposes jailing those who drop out, work in bad jobs, or make poor marriage decisions. The idea of doing so would seem ridiculous, clearly beyond the state's prerogatives.

(3) Another suggestion is that drug use harms users in a *different way* than the other listed activities. Well, what sorts of harms do drugs cause? First, illicit drugs may worsen users' health and, in some cases, entail a risk of death. But many other activities—including the consumption of alcohol, tobacco, and fatty foods; sex; and (on a broad construal of "health") driving automobiles—entail health risks, and yet almost no one believes those activities should be criminalized.

Second, drugs may damage users' relationships with others— particularly family, friends, and lovers—and prevent one from developing more satisfying personal relationships.[7] Being rude to others can also have this effect, yet no one believes you should be put in jail for being rude. Moreover, it is very implausible to suppose that people should be subject to criminal sanctions for ruining their personal relationships. I don't have a general theory of what sort of things people should be punished for, but consider the following example: suppose that I decide to break up with my girlfriend, stop calling my family, and push away all my friends. I do this for no good reason—I just feel like it. This would damage my personal relationships as much as anything could. Should the police now come and arrest me, and put me in jail? If not, then why should they arrest me for doing something that has only a *chance* of indirectly bringing about a similar result? The following seems like a reasonable political principle: if it would be wrong (because not part of the government's legitimate functions) to punish people for *directly bringing about* some result, then it would also be wrong to punish people for doing some other action on the grounds that the action has a *chance* of bringing about that result indirectly. If the state may not prohibit me from directly cutting off my relationships with others, then the fact that my drug use might have the result of damaging those relationships does not provide a good reason to prohibit me from using drugs.

Third, drugs may harm users' financial lives, costing them money, causing them to lose their jobs or not find jobs, and preventing them from getting promotions. The same principle applies here: if it would be an abuse of government power to prohibit me from directly bringing about those sorts of negative financial consequences, then surely the fact that drug use might indirectly bring them about is not a good reason to prohibit drug use. Suppose that I decide to quit my job and throw all my money out the window, for no reason. Should the police come and arrest me, and put me in prison?

Fourth and finally, drugs may damage users' moral character, as James Q. Wilson believes:

> [I]f we believe—as I do—that dependency on certain mind-altering drugs *is* a moral issue and that their illegality rests in part on their immorality, then legalizing them undercuts, if it does not eliminate altogether, the moral message. That message is at the root of the distinction between nicotine and cocaine. Both are highly addictive; both have harmful physical effects. But we treat the two drugs differently not simply because nicotine is so widely used as to be beyond the reach of effective prohibition, but because

its use does not destroy the user's essential humanity. Tobacco shortens one's life, cocaine debases it. Nicotine alters one's habits, cocaine alters one's soul. The heavy use of crack, unlike the heavy use of tobacco, corrodes those natural sentiments of sympathy and duty that constitute our human nature and make possible our social life.[8]

In this passage, Wilson claims that the use of cocaine (a) is immoral, (b) destroys one's humanity, (c) alters one's soul, and (d) corrodes one's sense of sympathy and duty. One problem with Wilson's argument is the lack of evidence supporting claims (a)–(d). Before we put people in prison for corrupting their souls, we should require some objective evidence that their souls are in fact being corrupted. Before we put people in prison for being immoral, we should require some argument showing that their actions are in fact immoral. Perhaps Wilson's charges of immorality and corruption all come down to the charge that drug users lose their sense of sympathy and duty—that is, claims (a)–(c) all rest upon claim (d). It is plausible that *heavy* drug users experience a decreased sense of sympathy with others and a decreased sense of duty and responsibility.[9] Does this provide a good reason to prohibit drug use?

Again, it seems that one should not prohibit an activity on the grounds that it may indirectly cause some result, unless it would be appropriate to prohibit the direct bringing about of that result. Would it be appropriate, and within the legitimate functions of the state, to punish people for being unsympathetic and undutiful, or for behaving in an unsympathetic and undutiful way? Suppose that Howard—though not a drug user—doesn't sympathize with others. When people try to tell Howard their problems, he just tells them to quit whining. Friends and co-workers who ask Howard for favors are rudely rebuffed. Furthermore—though he does not harm others in ways that would be against our current laws—Howard has a poor sense of duty. He doesn't bother to show up for work on time, nor does he take any pride in his work; he doesn't donate to charity; he doesn't try to improve his community. All around, Howard is an ignoble individual. Should he be put in jail?

If not, then why should someone be put in jail merely for doing something that would have a *chance* of causing them to become like Howard? If it would be an abuse of governmental power to punish people for being jerks, then the fact that drug use may cause one to become a jerk is not a good reason to prohibit drug use.

II. Drugs and Harm to Others

Some argue that drug use must be outlawed because drug use harms the user's family, friends and co-workers, and/or society in general. A report produced by the Office of National Drug Control Policy (ONDCP) states:

> Democracies can flourish only when their citizens value their freedom and embrace personal responsibility. Drug use erodes the individual's capacity to pursue both ideals. It diminishes the individual's capacity to operate effectively in many of life's spheres—as a student, a parent, a spouse, an employee—even as a coworker or fellow motorist. And, while some claim it represents an expression of individual autonomy, drug use is in fact inimical to personal freedom, producing a reduced capacity to participate in the life of the community and the promise of America.[10]

At least one of these alleged harms—dangerous driving—*is* clearly the business of the state. For this reason, I entirely agree that people should be prohibited from driving while under the influence of drugs. But what about the rest of the alleged harms?

Return to our hypothetical citizen Howard. Imagine that Howard—again, for reasons having nothing to do with drugs—does not value freedom, nor does he embrace personal responsibility. It is unclear exactly what this means, but, for good measure, let us suppose that Howard embraces a totalitarian political ideology and denies the existence of free will. He constantly blames other people for his problems and tries to avoid making decisions. Howard is a college student with a part-time job. However, he is a terrible student and worker. He hardly ever studies and frequently misses assignments, and, as a result, he gets poor grades. As we mentioned earlier, Howard comes to work late and takes no pride in his work. Though he does nothing against our current laws, he is an inattentive and inconsiderate spouse and parent. Nor does he make any effort to participate in the life of his community, or the promise of America. He would rather lie around the house, watching television and cursing the rest of the world for his problems. In short, Howard does all the bad things to his family, friends, co-workers, and society that the ONDCP says *may* result from drug use. And most of this is voluntary.

Should Congress pass laws against what Howard is doing? Should the police then arrest him, and the district attorney prosecute him, for being a loser?

Once again, it seems absurd to suppose that we would arrest and jail someone for behaving in these ways, undesirable as they may be. Since drug use has only a *chance* of causing one to behave in each of these ways, it is even more absurd to suppose that we should arrest and jail people for drug use on the grounds that drug use has these potential effects.

III. The Injustice of Drug Prohibition

Philosopher Douglas Husak has characterized drug prohibition as the greatest injustice perpetrated in the United States since slavery.[11] This is no hyperbole. If the drug laws are unjust, then we have 450,000 people unjustly imprisoned at any given time.[12]

Why think the drug laws are *unjust*? Husak's argument invokes a principle with which few could disagree: it is unjust for the state to punish people without having a good reason for doing so.[13] We have seen the failure of the most common proposed rationales for drug prohibition. If nothing better is forthcoming, then we must conclude that prohibitionists have no rational justification for punishing drug users. We have deprived hundreds of thousands of people of basic liberties and subjected them to severe hardship conditions, for no good reason.

This is bad enough. But I want to say something stronger. It is not just that we are punishing people for no good reason; we are punishing people for exercising their natural rights. Individuals have a right to use drugs. This right is neither absolute nor exceptionless. Suppose, for example, that there existed a drug which, once ingested, caused a significant proportion of users, without any further free choices on their part, to attack other people without provocation. I would think that stopping the use of this drug would be the business of the government. But no existing drug satisfies this description. Indeed, though I cannot take time to delve into the matter here, I think it is clear that the drug *laws* cause far more crime than drugs themselves do.

The idea of a right to use drugs derives from the idea that individuals own their own bodies. That is, a person has the right to exercise control over his own body—including the right to decide how it should be used, and to exclude others from using it—in a manner similar to the way one may exercise control over one's (other) property. This statement is somewhat vague; nevertheless, we can see the general idea embodied in common-sense morality. Indeed, it seems that if there is *anything* one would have rights to, it would be one's own body. This explains why we think others may not physically attack you or kidnap you. It explains why we do not accept the use of unwilling human subjects for medical experiments, even if the experiments are beneficial to society—the rest of society may not decide to use your body for its own purposes without your permission. It explains why some believe that women have a right to an abortion—and why some others do not. The former believe that a woman has the right to do what she wants with her own body; the latter believe that the fetus is a distinct person, and a woman does not have the right to harm *its* body. Virtually no one disputes that, *if* a fetus is merely a part of the woman's body, *then* a woman has a right to choose whether to have an abortion; just as virtually no one disputes that, *if* a fetus is a distinct person, *then* a woman lacks the right to destroy it. Almost no one disputes that persons have rights over their own bodies but not over other people's bodies.

The right to control one's body cannot be interpreted as implying a right to use one's body in *every* conceivable way, any more than we have the right to use our property in every conceivable way. Most importantly, we may not use our bodies to harm others in certain ways, just as we may not use our property to harm others. But drug use seems to be a paradigm case of a legitimate exercise of the right to control one's own body. Drug consumption takes place in and immediately around the user's own body; the salient effects occur *inside* the user's body. If we consider drug use merely as altering the user's own body and mind, it is hard to see how anyone who believes in rights at all could deny that it is protected by a right, for (a) it is hard to see how anyone who believes in rights could deny that individuals have rights over their own bodies and minds, and (b) it is hard to see how anyone who believes in such rights could deny that drug use, considered merely as altering the user's body and mind, is an example of the exercise of one's rights over one's own body and mind.

Consider two ways a prohibitionist might object to this argument. First, a prohibitionist might argue that drug use does not *merely* alter the user's own body and mind, but also harms the user's family, friends, co-workers, and society. I responded to this sort of argument in Section II. Not just *any* way in which an action might be said to "harm" other people makes the action worthy of criminal sanctions. Here we need not try to state a general criterion for what sorts of harms make an action worthy of criminalization; it is enough to note that there are some kinds of "harms" that virtually no one would take to warrant criminal sanctions, and that these include the "harms" I cause to others by being a poor student, an incompetent worker, or an apathetic citizen.[14] That said, I agree with the prohibitionists at least this far: no one should be permitted to drive or operate heavy machinery while under the influence of drugs that impair their ability to do those things; nor should pregnant mothers be permitted to ingest drugs, if it can be proven that those drugs cause substantial risks to their babies (I leave aside the issue of what the threshold level of risk should be, as well as the empirical questions concerning the actual level of risk created by illegal drugs—I don't know those things). But, in the great majority of cases, drug use does not harm anyone in any *relevant* ways—that is, ways that we normally take to merit criminal penalties—and should not be outlawed.

Second, a prohibitionist might argue that drug use fails to qualify as an exercise of the user's rights over his own body, because the individual is not truly acting freely in deciding to use drugs. Perhaps individuals use drugs only because they have fallen prey to some sort of psychological compulsion, because drugs exercise a siren-like allure that distorts users' perceptions, because users don't realize how bad drugs are, or something of that sort. The exact form of this objection doesn't matter; in any case, the prohibitionist faces a dilemma. If users do not freely choose to use drugs, then it is unjust to *punish* them for using drugs. For if users do not choose freely, then they are not morally responsible for their decision, and it is unjust to punish a person for something he is not responsible for. But if users *do* choose freely in deciding to use drugs, then this choice is an exercise of their rights over their own bodies.

I have tried to think of the best arguments prohibitionists could give, but in fact prohibitionists have remained puzzlingly silent on this issue. When a country goes to war, it tends to focus on its national interests, sparing little thought for the rights of the victims in the enemy country. Similarly, one effect of America's declaring "war" on drug users seems to have been that prohibitionists have given almost no thought to the rights of drug users. Most either ignore the issue or mention it briefly, only to dismiss it without argument.[15] In an effort to discredit legalizers, the Office of National Drug Control Policy produced the following caricature:

> The easy cynicism that has grown up around the drug issue is no accident. Sowing it has been the deliberate aim of a decades-long campaign by proponents of legalization, critics whose mantra is "nothing works," and whose central insight appears to be that they can avoid having to propose the unmentionable—a world where drugs are ubiquitous and where use and addiction would skyrocket—if they can hide behind the bland management critique that drug control efforts are "unworkable."[16]

This apparently denies the existence of the central issues I have discussed in this essay. It seems reasonable to assume that an account of the state's right to forcibly interfere with individuals' decisions regarding their own bodies is not forthcoming from these prohibitionists.

IV. Conclusion

Undoubtedly, the drug war has been disastrous in many ways that others can more ably describe—in terms of its effects on crime, on police corruption, and on other civil liberties, to name a few. But more than that, the drug war is morally outrageous in its very conception. If we are to retain some sort of respect for human rights, we cannot deploy force to deprive people of their liberty and property for whimsical reasons. The exercise of such coercion requires a powerful and clearly stated rationale. Most of the reasons that have actually been proposed in the case of drug prohibition would be considered feeble if advanced in other contexts. Few would take seriously the suggestion that people should be imprisoned for harming their own health, being poor students, or failing to share in the American dream. It is still less credible that we should imprison people for an activity that only *may* lead to those consequences. Yet these and other, similarly weak arguments form the core of prohibition's defense.

Prohibitionists are likewise unable to answer the argument that individuals have a right to use drugs. Any such answer would have to deny either that persons have rights of control over their own bodies, or that consuming drugs constitutes an exercise of those rights. We have seen that the sort of harms drug use allegedly causes to society does not make a case against its being an exercise of the user's rights over his own body. And the claim that drug users can't control their behavior or don't know what they are doing renders it even more mysterious why one would believe drug users deserve to be punished for what they are doing.

I will close by responding to a query posed by prohibition-advocate James Inciardi:

> The government of the United States is not going to legalize drugs anytime soon, if ever, and certainly not in this [the 20th] century. So why spend so much time, expense, and intellectual and emotional effort on a quixotic undertaking? ...[W]e should know by now that neither politicians nor the polity respond positively to abrupt and drastic strategy alterations.[17]

The United States presently has 450,000 people unjustly imprisoned. Inciardi may—tragically—be correct that our government has no intention of stopping its massive violations of the rights of its people any time soon. Nevertheless, it remains the duty of citizens and of political and social theorists to identify the injustice, and not to tacitly assent to it. Imagine a slavery advocate, decades before the Civil War, arguing that abolitionists were wasting their breath and should move on to more productive activities—such as arguing for incremental changes in the way slaves are treated—since the southern states had no intention of ending slavery any time soon. The institution of slavery is a black mark on our nation's history, but it would be even more shameful if no one at the time had spoken against it.

Is this comparison overdrawn? I don't think so. The harm of being unjustly imprisoned is qualitatively comparable (though it usually ends sooner) to the harm of being enslaved. The increasingly popular scapegoating and stereotyping of drug users and sellers on the part of our nation's leaders is comparable to the racial prejudices of previous generations. Yet very few seem willing to speak on behalf of drug users. Perhaps the unwillingness of those in public life to defend drug users' rights stems from the negative image we have of drug users and the fear of being associated with them. Yet these attitudes remain baffling. I have used illegal drugs myself. I know many decent and successful individuals, both in and out of my profession, who have used illegal drugs. We have had one United States President, one Vice-President, a Speaker of the House, and a Supreme Court Justice who have admitted to having used illegal drugs.[18] More than a third of all Americans over the age of 11 have used illegal drugs.[19] But now leave aside the absurdity of recommending criminal sanctions for all these people. My point is this: if we are convinced of the injustice of drug prohibition, then even if our protests should fall on deaf ears—we should not remain silent in the face of such a large-scale injustice in our own country. And, fortunately, radical social reforms *have* occurred, more than once in our history, in response to moral arguments.

Notes

1. Douglas Husak (*Legalize This! The Case for Decriminalizing Drugs*, London: Verso, 2002, pages 7 and 101–103) makes this sort of argument (I have added my own examples of harmful activities to his list).

2. Office of National Drug Control Policy (ONDCP), "Drug Use Consequences," www.whitehousedrugpolicy.gov/publications/policy/03ndcs/table19.html. The statistic includes both prescription and illegal drugs.

3. Centers for Disease Control (CDC), "Annual Smoking-Attributable Mortality, Years of Potential Life Lost, and Economic Costs—United States, 1995–1999," *Morbidity and Mortality Weekly Report* 51, 2002, www.cdc.gov/mmwr/PDF/wk/mm5114.pdf, page 300.

4. James A. Inciardi ("Against Legalization of Drugs" in Arnold Trebach and James Inciardi, *Legalize It? Debating American Drug Policy*, Washington, D.C.: American University Press, 1993, pages 161 and 165) makes this point, accusing drug legalizers of "sophism." He does not go on to calculate the number of deaths per user, however.

5. Based on the assumption of 29.7 million smokers in 1999 and 7.0 million users of illicit drugs (U.S. Census Bureau, *Statistical Abstract of the United States* 2001, Washington, D.C.: Government Printing Office, page 122). However, these figures may be off by quite a bit. CDC ("Annual Smoking-Attributable Mortality, Years of Potential Life Lost, and Economic Costs—United States, 1995–1999,"

Morbidity and Mortality Weekly Report 51, 2002, www.cdc.gov/mmwr/PDF/wk/mm5114.pdf, page 303) reports 46.5 million smokers in the same year, based on a different survey. The Substance Abuse and Mental Health Services Administration reports, "An estimated 14.8 million Americans were current users of illicit drugs in 1999, meaning they used an illicit drug at least once during the 30 days prior to the interview" for the *National Household Survey* (www.samhsa.gov/news/newsreleases/000831 nrhousehold.htm).

6. Based on the assumptions of 240,000 premature deaths caused by obesity in 1991 (David B. Allison, *et al.*, "Annual Deaths Attributable to Obesity in the United States," *Journal of the American Medical Association*, Volume 282, Number 16, 1999, pages 1530–1538), a 61% increase in the prevalence of obesity between 1991 and 2000 (CDC, "Prevalence of Obesity Among U.S. Adults, by Characteristics," www.cdc.gov/nccdphp/dnpa/obesity/trend/prev_char.htm), a 9% increase in population between 1991 and 2000 (U.S. Census Bureau, page 8), and 38.8 million obese Americans in 2000 (CDC, "Overweight and Obesity: Frequently Asked Questions," www.cdc.gov/nccdphp/dnpa/obesity/faq.htm). These figures may also be off—different sources give different estimates for each of these quantities.

7. Inciardi, pages 167 and 172.

8. James Q. Wilson, "Against the Legalization of Drugs," *Commentary* 89, 1990, page 26.

9. As Jacob Sullum has shown (*Saying Yes: In Defense of Drug Use*, New York: Tarcher/Putnam, 2003), many drug users have normal and successful lives, and it is widely known that most users are not addicts.

10. ONDCP, *National Drug Control Strategy 2002*, Washington, D.C.: Government Printing Office, www.whitehousedrugpolicy.gov/publications/policy/03ndcs/, pages 1–2.

11. Husak, page 2.

12. Based on 73,389 drug inmates in federal prison in 2000 (U.S. Department of Justice (U.S. DOJ), "Prisoners in 2001," Washington, D.C.: Government Printing Office, 2002, www.ojp.usdoj.gov/bjs/pub/pdf/p01.pdf, page 14), 251,000 drug inmates in state prisons in 2000 (U.S. DOJ, "Prisoners in 2001," page 13), and 137,000 drug inmates in local jails. The last statistic is based on the 2000 jail population of 621,149 (U.S. DOJ, "Prisoners in 2001," page 2) and the 1996 rate of 22% drug offenders in local jails (U.S. DOJ, "Profile of Jail Inmates 1996," Washington, D.C.: Government Printing Office, 1998, www.ojp.usdoj.gov/bjs/pub/pdf/pji96.pdf, page 1). The numbers have probably increased since then.

13. Husak, page 15; see his chapter two for an extended discussion of various proposed rationales for drug prohibition, including many issues that I lack space to discuss here.

14. Husak (*Drugs and Rights*, Cambridge University Press, 1992, pages 166–168), similarly, argues that no one has a right that I be a good neighbor, proficient student, and so on, and that only "harms" that violate rights can justify criminal sanctions.

15. See Inciardi for an instance of ignoring and Lungren (page 180) for an instance of dismissal without argument. Wilson (page 24) addresses the issue, if at all, by arguing that drug use makes users worse parents, spouses, employers, and co-workers. This fails to refute the contention that individuals have a right to use drugs.

16. ONDCP, *National Drug Control Strategy 2002*, page 3.

17. Inciardi, page 205.

18. Bill Clinton, Al Gore, Newt Gingrich and Clarence Thomas (reported by David Phinney, "Dodging the Drug Question," ABC News, August 19, 1999, http://abcnews.go.com/sections/politics/DailyNews/prez_questions990819.html). George W. Bush has refused to state whether he has ever used illegal drugs.

19. U.S. Census Bureau, page 122.

15. Drugs and Terror

BY ARI ARMSTRONG

Ari Armstrong edits the Colorado Freedom Report *at www.FreeColorado.com. His work has also been published in various newspapers and libertarian publications.*

The illegal drug trade supports terror. Following the terrorist attack of September 11, 2001, the Office of National Drug Control Policy launched a media campaign to convince Americans of that fact and to persuade them to stop buying illegal drugs. President George W. Bush said, "If you quit drugs, you join the fight against terror in America."

A lesson plan developed for high school teachers explains:

> To be effective, the War on Terrorism will require new levels of cooperation between allies, and to disable terrorist groups it will demand new skill at decoding international alliances. Even more demanding will be tracking the money connections that fund and support terrorism, and blocking the sources. In today's world, that means drugs. Already investigators are honing in on the connections of what is called "narco-terrorism." Drug and intelligence agencies have documented links to illicit drug activities for many of the international terrorist organizations identified by the U.S. State Department in its report of October 2001. The deposed Taliban regime has been tied to the opium trade in Afghanistan. During the period the Taliban were in power, opium production increased rapidly until 2000... In other parts of the world, terrorist

organizations are benefiting from drug profits. For example, the Revolutionary Armed Forces of Colombia (FARC) receives about $300 million from drug sales annually... But terror associated with drugs goes beyond the acts of terrorist organizations. Many drug trafficking organizations engage in acts that most people would consider terror. These include gruesome public killing of innocents, large scale bombings intended to intimidate governments, kidnapping and torture.[1]

What is the magnitude of the problem? Again, the U.S. government offers some idea: "Twelve of the 28 listed terror organizations identified by the U.S. State Department in October 2001 traffic in drugs. Drug income is the primary source of revenue of some of the more powerful groups."[2]

One approach to the problem would be to encourage people to buy their drugs only from non-terrorists. For instance, marijuana grown on one's own property would not fund terrorists or other violent criminals. For obvious but unstated reasons, the U.S. government didn't promote such a policy.

"Not That Complicated"

The arguments against buying illegal drugs were summed up in a series of television and radio advertisements. One typical TV ad portrayed a conversation between two men:

> *Norm*: This drugs and terror thing. I mean, it's a very complicated issue.
> *Nick*: A complicated issue?
> *Norm*: Complicated...very complicated.
> *Nick*: No drug buyers, no drug money. No drug money, no drug dealers. No drug dealers, no drug murders, shootings, bribery, corruption.
> *Norm*: Not that complicated.[3]

While it might be tempting to dismiss such a message out of hand as government-sponsored propaganda, we need to take the argument seriously. The truth or falsehood of a statement may be evaluated independently of the motives of those making the statement.

The government ads conflate the violence associated strictly with terrorism with the general violence associated with the illegal drug trade. Most drug sellers who use violence aren't interested in terrorism *per se*. They are not trying to change government policy or intimidate a population.

Instead, they are interested in making a lot of money for themselves. I will follow the government in discussing both sorts of violence as a package, but it benefits us to remember the distinction: some terrorist groups use profits obtained by selling illegal drugs in order to further violent ends, whereas most sellers of illegal drugs who use violence do so as a means to promote their trade. (Of course, many drug sellers don't resort to violence at all.)

The argument against buying illegal drugs can be described as a "but for" argument: but for drug buyers, there would be no drug-funded murder, etc. And that argument is true. If everybody suddenly stopped buying illegal drugs, terrorist groups would no longer profit from selling illegal drugs.

But the same "but for" argument immediately poses a problem for the advocates of prohibition: but for prohibition, there would be no drug-funded murder, etc.

The criminal black market is created by prohibitionist laws, and if those laws were lifted, the black market in drugs would almost immediately disappear. Americans experienced the same phenomenon with respect to the prohibition of another drug, alcohol. ("No alcohol buyers, no alcohol money…") A number of scholars, such as economist Jeffrey Miron, argue that in order to eliminate the violence associated with drug prohibition, the appropriate policy conclusion is to lift the prohibitionist laws.[4] The Libertarian Party even "ran full-page ads in *USA Today* and *The Washington Times* that accused America's drug warriors of financially supporting terrorism."[5]

Absent the illegal market in drugs created (in part) by prohibitionist laws, the high profits associated with the trade of illegal drugs would disappear. Drug sales would be no more profitable than those of any other commodity.

Thus, if the government's "but for" argument trumps, then obviously the government agents involved in passing and enforcing prohibitionist laws are exactly as morally culpable for the violence associated with the illegal drug trade as are the buyers of illegal drugs.

Moral Arguments

But, of course, moral culpability is not properly assigned by such "but for" arguments. A simple example amply illustrates this point. "Bank robbery is a bad thing. But for the existence of banks, there would be no bank robbers. No bank tellers, no bank money. No bank money, no bank robbers. No bank robbers, no bank murders, shootings, bribery, corruption." Hopefully readers will agree the appropriate conclusion is not that bank tellers are morally culpable for bank robberies. To generalize, if we relied on "but for" arguments to assign moral blame, almost every victim of crime would be as culpable as the perpetrator. Obviously, such a standard will not do.

Where does that leave us, then? If both the buyers of illegal drugs and the advocates of prohibitionist laws have some causal connection with the violence associated with the illegal drug trade, can we assign moral blame to one group or the other, or to both groups?

One way to resolve the dilemma is to turn to other moral arguments. If we could establish either that people have a right to buy drugs, or that government agents are morally wrong to impose prohibitionist laws, then that might give us a way to assign moral blame for the associated violence.

I believe both propositions are true. People have a right to buy drugs, and government agents have a moral responsibility to restrict the functions of government to protecting people and their property from violence and fraud, an arena that necessarily precludes drug prohibition. But my goal here is merely to point to such arguments, not flesh them out fully. (Michael Huemer offers a convincing case elsewhere in this volume.)

Of course, to say that people have a right to do something is not to imply that it is a moral activity. Obviously, some drug buyers use drugs in immoral ways, and this point applies to prohibited drugs as well as to legal drugs like alcohol and nicotine. Most people will grant others have a legal right to drink too much alcohol (though not drive drunk, harm others, or trespass), gamble excessively, practice unsafe sex (though not neglect to tell partners about existing transmissible diseases), lie to their mothers (though not commit fraud), and argue in an intellectually dishonest manner (again excepting fraud). We don't usually haul people off to prison for doing those immoral things. We do arrest buyers of some drugs and send them to prison, even though most people who buy illegal drugs do not use them in ways that are terribly (or even noticeably) self-destructive.[6] Obviously a few types of inherently evil activities—like murder, rape, robbery, child abuse, and fraud—should be outlawed. Other activities, even if they are or can be immoral, should not be outlawed.

To review, if one believes that people have a right to buy drugs, or that government agents may not morally impose prohibitionist laws, or both propositions, then a pretty good case can be made that the violence associated with illegal drug sales is the fault of the prohibitionists.

On the other hand, if one concludes drug use is inherently evil as well as something the government may properly outlaw, a case might be made that prohibitionist laws are appropriate and the resulting violence associated with the illegal drug trade is the fault of drug buyers. In order to be consistent, though, the prohibitionist would also have to advocate the complete prohibition of alcohol and tobacco, even if one result was a massive escalation of violence associated with the trade of those drugs. A simplistic distinction of "good drug/bad drug" will not do, given the magnitude of death and abuse associated with alcohol and tobacco. A distinction between "medicinal drugs" and "recreational drugs" might be made, although alcohol and tobacco would clearly fall in the second category, whereas marijuana and other drugs that are currently prohibited are sometimes used for medical purposes.

The Pragmatic Approach

Another approach, besides the moral one, is to argue along pragmatic (or utilitarian, or consequentialist) lines. No matter what one concluded about the morality of buying drugs, using drugs, or advocating prohibitionist laws, one might still argue that pragmatic concerns trump.

One pragmatist avenue is to argue that it's possible to repeal drug prohibition, whereas it is impossible to stop drug users from buying drugs. Most of America's history has been free of prohibition, indicating it's possible to lift prohibition in the modern era. On the other hand, decades of prohibitionist policies have proven largely ineffective (and in many ways have worsened the problems associated with drug use).

The economic concept of the "free rider" also suggests the only practical route is to repeal prohibition. True enough, if every drug user stopped buying illegal drugs, the profits relating to criminal activity would disappear. The problem is, the behavior of any individual drug user is inconsequential, so the individual has little incentive to change his or her behavior unilaterally. The free-rider problem also applies to the enforcers of prohibition: no single actor has much incentive to change the system (which, after all, redistributes billions of dollars every year to the enforcers). However, the free-rider problem is much more easily solved on the prohibitionist side, as it involves fewer individuals and the policy is subject to legislative action.

Another pragmatic approach is to argue the relative merits and demerits of repealing prohibition. The ads promoted by the U.S. government have anticipated this move. The conversation presented in one ad runs as follows:

Norm: Okay, let's say drug money does support terrorism.
Nick: And murder.
Norm: And murder.
Nick: And torture.

Norm: And torture.
Nick: Corruption…bribery…
Norm: Whatever.
Nick: What's your point.
Norm: Change the law.
Nick: I got you. Make 'em cheap. More available. Everywhere…
    Like soda or cheesy puffs.
Norm: Exactly.
Nick: Cocaine on the playground. Crack stands at the laundromat,
    heroin at the mini-mart, like that?
Norm: Yeah, that doesn't sound so good, does it.[7]

What's interesting about this ad is that it implicitly recognizes the link between prohibition and terror, yet it suggests such violence is an acceptable cost of attempting to keep the flow of drugs down. Perhaps the prohibitionists hope or imagine their laws will somehow reduce drug consumption sufficiently to alleviate the problem of violence, but after decades of drug wars and hundreds of billions of dollars devoted to the problem, surely that is a pipe dream at best.

The pragmatic argument of the ad's sponsors, then, can be interpreted, "We acknowledge prohibitionist laws help cause violence associated with the trade of illegal drugs, but the only alternative is to allow drugs to be more readily available in the U.S., and that's unacceptable. Thus, we continue to blame drug buyers for the violence associated with prohibition, and we continue our efforts to get people to stop using drugs."

But once we begin to look at pragmatic concerns, as the ad encourages us to do, where does the evaluation lead? Is international terrorism and violence worth the trade-off? Is the actual trade-off the one suggested by the government?

The ad is ironic almost to the point of self-parody. Alcohol, once a prohibited drug, today is not sold on playgrounds or in laundromats (though it is available at some mini-marts). The very drugs currently available on playgrounds and in laundromats (as well as at mini-marts and even in prisons) are the illegal ones.

Yes, once prohibition is lifted, the price of now-illegal drugs will fall dramatically. Yet reformers argue this is a primary virtue of changing the laws. A decline in prices will wipe out the criminal monopoly over drug sales, and it will also reduce thefts associated with drug habits. Whereas a reduction in price, other things being equal, will tend to increase the quantity of drugs demanded, other things will *not* be equal, and other factors will tend to reduce the demand for drugs. Crime rings will no longer thrive by promoting drug use in their communities, and treatment will be more accessible.[8] At the same time, lifting prohibition will free up billions of dollars and millions of work hours every year to deal with other pressing problems (such as the threat of terrorism).

The Prohibitionist Straddle

The advocates of prohibition have failed to sustain either a moral argument or a pragmatic one to justify their policies. Yet they tend to oscillate between both types of argumentation when defending their case.

There clearly seems to be a "prohibitionist straddle."[9] On one hand, prohibitionists argue that using drugs is immoral. When the weakness of the moral case against drug use is pointed out, the prohibitionists immediately invoke the pragmatic horrors that allegedly would accompany the lifting of prohibition. And when the pragmatic case is made that lifting prohibition would massively reduce violence, curb police corruption and abuse, reduce health problems associated with drug use, and so on, the prohibitionists turn again to moralistic denunciations. Thus the case for prohibition, though invalid, can avoid real criticism indefinitely.

Of course, a prohibitionist could argue that either the moral case or the pragmatic case in favor of prohibition stands alone, or that both arguments together support the policy of prohibition. That is, a prohibitionist could argue there's no "straddle" at all. A prohibitionist might further argue I am the one who is straddling the arguments against prohibition. My short answer is that it would be a wonderful step forward if the prohibitionists earnestly entered into such a debate.[10] Ultimately, what should concern us is the soundness of the respective cases. What makes me believe the prohibitionists are straddling is simply that their case is weak; they often seem to attempt to compensate for this weakness with denunciations rather than arguments, and they tend to pace between pseudo-moralistic (but quite stern) rhetoric and implausible (and sometimes wildly hysterical) stories about the imagined consequences of lifting prohibition.

The previously cited teachers' lesson contains a gem of advice: "Understanding the connection between drugs and terror requires critical thinking about information as it becomes available. Critical thinking means reading something carefully, weighing the information presented and asking questions that would clarify what is being said." The apparent failure of the government's advertising campaign against drug use[11] may indicate that critical thinkers have evaluated the information linking drugs and terror, and they have concluded prohibitionist policies are at fault. If that is the case, the ad campaign may well have been the best use of tax dollars relating to the drug war in its entire history.

Notes

1. Office of National Drug Control Policy (ONDCP), National Youth Anti-Drug Media Campaign, "Drugs and Terror: Teacher Lesson," www.theantidrug.com/drugs_terror/teachers_lessonplan.html.

2. ONDCP, National Youth Anti-Drug Media Campaign, "Drug Sources," www.theantidrug.com/drugs_terror/drug_sources.html. For some specific instances of violence related to illegal drug trafficking, see also ONDCP, National Youth Anti-Drug Media Campaign, "I Helped," www.theantidrug.com/drugs_terror/ihelp.html.

3. ONDCP, National Youth Anti-Drug Media Campaign, "Not That Complicated," www.mediacampaign.org/mg/transcripts/tr_complicated.html. In the audio-video file at www.mediacampaign.org/multimedia/complicated.mov, the characters "Nick and Norm" use slightly different language. Other television ads are available via internet at www.mediacampaign.org/mg/television.html. Notably, though the character "Norm" appears to be a drug user in this and other ads, the character "Nick" shows no interest in turning Norm in to the police.

4. Professor Miron's Web page at http://econ.bu.edu/miron/ contains a number of related essays and studies.

5. Libertarian Party, "LP's anti-Drug War advertisements reach millions in *USA Today, Washington Times,*" www.lp.org/lpnews/0204/ads.html.

6. Jacob Sullum, *Saying Yes: In Defense of Drug Use*, New York: Tarcher/Putman, 2003.

7. ONDCP, National Youth Anti-Drug Media Campaign, "Mini-Mart," www.mediacampaign.org/mg/transcripts/tr_minimart.html. The audi-video file is available at www.mediacampaign.org/multimedia/minimart.mov.

8. Sheriff Bill Masters discusses these and other factors in *Drug War Addiction: Notes from the Front Lines of America's #1 Policy Disaster*, St. Louis: Accurate Press (1.800.374.4049), 2001, pages 62–67.

9. Jeffrey Friedman describes the "straddle" in another context ("What's Wrong with Libertarianism," *Critical Review*, Volume 11, Number 3, Summer 1997; and "The Libertarian Straddle: Rejoinder to Palmer and Sciabarra," *Critical Review*, Volume 12, Number 3, Summer 1998). While Friedman's discussion of the "straddle" is limited to one specific matter of intellectual history, I believe the problem he describes is pervasive. I discuss a few other examples at www.freecolorado.com/2003/05/comemes.html.

10. My long answer begins with the view that a theory of rights ultimately should be grounded in (rule) consequentialism.

11. Drug Reform Coordination Network, "Drug Czar Gives Up on Drugs and Terror Ad Campaign, Also Cancels Studies to Track Ads' Effectiveness," *The Week Online with DRCNet*, Issue 281, April 4, 2003, www.stopthedrugwar.org/chronicle/281/drugczargivesup.shtml.

16. Your Government Is Lying To You (Again) About Marijuana

BY PAUL ARMENTANO AND KEITH STROUP

Paul Armentano is an author and senior policy analyst for The National Organization for the Reform of Marijuana Laws (NORML, www.norml.org) and the NORML Foundation. His work has appeared in numerous newspapers, magazines, and anthologies, including Drug Abuse: Opposing Viewpoints; You Are Being Lied To: The Disinformation Guide to Media Distortion, Historical Whitewashes and Cultural Myths; *and* Busted: Stone Cowboys, Narco-Lords and Washington's War on Drugs. *Keith Stroup, J.D., is the founder and executive director of NORML.*

It will come as no surprise to most Americans to learn that federal officials often exaggerate the potential dangers of marijuana in order to justify our nation's criminal drug policies. This technique is nothing new and may be traced back to the earliest days of marijuana prohibition—a period of time now known as "Reefer Madness."

Alarmingly, in recent years federal officials have reverted to the rhetoric of this bygone era, the White House's prominent ad campaign alleging that recreational pot use funds international terrorism being but one example. Like the outright propaganda of the 1930s, the Bush administration's new "Reefer Madness" does not qualify as a mere exaggeration; they are flat-out lying to the American public in an attempt to justify the nation's criminal pot laws, laws that now result in the arrests of more than 700,000 U.S. citizens each year.

In the fall of 2001, the White House Office of National Drug Control Policy (better known as the "drug czar's office") mailed an open letter to every prosecutor in America warning, "Nationwide, no drug matches the threat posed by marijuana."[1] The text of the letter, much of which has since been reprinted verbatim in newspapers nationwide, is a template for the Administration's resurrected "Reefer Madness" campaign. In response to these allegations,[2] we offer the following rebuttal.

Allegations and Rebuttals

Allegation #1: "There is a serious drug problem in this country."

Truth: America does have a serious drug problem, and our public policy needs to better address this issue with health and science-based educational programs, and by providing more accessible treatment to those who are drug-dependent. Unfortunately, the bulk of our nation's current anti-drug efforts and priorities remain fixated on arresting and jailing drug consumers—particularly recreational marijuana smokers.

In this sense, there is a serious drug *enforcement* problem in this country. Despite the notion that America's drug war focuses primarily on targeting so-called hard drugs and hard drug dealers, data compiled by the FBI reports that nearly half of all drug arrests in America are for marijuana only.[3]

In 2001, the last year for which statistics are available, law enforcement arrested an estimated 723,627 persons for marijuana violations.[4] This total far exceeds the total number of arrests for all violent crimes combined, including murder, manslaughter, forcible rape, robbery, and aggravated assault.[5] Today, it is estimated that taxpayers spend between 7.5 and $10 billion annually arresting and prosecuting individuals for marijuana violations[6]—monies that would be far better served targeting violent crime, including terrorism.

Since 1992, approximately six million Americans have been arrested on marijuana charges, a greater number than the entire populations of Alaska, Delaware, the District of Columbia, Montana, North Dakota, South Dakota, Vermont, and Wyoming combined.[7] Nearly 90% of these arrests were for simple possession, not cultivation or sale.[8] During these same years, arrests for cocaine and heroin have declined sharply,[9] indicating that increased enforcement of marijuana laws is being achieved at the expense of enforcing laws against the possession and trafficking of more dangerous drugs.

Allegation #2: "Nationwide, no drug matches the threat posed by marijuana."

Truth: This statement is pure hyperbole. In fact, almost all drugs— including those that are legal—pose greater threats to individual health and/or society than does marijuana. According to the Centers for Disease Control, approximately 46,000 people die each year from alcohol-induced deaths (not including motor vehicle fatalities where alcohol impairment was a contributing factor), such as overdose and cirrhosis.[10] Similarly, more than 440,000 premature deaths annually are attributed to tobacco smoking.[11] By comparison, marijuana is nontoxic and cannot cause death by overdose.[12] In a large-scale population study of marijuana use and mortality published in the *American Journal of Public Health*, marijuana use, even long-term, "showed little if any effect...on non-AIDS mortality in men and on total mortality in women."[13]

After an exhaustive, federally-commissioned study by the National Academy of Sciences Institute of Medicine (IOM) in 1999 examining all of marijuana's potential health risks, authors concluded, "Except for the harms associated with smoking, the adverse effects of marijuana use are within the range tolerated for other medications."[14] (It should be noted that many risks associated with marijuana and smoking may be mitigated by alternative routes of administration such as vaporization.) The IOM further added, "There is no conclusive evidence that marijuana causes cancer in humans, including cancers usually related to tobacco use."[15] A recent, large-scale, case-controlled study affirmed this finding, concluding that "the balance of evidence...does not favor the idea that marijuana as commonly used in the community is a major causal factor for head, neck, or lung cancer."[16]

Numerous studies and federally commissioned reports have endorsed marijuana's relative safety compared to other drugs, and recommended its decriminalization or legalization.[17] Virtually all of these studies have concluded that the criminal "classification of cannabis is disproportionate in relation both to its inherent harmfulness, and to the harmfulness of other substances."[18] Even a pair of editorials by the premier British medical journal, *The Lancet*, acknowledge: "The smoking of cannabis, even long-term, is not harmful to health.[19] ...It would be reasonable to judge cannabis as less of a threat...than alcohol or tobacco."[20] Indeed, by far the greatest danger to health posed by the use of marijuana stems from a criminal arrest and/or conviction.

Allegation #3: "Sixty percent of teenagers in treatment have a primary marijuana diagnosis. This means that the addiction to marijuana by our youth exceeds their addiction rates for alcohol, cocaine, heroin, methamphetamine, ecstasy and all other drugs combined."

Truth: This statement is purposely misleading. Although admissions to drug rehabilitation clinics among adolescent marijuana users have increased dramatically since the mid-1990s, this rise in marijuana admissions is due exclusively to a proportional increase in teens referred to drug treatment by the criminal justice system.[21] Primarily, these are teens arrested for pot possession, brought before a criminal judge (or drug court), and ordered to rehab in lieu of jail or juvenile detention.

As such, these data are in no way indicative of whether the person referred to treatment is suffering from any symptoms of dependence associated with marijuana use; most individuals admitted to treatment do so simply to avoid jail time. In fact, since 1995, the proportion of admissions from all sources other than the criminal justice system has actually *declined*, according to the federal Drug and Alcohol Services Information System (DASIS).[22] Consequently, DASIS reports that today, "over half (54%) of all adolescent marijuana admissions [are] through the criminal justice system," while an additional 25% come from referrals from schools and/or substance abuse providers.[23]

Allegation #4: "We may never rid this country of every crack pipe or marijuana plant. However, research proves that we have made substantial success in reducing drug use in this country."

Truth: In fact, marijuana enforcement has had no discernable long-term impact on marijuana availability or use. According to the most recent survey by the National Center on Addiction and Substance Abuse (CASA) at Columbia University, teenagers report that marijuana has surpassed tobacco and alcohol as the easiest drug to obtain.[24] This result is hardly surprising, given that annual federal data compiled by the University of Michigan's Monitoring the Future project reports that an estimated 85% of 12th graders say that marijuana is "fairly easy" or "very easy to get."[25] This percentage has remained virtually unchanged since the mid-1970s[26]—despite remarkably increased marijuana penalties, enforcement, and the prevalence of anti-marijuana propaganda since that time.

The percentage of adolescents experimenting with marijuana has also held steady over the long term. According to annual data compiled by Monitoring the Future, 47.3% of 12th graders reported having used marijuana in 1975.[27] Despite billions of dollars spent on drug education efforts (such as the federally funded DARE program) since that time, today's percentage (for the Class of 2001) remains virtually unchanged at 49%.[28]

In addition, according to data compiled by the federal National Household Survey on Drug Abuse, an estimated 2.4 million Americans tried marijuana for the first time in the year 2000, up from 1.4 million in 1990 and 0.6 million in 1965.[29] Not surprisingly, nearly one out of every two

American adults now acknowledges they have used marijuana, up from fewer than one in three in 1983.[30]

Allegation #5: "The truth is that marijuana is not harmless."
   Truth: This statement is correct; marijuana isn't harmless. No substance is, including those that are legal. Nevertheless, any risk presented by marijuana smoking falls within the ambit of choice we permit the individual in a free society.[31] As such, marijuana's relative risk to the user and society does not support criminal prohibition or the continued arrest of more than 700,000 Americans on marijuana charges every year. As recently concluded by the Canadian House of Commons in their December, 2002, report recommending marijuana decriminalization, "The consequences of conviction for possession of a small amount of cannabis for personal use are disproportionate to the potential harm associated with the behavior."[32]

Allegation #6: "As a factor in emergency room visits, marijuana has risen 176% since 1994, and now surpasses heroin."
   Truth: This statement is also purposely misleading, as it wrongly suggests that marijuana use is a causal factor in an alarming number of emergency room visits. It is not.
   Federal statistics gathered by the Drug Abuse Warning Network (DAWN) do indicate an increase in the number of people "mentioning" marijuana during hospital emergency room visits. (This increase is hardly unique to marijuana, however, as the overall number of drug mentions has risen dramatically since the late 1980s—likely due to improved federal reporting procedures.)[33] However, a marijuana "mention" does not mean that marijuana caused the hospital visit or that it was even a factor in leading to the emergency room episode, only that the patient said that he or she had used marijuana previously.
   For every emergency room visit related to drug use (so-called "drug abuse episodes"), hospital staff list up to five drugs the patient reports having used recently, regardless of whether or not their use of the drug caused the visit. The frequency with which any drug is mentioned in such visits is generally proportional to its frequency of use, irrespective of its inherent dangers.
   It is foolish for anyone—especially those in the administration's anti-drug office—to suggest or imply that marijuana is in any way potentially more dangerous to one's health than heroin. Marijuana is mentioned to hospital staff more frequently than heroin, not becauseit's more dangerous, but simply because a far greater percentage of the population uses marijuana than uses heroin. (It is also worth noting that alcohol is by far the

drug most frequently reported to DAWN, even though it is reported only when present in combination with another reportable drug.)[34]

Moreover, marijuana is rarely mentioned independently of other drugs. In fact, marijuana mentions alone accounted for less than 4% of all drug-related hospital emergency department visits (a level on par with common household pain relievers like acetaminophen), and only about .025% of all emergency room visits.[35]

Allegation #7: "Smoked marijuana leads to changes in the brain similar to those caused by the use of cocaine and heroin."

Truth: Allegations that marijuana smoking alters brain function or has long-term effects on cognition are reckless and scientifically unfounded. Federally sponsored population studies conducted in Jamaica, Greece and Costa Rica found no significant differences in brain function between long-term smokers and non-users.[36]

Similarly, a 1999 study of 1,300 volunteers published in *The American Journal of Epidemiology* reported "no significant differences in cognitive decline between heavy users, light users, and nonusers of cannabis" over a 15-year period.[37] Most recently, a meta-analysis of neuropsychological studies of long-term marijuana smokers by the National Institute on Drug Abuse (NIDA) reaffirmed this conclusion.[38] In addition, a study published in the *Canadian Medical Association Journal* in April, 2002, reported that even former heavy marijuana smokers experience no negative measurable effects on intelligence quotient.[39]

Claims specifically charging that marijuana leads to brain changes similar to those induced by heroin and cocaine are based solely on the results of a handful of animal studies that demonstrated that THC (delta-9-tetrahydrocannabinol, the main psychoactive ingredient in marijuana) can stimulate dopamine production under certain extreme conditions, and that the immediate cessation of THC (via the administration of a chemical blocking agent) will initiate some mild symptoms of withdrawal. These findings have little relevance to humans because, according to the U.S. Institute of Medicine, "The long half-life and slow elimination from the body of THC...prevent substantial abstinence symptoms."[40] As a result, such symptoms have been identified only in rare, unique patient settings limited to adolescents in treatment for substance abuse, or in clinical research trials where volunteers are administered marijuana or THC daily.[41]

Allegation #8: "One recent study involving a roadside check of reckless drivers (not impaired by alcohol) showed that 45% tested positive for marijuana."

Truth: Although no specific citation is provided in the drug czar's letter, this claim appears to be derived from a lone 1994 study published in the *New England Journal of Medicine* examining marijuana prevalence, not marijuana-associated culpability, in drivers arrested for reckless driving.[42] It should be noted that the drivers who tested positive for "marijuana" in this and similar studies actually tested positive for traces of a non-psychoactive marijuana metabolite during a urinalysis performed at the scene. Since marijuana metabolites remain present in the urine for days or even weeks after past use,[43] their detection is not indicative of intoxication or impairment, and it is misleading for the ONDCP to imply otherwise. While it is never safe or appropriate to drive under the influence of any substance—including marijuana—neither is it sound public policy to punish sober drivers as if they are impaired based solely on the presence of inactive metabolites.

As to the broader question of marijuana's acute impact on driving performance, evidence of marijuana's culpability in on-road driving accidents is not yet convincing.

Although marijuana intoxication has been shown to mildly impair psychomotor skills, this impairment does not appear to be severe or long-lasting.[44] In driving simulator tests, this impairment is typically manifested by subjects decreasing their driving speed and requiring greater time to respond to emergency situations.[45]

Nevertheless, this impairment does not appear to play a significant role in on-road traffic accidents. A 2002 review of seven separate crash culpability studies involving 7,934 drivers reported, "Crash culpability studies have failed to demonstrate that drivers with cannabinoids in the blood are significantly more likely than drug-free drivers to be culpable in road crashes."[46] This result is likely because subjects under the influence of marijuana are aware of their impairment and compensate for it accordingly, such as by slowing down and by focusing their attention when they know a response will be required. This reaction is the opposite of that exhibited by drivers under the influence of alcohol, who tend to drive in a more risky manner proportional to their intoxication.[47]

Today, a large body of research exists analyzing the impact of marijuana on psychomotor skills and actual driving performance. This research consists of driving simulator studies, on-road performance studies, crash culpability studies, and summary reviews of the existing evidence. The results of this data are fairly consistent: marijuana has a measurable yet relatively mild effect on psychomotor skills, yet it does not appear to play a significant role in vehicle crashes, particularly when compared to alcohol.

As summarized by the Canadian Senate's exhaustive 2002 report, "Cannabis: Our Position for a Canadian Public Policy," "Cannabis alone, particularly in low doses, has little effect on the skills involved in automobile driving."[48]

Allegation #9: "The truth is that marijuana is addictive... Marijuana users have an addiction rate of about 10%, and of the 5.6 million drug users who are suffering from illegal drug dependence or abuse, 62% are dependent on or abusing marijuana."

Truth: Marijuana use is not marijuana abuse. According to the U.S. Institute of Medicine, "Millions of Americans have tried marijuana, but most are not regular users... [and] few marijuana users become dependent on it."[49] In fact, less than 10% of marijuana users ever exhibit symptoms of dependence (as defined by the American Psychiatric Association's DSM-III-R criteria.)[50] By comparison, 15% of alcohol users, 17% of cocaine users, and a whopping 32% of cigarette smokers statistically exhibit symptoms of drug dependence.[51]

Marijuana is well-recognized as lacking the so-called "dependence liability" of other substances. According to the IOM, "Experimental animals that are given the opportunity to self-administer cannabinoids generally do not choose to do so, which has led to the conclusion that they are not reinforcing or rewarding."[52] Among humans, most marijuana users voluntarily cease their marijuana smoking by their late 20s or early 30s—often citing health or professional concerns and/or the decision to start a family.[53] Contrast this pattern with that of the typical tobacco smoker—many of whom begin as teens and continue smoking daily the rest of their lives.

That's not to say that some marijuana smokers do not become psychologically dependent on marijuana or find quitting difficult. But a comprehensive study released in 2002 by the Canadian Senate concluded that this dependence "is less severe and less frequent than dependence on other psychotropic substances, including alcohol and tobacco."[54] Observable withdrawal symptoms attributable to marijuana are also exceedingly rare. According to the Institute of Medicine, these symptoms are "mild and short lived"[55] compared to the profound physical withdrawal symptoms of other drugs, such as alcohol or heroin, and unlikely to persuade former smokers to reinitiate their marijuana use.[56]

Allegation #10: "Average THC levels rose from less than 1% in the late 1970s to more than 7% in 2001, and sinsemilla potency increased from 6% to 13%, and now reach as high as 33%"

Truth: This statement is both factually inaccurate and purposefully misleading. No population *en masse* has ever smoked marijuana averaging less than 1% THC, since such low potency marijuana would not induce euphoria. In fact, in many nations, marijuana of 1% THC or less is legally classified as an agricultural fiber crop.

Although annual marijuana potency data compiled by the University of Mississippi's Research Institute of Pharmaceutical Sciences does show a slight increase in marijuana's strength through the years (from about 3% to 5%), this increase is not nearly as dramatic as purported by the White House Office of National Drug Control Policy.[57] In addition, quantities of exceptionally strong strains of marijuana or sinsemilla (seedless marijuana) are inordinately expensive, comprise only a small percentage of the overall marijuana market, and are seldom used by the population at large— particularly younger adults.

It's worth noting, however, that more potent marijuana is not necessarily more dangerous. Marijuana poses no risk of fatal overdose, regardless of THC content, and since marijuana's greatest potential health hazard stems from the user's intake of carcinogenic smoke, it may be argued that higher potency marijuana may be slightly less harmful because it permits people to achieve desired psychoactive effects while inhaling less burning material.[58] In addition, studies indicate that marijuana smokers distinguish between high and low potency marijuana and moderate their use accordingly,[59] just as an alcohol consumer would drink fewer ounces of (high potency) bourbon than they would ounces of (low potency) beer.

Allegation #11: "The truth is that marijuana and violence are linked."

Truth: Absolutely not. No credible research has shown marijuana use to play a causal factor in violence, aggression or delinquent behavior, dating back to former President Richard Nixon's "First Report of the National Commission on Marihuana and Drug Abuse" in 1972, which concluded, "In short, marihuana is not generally viewed by participants in the criminal justice community as a major contributing influence in the commission of delinquent or criminal acts."[60]

Most recently, the Canadian Senate's 2002 "Discussion Paper on Cannabis" reaffirmed, "Cannabis use does not induce users to commit other forms of crime. Cannabis use does not increase aggressiveness or anti-social behavior."[61] In contrast, research has demonstrated that certain legal drugs, such as alcohol, do induce aggressive behavior.

"Cannabis differs from alcohol...in one major respect. It does not seem to increase risk-taking behavior," the British Advisory Council on the

Misuse of Drugs concluded in its 2002 report recommending the decriminalization of marijuana. "This means that cannabis rarely contributes to violence either to others or to oneself, whereas alcohol use is a major factor in deliberate self-harm, domestic accidents and violence."[62]

Allegation #12: "The truth is that we aren't imprisoning individuals for just 'smoking a joint.'... Nationwide, the percentage of those in prison for marijuana possession as their most serious offense is less than half of one percent (0.46%), and those generally involved exceptional circumstances."

Truth: This statement is both inaccurate and misleading. Police have arrested some six million Americans for marijuana violations since 1992 and now average more than 700,000 arrests per year.[63] The overwhelming majority of these arrests—approximately 88%—are for simple possession only, not marijuana cultivation or sale.[64]

While not all of those individuals arrested are eventually sentenced to long terms in jail, the fact remains that the repercussions of a marijuana conviction are significant—including (but not limited to) probation and mandatory drug testing, loss of driving privileges, loss of federal college aid, asset forfeiture, revocation of professional driver's license, loss of certain welfare benefits such as food stamps, removal from public housing, loss of child custody, and loss of employment.

Whether or not marijuana offenders ultimately serve time in jail, the fact is that hundreds of thousands of otherwise law-abiding citizens are having their lives needlessly destroyed each year for nothing more than smoking marijuana.

Specific totals on marijuana offenders behind bars are seldom available because federal statistics do not categorize drug offenders by drug type or drug offense. However, according to a 1997 Bureau of Justice Statistics survey of federal and state prisoners, approximately 19% of federal and 13% of state drug offenders are incarcerated for marijuana offenses.[65] Based on those statistics, a 1999 paper published by the Federation of American Scientists estimated that nearly 60,000 inmates (roughly one in every seven drug prisoners) were incarcerated for marijuana offenses at that time.[66] Since then, some experts estimate that this number has grown to more than 75,000 marijuana prisoners.[67]

Allegation #13: "The truth is that marijuana is a gateway drug... People who used marijuana are 8 times more likely to have used cocaine, 15 times more likely to have used heroin, and 5 times more likely to develop a need for treatment of abuse or dependence on ANY drug."

Truth: Nonsense. According to the Canadian Senate's 2002 study,

"Cannabis: Our Position for a Canadian Public Policy," "Cannabis itself is not a cause of other drug use."[68] This finding concurs with the conclusions of the U.S. National Academy of Science's Institute of Medicine 1999 study, which stated that marijuana is not a "gateway drug to the extent that it is a cause or even that it is the most significant predictor of serious drug abuse."[69] Statistically, for every 104 Americans who have tried marijuana, there is only one regular user of cocaine and less than one user of heroin, according to annual data compiled by the federal National Household Survey on Drug Abuse.[70] Clearly, for the overwhelming majority of marijuana smokers, pot is a "terminus" rather than a gateway.[71]

However, among the minority of marijuana smokers who do graduate to harder substances, it's arguably marijuana prohibition rather than the use of marijuana itself that often serves as a doorway to the world of hard drugs. The more users become integrated in an environment where, apart from marijuana, more dangerous drugs can also be obtained, the greater the chances they will experiment with those harder substances. Therefore, if the Office of National Drug Control Policy truly wished to address the limited association between marijuana and the use of other drugs, it would support policies separating marijuana from the criminal black market.

Allegation #14: "The truth is that marijuana legalization would be a nightmare in America. After Dutch coffee shops started selling marijuana in small quantities, use of the drug nearly tripled…between 1984 and 1996. While our nation's cocaine consumption has decreased by 80% over the past 15 years, Europe's has increased…and the Dutch government has started to reconsider its policy."

Truth: This statement is inaccurate and greatly distorts the well-documented European drug policy experience. Most European countries—including Belgium, Germany, Italy, Luxembourg, the Netherlands, Portugal, Spain, Switzerland—do not criminally arrest marijuana users.[72] Yet virtually every European nation, including the Netherlands, has drastically lower rates of marijuana and drug use among their adult and teen population compared to the United States.[73] In fact, the national drug policy trends in Europe are currently moving toward more liberal marijuana laws and away from U.S.-styled drug policy.[74] For example, Great Britain recently announced that Parliament would formally downgrade marijuana so that its possession is no longer an arrestable offense.[75]

As to the White House's specific claim regarding Dutch marijuana use, the truth is that lifetime reported use of marijuana by Dutch citizens aged 12 and older is less than half of what is reported in America.[76] In addition, Dutch policy-makers downgraded marijuana offenses in the mid-1970s; this

163

makes it unlikely that any purported increase in Dutch marijuana use during the 1980s was directly attributable to the change in law. In fact, most experts agree that marijuana's illegality has little impact on marijuana use.[77] According to a 2001 study published in *The British Journal of Psychiatry*, "The Dutch experience, together with those of a few other countries with more modest [marijuana] policy changes, provides a moderately good empirical case that removal of criminal prohibitions on cannabis possession (decriminalization) will not increase the prevalence of marijuana or any other illicit drug; the argument for decriminalization is thus strong."[78]

Allegation #15: "The truth is that marijuana is not a medicine, and no credible research suggests that it is."

Truth: This allegation is a lie, plain and simple. According to a 2001 national survey of U.S. physicians conducted for the American Society of Addiction Medicine, nearly half of all doctors with opinions support legalizing marijuana as a medicine.[79] Moreover, no less than 80 state and national health care organizations—including the American Public Health Association[80] and *The New England Journal of Medicine*[81]—support immediate, legal patient access to medical marijuana.[82] The medical community's support for medical marijuana is not based on "pseudo-science," but rather on the reports of thousands of patients and scores of scientific studies affirming pot's therapeutic value.

Modern research suggests that cannabis is a valuable aid in the treatment of a wide range of clinical applications. These include pain relief—particularly of neuropathic pain (pain from nerve damage)—nausea, spasticity, glaucoma, and movement disorders.[83] Marijuana is also a powerful appetite stimulant, specifically for patients suffering from HIV, the AIDS wasting syndrome, or dementia.[84] Emerging research suggests that marijuana's medicinal properties may protect the body against some types of malignant tumors and are neuroprotective.[85]

Recent scientific reviews supporting marijuana's use as a therapeutic agent include a 1998 report by Britain's House of Lords Science and Technology Committee that concludes, "The government should allow doctors to prescribe cannabis for medical use… Cannabis can be effective in some patients to relieve symptoms of multiple sclerosis, and against certain forms of pain… This evidence is enough to justify a change in the law."[86]

A 1999 review by the U.S. Institute of Medicine added, "The accumulated data indicate a potential therapeutic value of cannabinoid drugs, particularly for symptoms such as pain relief, control of nausea and vomiting, and appetite stimulation,"[87] and recommended the U.S. government allow immediate single-patient clinical trials whereupon patients could legally use inhaled marijuana medicinally in a controlled setting.[88] It should be noted that the IOM also reviewed the medical efficacy of the legal synthetic THC drug Marinol, which it found to have "poor bioavailability," slow onset, and adverse effects such as "anxiety, depersonalization, dizziness, euphoria, dysphoria, [and] somnolence" in approximately one-third of patients who use it.[89] As such, the authors noted that many patients prefer whole smoked marijuana rather than this legal alternative.

The most recent overview of marijuana's medical efficacy was conducted by the Canadian Senate's Special Committee on Illegal Drugs in 2002. The authors concluded, "There are clear...indications of the therapeutic benefits of marijuana in the following conditions: analgesic for chronic pain, antispasm for multiple sclerosis, anticonvulsive for epilepsy, antiemetic for chemotherapy and appetite stimulant for cachexia,"[90] and advised Parliament to revise existing federal regulations so that any "person affected by one of the following [medical conditions]: wasting syndrome; chemotherapy treatment; fibromyalgia; epilepsy; multiple sclerosis; accident-induced chronic pain; and some physical conditions including migraines and chronic headaches, whose physical state has been certified by a physician or an individual duly authorized by the competent medical association of the province or territory in question, may choose to buy cannabis and its derivatives for therapeutic purposes."[91]

Commentary

From an ethical standpoint, the federal government's return to "Reefer Madness" is obviously disturbing. Equally troublesome, however, is the fact that from a strictly public health and safety standpoint, this campaign is inherently self-defeating. There is nothing to be gained by exaggerating marijuana's harmfulness. On the contrary, by overstating marijuana's potential dangers, the government seriously undermines its credibility— including its ability to effectively educate people about the harms associated with more dangerous drugs.

How much damage has already been done? A 2002 federally commissioned review of the White House's National Youth Anti-Drug Media Campaign had this to say, and it's not encouraging. "There is little evidence of direct favorable Campaign effects on youth," the authors determined. "There is no statistically significant decline in marijuana use or improvement in beliefs or attitudes about marijuana use."[92] In fact, the only statistical association researchers found between the government's anti-marijuana ads (the most visible part of its new "Reefer Madness" campaign) and viewers' use habits was that teens who were exposed most often to the ads were more likely to use marijuana at levels higher than their peers.

Testifying before Congress in June of 2002, one of the report's authors labeled the government's anti-marijuana effort the worst large-scale public ad campaign in history.[93] The federal government's response? Simply up the ante with more frequent ads and even harsher rhetoric. Call it the new, "New Reefer Madness" campaign.

It doesn't have to be this way. Rather than stay this failing course, our federal officials ought to tear a page from their more successful public health campaigns discouraging teen pregnancy, drunk driving, and adolescent tobacco smoking—all of which have been significantly reduced in recent years. America has not achieved these results by banning the use of alcohol or tobacco, or by targeting and arresting adults who engage in these behaviors responsibly, but through honest, fact-based public education campaigns. Until the federal government applies these same common-sense principles and strategies to address marijuana policy, their efforts are doomed to fail, and no amount of "Reefer Madness" can change that.

Notes

1. S. Burns, White House Office of National Drug Control Policy (ONDCP), "An Open Letter to America's Prosecutors," Washington, D.C., November 1, 2002.

2. Excerpts from the drug czar's letter are included here. The full text is available at www.norml.org/index.cfm?Group_ID=5513.

3. U.S. Department of Justice (U.S. DOJ), Federal Bureau of Investigation (FBI), *Uniform Crime Report: Crime in the United States 2001*, Washington, D.C., 2002, page 232, Table 4.1: Arrest for Drug Abuse Violations.

4. *Ibid.*

5. *Ibid.*, Table 4.1: Arrest for Drug Abuse Violations and Table 29: Estimated Arrests, United States, 2001.

6. National Organization for the Reform of Marijuana Laws (NORML), *Still Crazy After All These Years: Marijuana Prohibition 1937–1997: A report prepared by the National Organization for the Reform of Marijuana Laws (NORML) on the occasion of the sixtieth anniversary of the adoption of the Marijuana Tax Act of 1937*, Washington, D.C., 1997.

7. U.S. DOJ, FBI, combined *Uniform Crime Reports, 1993–2002*, Washington, D.C. U.S. Census Bureau, April 1, 2000. State population data available at www.census.gov/population/cen2000/tab05.txt.

8. U.S. DOJ, FBI, combined *Uniform Crime Reports, 1993–2002*, Washington, D.C.

9. U.S. DOJ, Bureau of Justice Statistics, *Drugs and Crime Facts*, Table: Number of Arrests by Drug Type, 1982-1999, Washington, D.C., 2000. NORML, *Drug War Priorities Shift From Hard Drugs To Marijuana Arrest Figures Reveal*, July 8, 1999, www.norml.org/index.cfm?Group_ID=4015.

10. Centers for Disease Control (CDC), *National Vital Statistics Report*, September 16, 2002.

11. CDC, *Morbidity and Mortality Weekly Report*, April, 2002, www.cdc.gov/mmwr/preview/mmwrhtml/mm5114a2.htm#tab1.

12. Australian National Drug and Alcohol Research Centre, *The Health and Psychological Consequences of Cannabis Use*, Canberra: Australian Government Publishing Service, 1994; see specifically Chapter 9, Section 9.3.1, Acute Effects: "There are no recorded cases of fatalities attributable to cannabis, and the extrapolated lethal dose from animal studies cannot be achieved by recreational users." National Academy of Sciences, Institute of Medicine (IOM), *Marijuana and Medicine: Assessing the Science Base*, Washington D.C.: National Academy Press, 1999.

13. S. Sidney *et al.*, "Marijuana Use and Mortality," *American Journal of Public Health* 87, 1997, pages 1–4.

14. National Academy of Sciences, page 5.

15. *Ibid.*, page 199.

16. D. Ford *et al.*, National Institutes of Health, "Marijuana use is not associated with head, neck or lung cancer in adults younger than 55 years: Results of a case cohort study," *National Institute on Drug Abuse Workshop on Clinical Consequences of Marijuana: Program Book*, Rockville, MD, 2001, page 10.

17. Studies include but are not limited to the following. Canadian House of Commons Special Committee on the Non-Medical Use of Drugs, *Policy for the New Millennium: Working Together to Redefine Canada's Drug Strategy*, Ottawa, 2002. Canadian Special Senate Committee on Illegal Drugs, *Cannabis: Our Position for a Canadian Public Policy*, Ottawa, 2002. United Kingdom's Advisory Council on the Misuse of Drugs, *The Classification of Cannabis Under the Misuse of Drugs Act of 1971*, London, 2002. British House of Commons Home Affairs Committee, *Third Report*, London, 2002. Jamaican National Commission on Ganja, *A Report of the National Commission on Ganja*, Kingston, 2001. Australian National Drug and Alcohol Research Centre, *The Health and Psychological Consequences of Cannabis Use*, 1994. First Report of the National Commission on Marihuana and Drug Abuse, *Marihuana: A Signal of Misunderstanding*, Washington, D.C.: U.S. Government Printing Office, 1972.

18. House of Commons Home Affairs Committee, see specifically note 118.

19. "Editorial: Deglamorising Cannabis," *The Lancet*, November 11, 1995, page 346.

20. "Editorial: Dangerous Habits," *The Lancet*, November 14, 1998, page 352.

21. U.S. Office of Applied Studies, Substance Abuse and Mental Health Services Administration (SAMHSA), "Treatment Referral Sources for Adolescent Marijuana Users," *The DASIS (Drug and Alcohol Services Information System) Report*, Washington, D.C., March 29, 2002.

22. *Ibid.*, Figure 1: Number of Adolescent Marijuana Admissions, by Referral Source, 1992–1999.

23. *Ibid.*

24. Associated Press, *Teens Say Buying Dope Is Easy*, August 19, 2002.

25. Monitoring the Future, *2002 Data From In-School Surveys of 8th, 10th, and 12th Grade Students*, Ann Arbor, Michigan; see specifically Drug and Alcohol Press Release and Tables, Specific Drugs—Figure 2: Marijuana: Trends in Annual Use, Risk, Disapproval, and Availability for 8th, 10th, and 12th Graders, 2002, http://monitoringthefuture.org/data/02data.html#2002data-drugs.

26. *Ibid.*

27. Monitoring the Future, *2001 Data From In-School Surveys of 8th, 10th, and 12th Grade Students*, Ann Arbor, Michigan. See specifically Drug and Alcohol Press Release and Tables, Data Tables—Figure 4: Long-Term Trends in Lifetime Prevalence of Use of Various Drugs for 12th Graders, 2001, http://monitoringthefuture.org/data/01data.html.

28. *Ibid.*

29. SAMHSA, *2001 National Household Survey on Drug Abuse*, Washington, D.C., 2002; see specifically Chapter 5, Trends in Initiation of Substance Use: Marijuana, www.samhsa.gov/oas/nhsda/2k1nhsda/vol1/CHAPTER5.HTM#fig5.1.

30. Results from a *Time/CNN* telephone poll of 1,007 adult Americans age 18 or older, conducted October 23–24, 2002.

31. Jimmy Carter, Presidential address to Congress, August 2, 1977, "Penalties against drug use should

not be more damaging to an individual than use of the drug itself. Nowhere is this more clear than in the laws against the possession of marijuana in private for personal use."

32. Canadian House of Commons Special Committee on the Non-Medical Use of Drugs, page 131.

33. John P. Morgan and Lynn Zimmer, *Marijuana Myths, Marijuana Facts: A Review of the Scientific Evidence*, New York: The Lindesmith Center, 1997, page 131.

34. SAMHSA, Drug Abuse Warning Network (DAWN), *Detailed Emergency Department Tables From the Drug Abuse Warning Network, 2001*, Washington, D.C., 2002.

35. Analysis of 2001 DAWN data by Richard Cowan, www.marijuananews.com/news.php3?sid=575.

36. E. Russo *et al.*, "Chronic cannabis use in the Compassionate Investigational New Drug Program: an examination of benefits and adverse effects of legal clinical cannabis," *Journal of Cannabis Therapeutics* 2, 2002, pages 3–57; see specifically "Previous Chronic Cannabis Use Studies."

37. C. Lyketsos *et al.*, "Cannabis use and cognitive decline in persons under 65 years of age," *American Journal of Epidemiology* 149, 1999, pages 794–800.

38. I. Grant *et al.*, "Long-Term neurocognitive consequences of marijuana: a meta-analytic study," *National Institute on Drug Abuse Workshop on Clinical Consequences of Marijuana: Program Book*, National Institutes of Health, Rockville, MD, 2001, page 12; see specifically Abstract: "The 13 studies that met our criteria yielded no basis for concluding that long-term cannabis use is associated with generalized neurocognitive decline, with the possible exception of slight decrements in the area of learning new information."

39. P. Fried *et al.*, "Current and former marijuana use: preliminary findings of a longitudinal study of effects on IQ in young adults," *Canadian Medical Association Journal* 166, 2002, pages 887–891; see specifically Abstract: "A negative effect was not observed among subjects who had previously been heavy users but were no longer using the substance. We conclude that marijuana does not have a long-term negative impact on global intelligence."

40. National Academy of Sciences, page 58.

41. *Ibid.*, page 91.

42. D. Brookoff *et al.*, "Testing reckless drivers for cocaine and marijuana," *The New England Journal of Medicine* 331, 1994, pages 518–522.

43. C. Dackis *et al.*, "Persistence of urinary marijuana levels after supervised abstinence," *American Journal of Psychiatry* 139, 1982, pages 1196–1198; see specifically Discussion: "Urinary excretion of cannabinoids persist for roughly three weeks after supervised abstinence."

44. Studies include but are not limited to the following. Canadian Special Senate Committee on Illegal Drugs, *Cannabis: Our Position for a Canadian Public Policy*, 2002; see specifically Chapter 5, "Driving Under the Influence of Cannabis." UK Department of Environment, Transport and the Regions (Road Safety Division), *Cannabis and Driving: A Review of the Literature and Commentary*, Crowthorne, Berks: TRL Limited, 2000. A. Smiley, "Marijuana: On-Road and Driving Simulator Studies," H. Kalant *et al.* (editors), *The Health Effects of Cannabis*, Toronto: Center for Addiction and Mental Health, 1999, pages 173–191. House of Lords Select Committee on Science and Technology, *Ninth Report, Cannabis: The Scientific and Medical Evidence*, London: The Stationary Office, 1998; see specifically Chapter 4, Section 4.7.

45. B. Sexton *et al.*, *The influence of cannabis on driving: A report prepared for the UK Department of the Environment, Transport and the Regions (Road Safety Division)*, Crowthorne, Berks: TRL Limited, 2000. UK Department of Environment, Transport and the Regions (Road Safety Division), *Cannabis and Driving: A Review of the Literature and Commentary*, 2000. Smiley.

46. G. Chesher and M. Longo, *2002 Cannabis and alcohol in motor vehicle accidents*, Grotenhermen and E. Russo (editors), *Cannabis and Cannabinoids: Pharmacology, Toxicology, and Therapeutic Potential*, New York: Haworth Press, pages 313–323.

47. *Ibid.* Smiley. United Kingdom's Advisory Council on the Misuse of Drugs, *The Classification of*

Cannabis Under the Misuse of Drugs Act of 1971, 2002; see specifically Chapter 4, Section 4.3.5: "Cannabis differs from alcohol;…it seems not to increase risk-taking behavior. This may explain why it appears to play a smaller role than alcohol in road traffic accidents."

48. Canadian Special Senate Committee on Illegal Drugs, *Cannabis: Our Position for a Canadian Public Policy*, page 18.

49. National Academy of Sciences, pages 92–96.

50. *Ibid.*, page 95, Table 3.4: Prevalence of Drug Use and Dependence in the General Population.

51. *Ibid.*

52. *Ibid.*, page 57.

53. *Ibid.*, page 92. Canadian Special Senate Committee on Illegal Drugs, *Cannabis: Our Position for a Canadian Public Policy*, page 16.

54. Canadian House of Commons Special Committee on the Non-Medical Use of Drugs, page 17.

55. National Academy of Sciences, page 6.

56. *Ibid.*, pages 83–101.

57. University of Mississippi Potency Monitoring Project Quarterly Reports, Oxford. Dan Forbes, "The Myth of Potent Pot," *Slate*, November 19, 2002.

58. John P. Morgan and Lynn Zimmer, page 139.

59. S. Heishman *et al.*, "Effects of tetrahydrocannabinol content on marijuana behavior, subjective reports, and performances," *Pharmacology, Biochemistry and Behavior* 34, 1989, pages 173–179.

60. First Report of the National Commission on Marihuana and Drug Abuse, *Marihuana: A Signal of Misunderstanding*, 1972, page 75.

61. Canadian Special Senate Committee on Illegal Drugs, *Discussion Paper on Cannabis*, Ottawa, 2002, page 4.

62. United Kingdom's Advisory Council on the Misuse of Drugs, Chapter 4, Section 4.3.6.

63. www.norml.org/index.cfm?Group ID=5513. FBI, *Uniform Crime Report: Crime in the United States 2001*, Table 4.1: Arrest for Drug Abuse Violations and Table 29: Estimated Arrests, United States, 2001.

64. FBI, *Uniform Crime Report: Crime in the United States 2001*, Table 4.1: Arrest for Drug Abuse Violations.

65. U.S. DOJ, Bureau of Justice Statistics, *Substance Abuse and Treatment of State and Federal Prisoners 1997*, Washington, D.C., 1999.

66. C. Thomas, Federation of American Scientists (FAS), "Marijuana arrests and incarceration in the United States," *FAS Drug Policy Analysis Bulletin* 7, 1999.

67. Marijuana Policy Project, *Marijuana Arrests Near All-Time High in 2001*, Washington, D.C., October 28, 2002.

68. Canadian Special Senate Committee on Illegal Drugs, *Cannabis: Our Position for a Canadian Public Policy*, page 15.

69. National Academy of Sciences, page 101.

70. Morgan and Zimmer, page 36, Figure 4–2: Very Few Marijuana Users Become Regular Users of Cocaine; see cited Federal Household data.

71. United Kingdom's Advisory Council, Chapter 4, Section 4.6.2: "Even if the gateway theory is correct, it cannot be a particularly wide gate as the majority of cannabis users never move on to Class A [hard] drugs."

72. European Monitoring Centre for Drugs and Drug Addiction, *European Legal Database on Drugs: Country Profiles*, 2002, http://eldd.emcdda.org/databases/eldd_country_profiles.cfm. NORML, *European Drug Policy: 2002 Legislative Update*, Washington, D.C., 2002, www.norml.org/index.cfm?Group_ID=5446.

73. European Monitoring Centre for Drugs and Drug Addiction, *2001 Annual Report on the State of the Drugs Problem in the European Union*, Lisbon. "Study Finds Teenage Drug Use Higher in U.S. Than in

Europe," *The New York Times*, February 21, 2001.

74. European Monitoring Centre for Drugs and Drug Addiction, *Decriminalisation in Europe: Recent developments in legal approaches to drug use*, Lisbon, 2001. "Europe Moves Drug War From Prisons to Clinics," *The Washington Post*, May 2, 2002.

75. United Press International, *UK Govt Downgrades Cannabis*, July 10, 2002.

76. R. MacCoun and Peter Reuter, "Evaluating alternative cannabis regimes," *British Journal of Psychiatry* 178, 2001, pages 123–128. R. MacCoun, "American distortions of Dutch drug statistics," *Society*, March/April, 2001, pages 23–26.

77. NORML, "Marijuana Decriminalization and Its Impact on Use: A Review of the Scientific Evidence," 2001, www.norml.org/index.cfm?Group_ID=3383. E. Single *et al.* "The Impact of Cannabis Decriminalisation in Australia and the United States," *Journal of Public Health Policy* 21, 2000, pages 157–186. National Academy of Sciences, page 104. E. Single, "The Impact of Marijuana Decriminalization: An Update," *Journal of Public Health* 10, 1989, pages 456–466. L. Johnson *et al.*, "Marijuana Decriminalization: The Impact on Youth 1975–1980," *Monitoring the Future, Occasional Paper Series*, Paper 13, Institute for Social Research, University of Michigan, Ann Arbor, 1981.

78. MacCoun and Reuter.

79. Reuters News Wire, *Physicians divided on medical marijuana*, April 23, 2001.

80. American Public Health Association (APHA) Resolution #9513, "Access to Therapeutic Marijuana/Cannabis." The resolution states, in part, that the APHA "encourages research of the therapeutic properties of various cannabinoids and combinations of cannabinoids, and...urges the Administration and Congress to move expeditiously to make cannabis available as a legal medicine."

81. "Editorial: Federal Foolishness and Marijuana," *New England Journal of Medicine* 336, January 30, 1997; "Federal authorities should rescind their prohibition of the medical use of marijuana for seriously ill patients and allow physicians to decide which patients to treat. The government should change marijuana's status from that of a Schedule I drug...to that of a Schedule II drug...and regulate it accordingly."

82. The complete list of health organizations endorsing legal access to medical marijuana is available at www.norml.org/index.cfm?Group_ID=3388.

83. Studies include but are not limited to the following. Canadian Special Senate Committee on Illegal Drugs, *Cannabis: Our Position for a Canadian Public Policy*. Jamaican National Commission on Ganja. National Academy of Sciences. House of Lords Select Committee on Science and Technology. IOM, *Marijuana and Health*, Washington, D.C.: National Academy Press, 1982.

84. *Ibid.*

85. National Academy of Sciences.

86. House of Lords Press Office, *Lords Say, Legalise Cannabis for Medical Use*, London, November 11, 1998.

87. National Academy of Sciences, page 3.

88. *Ibid.*, page 8.

89. *Ibid.*, page 203.

90. Canadian Special Senate Committee on Illegal Drugs, *Cannabis: Our Position for a Canadian Public Policy*, page 19.

91. *Ibid*, page 51, "Proposals for Implementing the Regulation of Cannabis for Therapeutic and Recreational Purposes,"

92. Westat & The Annenberg School for Communication, *Evaluation of the National Youth Anti-Drug Media Campaign: Fourth Semi-Annual Report of Findings*, Rockville, MD, 2002, page xi.

93. Robert Hornick, Written Testimony, Senate Committee on Appropriations, Subcommittee on Treasury and General Government, Hearing on the Effectiveness of the National Youth Anti-Drug Media Campaign, June 19, 2002.

Section V:

STRATEGIES FOR REFORM

17. Liberal Versus Libertarian Views on Drug Legalization

BY JEFFREY MIRON

Jeffrey Miron is a professor of economics at Boston University. He has written extensively about crime related to alcohol and drug prohibition (http://econ.bu.edu/miron/). Miron earned his doctorate at MIT in 1984.

To most observers of the drug-policy debates, all drug legalizers are alike. The reality, however, is that legalizers come in two distinct flavors. Most legalizers are liberals, and their views on drug policy are consistent with liberal views on other issues. A minority of legalizers are libertarians, however, and their views on drug policy reflect libertarian perspectives on policy generally. There is ample overlap in the views espoused by these two camps. But there are also substantial differences in their views on legalization and related matters.

In this piece I compare the liberal and libertarian views on drug legalization. Most advocacy on behalf of legalization comes from liberal supporters of this policy, so most persons familiar with the issue have been exposed mainly to this perspective. My goal here is to outline the libertarian defense of drug legalization and explain how it differs from the more common approach.

The discussion does not suggest that the libertarian defense is "better" or "more correct" than the liberal perspective; instead, it clarifies the implicit assumptions underlying both views. In addition, the analysis suggests that some aspects of the libertarian perspective can make legalization appealing to a segment of the population that finds the liberal defense unpersuasive; thus, incorporating components of the libertarian perspective potentially strengthens the case for legalization.

In presenting this analysis, I have oversimplified both liberal and libertarian views on legalization. There is enormous diversity within both camps, so the generalizations offered here may not reflect the views of everyone in either camp. But I believe the characterizations presented capture the essential elements in the two perspectives and thus allow an accessible discussion of the differences.

Overview

The fundamental tenet of the libertarian perspective on drug legalization is that individuals, not governments, should decide who consumes drugs. This stems in part from the libertarian assumption that most individuals make reasonable choices about drug use. It also reflects the libertarian view that, even when individuals make bad decisions about drug use, government attempts to "improve" these decisions create more problems than they solve.

Thus, libertarians accept that some drug use seems irrational and self-destructive, but they believe prohibition creates far more harm than does drug use itself. Moreover, they do not think reducing drug use is an appropriate goal for government policy except in situations where such use has direct and substantial costs to innocent third parties. In both these senses, the libertarian view on drug policy is consistent with the libertarian attitude toward prohibitions generally.

The liberal view on drug legalization stems from somewhat different considerations. Liberals do not generally trust individuals to make reasonable choices about drug use, and they think government should adopt policies that attempt to discourage drug use. But liberal legalizers do not like using police power to achieve this goal, especially when that power is directed at drug users as opposed to drug sellers. Thus, although liberal legalizers want government to reduce the harms from drug abuse, they prefer approaches other than prohibition.

The liberal view on legalization reflects an assessment of the relative harms of drug use versus drug prohibition, and in that sense is similar to the libertarian calculus. But liberals put less weight on consumer sovereignty, and they are not as fundamentally suspicious of government prohibitions as are libertarians. Thus, for commodities viewed as substantially harmful (e.g., tobacco), liberals are willing to consider prohibition, but for commodities viewed as relatively benign (e.g., marijuana), they find prohibition excessive.

Liberals and libertarians are in close agreement on the fact that prohibition has many undesired consequences. These include the infringements on civil liberties that are an inevitable consequence of attempts to sanction victimless crimes; the corruption and violence fostered in foreign countries by U.S. attempts to enforce prohibition; the increased frequency of overdoses and accidental poisonings that result from the poor quality control in black markets; the increased property crime that results from elevated drug prices; and the violence that results because participants in black markets settle disagreements with guns rather than lawyers.

Liberal and libertarian legalizers agree, therefore, that the arrest and prosecution of drug users is ill-advised and that current enforcement of prohibition against drug suppliers is excessive. On the question of whether drugs should be legalized outright, however, and on a broad range of other drug policy issues, they disagree considerably. In the remainder of this piece, I outline the main areas of disagreement.

Legalization or Decriminalization

Perhaps the most fundamental difference between libertarian and liberal legalizers is that libertarians favor outright legalization, while liberals prefer decriminalization or other partial measures. Under full legalization, the production, distribution, sale, and possession of drugs are all legal; the law treats drugs like any other commodity. Under decriminalization, the possession of drugs is not subject to criminal sanctions, but penalties against production, distribution, and sale remain in place. Thus, drugs are not legal commodities.

This liberal preference for decriminalization derives from several sources. Liberals regard freedoms practiced by individuals as more important than freedoms practiced by businesses; thus, they defend the right to consume drugs more ardently than the right to sell drugs. Liberals also regard the pursuit of profits with skepticism, which makes them more hostile toward drug sellers than toward drug users. And focus on decriminalization is consistent with the liberal view that the main negative of prohibition is its adverse treatment of drug users.

Many liberal legalizers do advocate more than just decriminalizing possession. The specific proposals, however, involve substantial government control over the production, distribution, and sale of drugs. Some proposals, for example, permit the sale of drugs only through government-owned stores, as occurs for liquor in certain places. Other proposals require consumers to have special government IDs in order to buy drugs. Still other proposals retain much of the current legal regime while allowing freer distribution of drugs through medical channels, as in the British system of narcotic maintenance, or via clinics, as in methadone maintenance.

Libertarians regard the decriminalization approach as odd. They note that for every buyer there must be a seller, so it makes little sense to criminalize one side of the market but not the other. And libertarians have no objection to the vigorous pursuit of profits, so long as this occurs within the law.

Even more importantly, libertarians emphasize that decriminalization does little to reduce prohibition-generated ills other than those directly related to the adverse legal treatment of drug users. Decriminalization maintains the illegal status of production, distribution, and sale of drugs, so the industry still operates underground. This means the negative side effects of prohibition (crime, corruption, infringements on civil liberties, poor quality control, wealth transfers to criminals, disruption of other countries) all continue under decriminalization. The only benefit of decriminalization relative to prohibition is that drug users face limited legal penalties from drug use.

Liberals might respond to this perspective by suggesting that several European countries have minimized the harms from drugs and drug prohibition by decriminalizing without legalizing. This conclusion is unwarranted, however, because it confounds the prohibition of drugs with the degree to which prohibition is enforced. Countries that have decriminalized are, by and large, countries with minimal enforcement of their drug laws generally, including those directed at the supply side. This low level of enforcement mitigates the effects of prohibition on crime, corruption, and other prohibition-generated ills, even though drugs are still prohibited.

Thus, libertarians advocate outright legalization rather than decriminalization, although they agree that decriminalization is preferable to current practice. They also agree that expanded medical provision of drugs, or the supply of drugs via government stores, diminishes many prohibition-induced ills by bringing some or all of the drug market above ground. Libertarians nevertheless regard these partial approaches as less desirable than full legalization.

Legalization of Marijuana Only Versus Legalization of All Drugs

A second important difference between liberal and libertarian positions on legalization is whether to legalize all drugs or just marijuana.

For libertarians, the answer is to legalize all drugs. Libertarians view individuals as competent to make reasonable decisions about commodities that have modest risks, such as marijuana, and about commodities that have more serious risks, such as cocaine or heroin. They view the evils of prohibition as arising from the nature of prohibition itself, independent of the qualities of the product being prohibited.

For many liberals, the answer is to legalize marijuana only. Since liberals are not convinced individuals make reasonable decisions on their own, their views on which drugs to legalize reflect their views on which drugs are relatively benign and which drugs are relatively harmful. Most observers regard marijuana as far less dangerous than cocaine, heroin, or other illegal drugs, which means liberals see legalization as obvious for marijuana but less compelling with respect to other drugs.

The libertarian versus liberal perspective on addiction leads to the same conclusion about legalizing marijuana versus legalizing other drugs. By all reasonable accounts, marijuana is far less addictive than cocaine, heroin, and other prohibited drugs. To liberals, this is an important factor in determining the appropriate legal status, since liberals view addiction as a disease that invalidates users' ability to make rational choices about drug consumption.

Libertarians do not accept this perspective. They agree that some commodities are reasonably characterized as habit-forming, but they do not regard addiction as a problem *per se*. Moreover, they believe those addicted to drugs bear responsibility for their actions, whatever the pharmacological properties of the drugs. Thus, again, they prefer legalization of all drugs.

Subsidizing Drug Abuse Treatment

Another issue that separates liberal and libertarian views on drug policy is government-funded treatment for drug abuse. The typical liberal view is that government expenditure on interdiction should be scaled back or eliminated, with these funds transferred to the budget for drug-abuse treatment. The libertarian view is that interdicting drugs and subsidizing treatment are, at a minimum, separate issues. Governments can scale back interdiction without necessarily increasing treatment budgets, and the question of whether to subsidize treatment arises with or without legalization.

In addition, libertarians doubt that expenditure for drug-abuse treatment is a good use of government funds. This perspective again derives from the view that most individuals make informed, voluntary decisions about whether to use drugs and that reducing drug use is not an appropriate goal of government policy. This is not a criticism of treatment for persons who wish to curtail their drug use; rather, it is a view that treatment should be paid for by those obtaining the treatment.

Moreover, libertarians believe government subsidy of drug-abuse treatment has several negatives. Perhaps most importantly, subsidizing treatment implicitly accepts the viewthat drug use is wrong; libertarians are agnostic on whether other persons' drug use is good or bad, so long as that use does not substantially harm innocent third parties. A different negative is that accepting a government role in subsidizing treatment is the first step down a slippery slope toward coercing treatment, which has alarming implications for civil liberties.

On top of these concerns, libertarians note that treatment is expensive, and there is little evidence that subsidized treatment produces long-term reductions in drug use. Plus, the demand for treatment would likely fall substantially under legalization, both because there would be less government coercion and because there would be less social pressure to abstain from drug use. Thus, whatever the case for subsidy, the appropriate amount would be far smaller under legalization.

The liberal support for government-funded drug-abuse treatment partly reflects the view that drug use should be reduced, although by means other than police power. It also reflects the view that drug addiction is a treatable disease that is not controllable by individuals.

Although support for subsidized treatment is widespread among liberal legalizers, this view is not uniform. Some liberals advocate legalization because they enjoy drug use and wish to do so without being hassled by the law. Many persons in this category view treatment as a waste of money that is perpetuated by the puritanical streak in U.S. society.

And there is considerably more agreement between liberal and libertarian legalizers about the value of drug treatment, subsidized or not, in the case of marijuana. Many liberals share the libertarian perspective that treatment for marijuana reflects coercion by the state, with few users deriving any benefit from such treatment. There is agreement on this point because liberal legalizers view marijuana as relatively benign and thus see no point in treatment, regardless of who pays.

The Regulation and Taxation of Legal Drugs

In addition to disagreement about how far to go in legalizing drugs, liberal and libertarian legalizers disagree about the parameters of a legalized regime for drugs, given that one occurs. Libertarians would treat legalized drugs like all other goods. Liberal legalizers assume that, even if legal, drugs should be subject to substantially more regulation and taxation than applies to most other commodities.

Sin Taxes: Liberal legalizers typically advocate heavy taxes for legalized drugs, as currently occurs for alcohol and tobacco. There are two main rationales. One is that drug use imposes negative effects on innocent third parties (e.g., by causing traffic accidents), so government policy should discourage use. The other is that many users make irrational decisions to consume drugs, so policy should again discourage use by imposing substantial taxes.

Libertarians are suspicious of using the tax code in this manner. Libertarians do not, contrary to some assertions, oppose all taxation. Libertarians are not anarchists; they simply believe government should be far smaller than it is today.

But libertarians oppose sin taxation and related tinkering because such measures are frequently manipulated for political reasons. Libertarians suggest it is hard to know which goods generate the biggest externalities, and given the perspective that individuals should make reasonable decisions about drug use or bear the consequences of their actions, libertarians do not endorse policies that discourage drug consumption. Plus, libertarians worry that sin taxation can increase to the point where it drives the drug market underground, which generates the same negatives as prohibition.

Libertarians agree that legalization combined with moderate sin taxation is a far better approach than prohibition. But their preference is to have drugs taxed at whatever rate applies to all other goods.

Age Restrictions on the Purchase of Legalized Drugs: Liberal legalizers typically assume that age restrictions similar to those currently in effect for alcohol and tobacco would apply to legalized drugs. They view current age restrictions as beneficial, assuming that these both restrict access by minors and send an appropriate message about consuming "adult" goods.

Libertarians suspect that age restrictions do more harm than good. They believe minors often evade these restrictions, which breeds contempt for the law by the minors who purchase the goods and by the merchants who sell them. They also note that legislating minimum purchase ages can encourage parents to supervise their children less diligently, under the (oft-mistaken) assumption that the law has addressed the problem. Again, libertarians would regard a legalized regime with age restrictions as an enormous improvement over total prohibition, and they would not object strongly to mild age restrictions for purchase of drugs. But their first choice would be no age restrictions whatsoever.

Advertising Restrictions on Legalized Drugs: Libertarians would impose few, if any, restrictions on advertising of legalized drugs. In part this reflects respect for the First Amendment; in part it reflects the view that advertising does not persuade people to consume goods but merely shifts preferences across brands. It also stems from the view that advertising can be beneficial: it provides consumers with information about different products, and it gives producers a way to attract business when they develop products that have good ratios of benefits to risks. Libertarians accept that legalization combined with advertising restrictions is preferable to prohibition, but their first choice is to avoid advertising restrictions as well.

Liberals view consumers as far more impressionable and easily manipulated than do libertarians. They do not think consumers consistently take available information and make reasonable choices. Thus, liberal legalizers fear advertising would persuade many persons to consume drugs who would not otherwise do so, and they argue or implicitly assume this is undesirable. They would therefore ban most or all advertising of legalized drugs, as currently occurs for tobacco products.

Needle Exchange Programs

Liberal legalizers often suggest that governments should operate needle exchange programs that provide clean syringes to drug users in order to reduce the spread of HIV. Libertarians do not think this is an appropriate function of government. Rather, they believe drug users should determine and accept the risks associated with drug use, and they assume the private sector can supply drugs with the degree of risk that consumers demand.

Although needle exchange programs again raise differences between liberal and libertarian legalizers, this disagreement becomes moot under legalization. A critical reason for these programs is prohibition-inspired restrictions on the sale of clean needles. Under legalization, such restrictions would soften or disappear, so drug users who wished to purchase and use syringes would find them both legal and inexpensive.

In addition, legalization would produce substantial declines in drug prices. This means users would have less incentive to seek the elevated "bang-for-the-buck" provided by injection. No doubt some users would still inject, but a substantial fraction would choose less risky consumption methods. And the range of such methods would increase under legalization. For example, drugs like heroin might be packaged with inexpensive, disposable syringes that would reduce the incidence of shared needles and thus diminish the spread of disease.

Drug Testing

Another critical difference between liberal and libertarian perspectives on drug policy concerns drug testing of job applicants and employees. Liberals generally regard such testing with suspicion, believing it an inappropriate invasion of privacy conducted by untrustworthy firms who hound their employees in the pursuit of profits.

Libertarians take a more nuanced view. They regard government policies that mandate drug testing as unwarranted intrusions in the marketplace. But they believe private employers have the right to use drug testing if they wish. Some employers might adopt testing because they believe drug use reduces productivity; others might adopt testing because they believe it identifies responsible employees. In the libertarian view, employers get to make this call, whether or not objective evidence substantiates their concerns.

Implications

This essay has discussed the differences between liberal and libertarian perspectives on drug legalization and related policies. The discussion makes clear that liberal and libertarian legalizers differ on a huge range of issues; indeed, they agree fully only on the relatively limited questions of whether prohibition should be applied to individual drug users and whether current enforcement against suppliers is excessive.

What are the lessons from considering the libertarian justification for drug legalization? In my view, there are two.

First, examination of the libertarian view helps indicate that some aspects of the drug policy debate are logically separable from the question of legalization. The main examples are subsidizing treatment and government promotion of, or restrictions on, drug testing. Whatever the merits of these policies, they are logically separate from the issue of legalization versus prohibition. This is not to say their effects are the same under the two regimes. But the view that prohibition is a bad idea does not mean subsidized treatment is a good idea nor that drug testing is a bad idea. These policies require a separate analysis.

Second, the libertarian perspective provides a defense of legalization that is potentially appealing to some citizens who find the liberal defense unpersuasive. In particular, the liberal perspective strikes some observers as "indulging" drug users, via subsidized treatment, government-funded needle exchanges, protection from drug tests, and the like. The libertarian view suggests instead that people should be free to use drugs, or abuse drugs, if they like, but that drug users must bear the consequences. For some persons, this is a more convincing rationale than the standard liberal perspective.

This is not to suggest the libertarian defense of drug legalization is an easy sell. Among liberal legalizers, it runs into difficulties because liberals do not accept the key libertarian assumption that most drug use is rational. And the libertarian view has difficulty even with "soft" libertarians because, in its pure form, it puts the entire onus for responsible drug use on individuals. In particular, most persons other than hard-core libertarians will, at least initially, prefer modifications in drug policy that focus on marijuana and incorporate auxiliary regulation such as sin taxes, minimum purchase ages, and advertising restrictions.

Nevertheless, some persons who find drug use distasteful, and who thus regard the liberal defense of legalization as too tolerant, might still accept legalization under certain conditions: that tax dollars are not spent on subsidized treatment or needle exchanges; that employers are free to use drug-testing, if they wish; and that drug users are held accountable for their actions.

The overall message, then, is that the libertarian defense of legalization has a potentially important role to play in the policy debates. This does not mean liberal and libertarian legalizers cannot agree on key arguments for legalization. But the analysis here suggests that a modest rethinking of the standard defense can broaden the impact of this message.

18. Medicalization as an Alternative to the Drug War

BY JEFFREY A. SINGER

Jeffrey A. Singer, M.D., is a general surgeon in private practice in Phoenix, Arizona. He served as Medical Spokesperson for Arizonans for Drug Policy Reform, the organization that drafted and promoted Arizona's Proposition 200 (The Drug Medicalization, Prevention, and Control Act of 1996). He is a contributor to AZMed, the journal of the Arizona Medical Association. This article is based upon a paper delivered at the Fraser Institute Symposium, "Sensible Solutions to the Urban Drug Problem," in Vancouver, BC, Canada, 1998.[1]

"Medicalization" is a new strategy for American drug policy reform that saw its first attempt at implementation in the mid-1990s. It approaches drug use as a public health issue, rather than a criminal justice issue. Its advocates consider it a more rational and humane alternative to the present militaristic approach of federal, state, and local law enforcement. Some would argue it respects and promotes human dignity and autonomy while realistically dealing with substance abuse. But advocates of *status quo* policy fear "medicalization" is a dangerous first step towards complete legalization of drugs proscribed by the state. Still others complain, however, that "medicalization" merely replaces the prison bed with the hospital bed. Worse, they see it as a dangerous extension of state power to the medical profession, an ominous enhancement of the therapeutic state. Yet more careful consideration of "medicalization" might lead to an alternative conclusion. "Medicalization" might not be incipient drug legalization, but might still respect and advance the autonomy of the individual. Neither classic prohibition nor decriminalization, "medicalization" might represent a third way to approach drug policy in the early 21st century—one that can move the ball closer to the ultimate goal of ending drug prohibition altogether.

In November, 1996, voters in California and Arizona approved ballot measures making "medicalization" a major policy reform option. California voters allowed people to possess and use marijuana for medical purposes with the recommendation of a medical doctor. Arizonans went further. With passage of Proposition 200, the "Drug Medicalization, Prevention, and Control Act of 1996," they permitted patients to possess and use any illicit drug, provided they receive a written prescription for its use from a licensed medical doctor, who, in turn, obtains a concurring second opinion from another doctor. In addition, the Arizona ballot measure gave recreational drug offenders probation and rehabilitation rather than prison time for the first two convictions. Prison is not an option for "nonviolent" drug offenders until the third conviction. On the other hand, those convicted of violent crimes while under the influence of an illicit drug must serve their entire sentence, without the opportunity for parole. Finally, the measure made eligible for release from prison all inmates serving time for "simple" drug possession with no other offenses, pending approval by the state Board of Executive Clemency.

Arizona Searches for a New Approach

A year earlier, business, professional, academic, political, and clerical leaders from Arizona met to explore alternatives to the drug policy in effect since the early 1970s. After 30 years of a war on drugs, they surveyed the results. Teenage drug use was back on the increase. America's prison population was at an all time high, with the overwhelming majority serving time for drug-related crimes. More people in the U.S. were incarcerated, *per capita*, than in any other country in the "free world."

Civil liberties of America's citizens were found under unprecedented assault. From search and seizure and asset forfeiture abuses; to wiretapping and other privacy invasions; to the Gestapo-like investigation of retailers' sales records, searching for customers who fit a drug dealer "profile," Americans were witnessing the steady erosion of constitutionally-guaranteed rights in the name of achieving a "drug-free America." Yet despite the threats to civil liberties—despite the explosion in the number of prisons and prisoners—despite the billions of dollars spent on surveillance, interdiction, prisons, and law enforcement—illicit drugs were more available and more potent than ever, while drug prices were steady or decreasing. America's inner cities became hellish war zones, overrun by drug-dealing gangs. And there was no evidence of the drug war having a significant effect on teenage drug use. This *ad hoc* group of Arizona leaders was interested in finding a way out of the box in which drug policy makers were trapped.

This took courage. The drug policy establishment has succeeded in putting in place an intense, state-driven education and propaganda machine. This makes it very difficult to challenge the prevailing doctrine without risking the epithets of "soft on drugs" or "pro-drug." At first, the group met in a clandestine manner. Participants were very cautious about expressing their views. As the group members became more comfortable with each other, they became more convinced of each other's sincerity and intentions. It was unanimously agreed that America's drug policy was a failure. It needed to be revamped. Reform was needed most acutely in policies dealing with the two principal categories of nonviolent drug offenders: those who possess drugs for recreational use, and those who do so for medicinal purposes. "Arizonans for Drug Policy Reform" was thus established.

I served as medical spokesperson for Arizonans for Drug Policy Reform, the group that developed and promoted the Drug Medicalization, Prevention, and Control Act of 1996 (Proposition 200). To start, we commissioned Celinda Lake to conduct focus group studies across Arizona to examine how citizens felt about the drug issue. Focus groups are different from polls, in that all questions are open-ended. The strategy behind focus groups is to let people freely express their opinions, rather than forcing them into a funnel, as often happens with polls. Lake developed her reputation as one of the nation's best focus group leaders by conducting the dozens of focus groups that helped Bill Clinton develop his 1992 presidential campaign message.

Two dispositions were immediately discerned from the focus groups: (1) people overwhelmingly felt the drug war was a failure; and (2) people strongly opposed the alternatives of decriminalization and legalization. Thus there appeared to be a paradox: people wanted a fundamental change in drug policy, but they could not accept the alternatives to prohibition, legalization or decriminalization. This did not mean, however, that they opposed significant drug policy reform. For example, focus group participants firmly opposed the drug war's "Do Drugs, Do Time" strategy.

They believed treatment was much more appropriate than punishment in prisons. Their belief that drug users should not be in prison was so strong that they were willing to parole existing offenders. Furthermore, they believed that when it came to prescribing drugs—even marijuana, heroin, and LSD—the patient/doctor relationship took precedence over government control. It was on the basis of these focus group findings that we designed Proposition 200. We were confident the people were ready to try a new way, a way that was neither classic zero-tolerance prohibition nor decriminalization.

Critics Attack Medicalization

The drug-war establishment opposed Proposition 200 from the outset. Critics claimed the initiative was a "smoke screen" for drug legalization. They warned that "medicalization" was the first step in the incremental legalization of all illicit drugs.

We countered that there was nothing inherent in our proposed reforms that in any way furthered the cause of legalization. The drugs in question were still prohibited for recreational use. But 30 years of experience with chemical dependency had taught Americans that drug users were not necessarily evil or dangerous people. In many cases, they were our friends and relatives. The crazed, malevolent dope fiend most Americans were warned about in earlier years now had a face—in many cases it was the face of a son or daughter, a brother or sister. Locking up these people like criminals was no longer a reasonable remedy for substance abuse. Rather, like alcohol abuse, illicit drug abuse was more of a medical problem than a "law and order" problem. We needed to "medicalize" our drug policy.

Further, we pointed out that political leaders such as former Senators Dennis DeConcini and Barry Goldwater—leaders on record as staunch opponents of illicit drug use—were our supporters.

Senator DeConcini appeared in television advertisements for the campaign. Former Reagan administration Deputy Secretary of Agriculture John R. Norton, then-president of the Goldwater Institute (a conservative public policy research institute), chaired Arizonans for Drug Policy Reform and was heard in radio ads. Former policeman and Deputy U.S. Attorney Steve Mitchell appealed to voters to support Proposition 200 in television ads, exclaiming that our current drug policy is "just not working...it's time to try another way." These spokesmen could not be accused of being symbols of the "drug culture."

The opposition argued that probation and treatment without incarceration for nonviolent drug users would remove the "hammer" (as the Maricopa county attorney put it) of prison as punishment for noncompliance. Therefore, medicalization would not work. But, we countered, teen drug use was on the increase, as we continued losing the drug war, despite the routine and frequent use of this "hammer." Further, the futures and lives of many youths were being destroyed by subjecting them to prison life—where studies have shown illicit drugs are often plentiful and readily available—and exposing them to violent sociopaths. Some drug abusers become drug addicts while in prison, where inmate-dealers team up with corrupt prison guards to provide drugs to convicts with nothing better to do while doing time than to get high. We cynically joked that our current drug policy was not really "Do Drugs, Do Time," but rather "Do Time, Do Drugs." A troubled youth experimenting with drugs might be forever placed on the path toward a life of crime and drugs by use of this "hammer."

Critics also argued that there was no recognized medical use for marijuana or other illicit drugs. Even if marijuana or other illicit substances had medically proven benefits, they believed the federal Food and Drug Administration should approve these drugs before permitting their medical use.

This last argument didn't hold water. For years, it has been common knowledge among Americans that marijuana has medicinal value. Many people know of a person whose misery from cancer chemotherapy, or malnutrition and wasting from AIDS, has been helped by smoking marijuana. In 1937, when the United States Congress banned marijuana with the Marijuana Tax Act, the American Medical Association testified in Congress against the ban, citing already-known medicinal applications for the drug. In addition, most Americans were well aware of and upset with the slow, bureaucratic, and often politicized methods employed by the Food and Drug Administration. Much publicity had been given to the plight of cancer and AIDS patients, who don't have time to spare and who were denied a chance at therapy because of the FDA's procrastination. Arizona's voters simply had no major problem with a severely ill person using a nonapproved drug, especially when under the guidance or recommendation of a doctor. The recent explosion in the popularity of alternative medicine in the U.S., with its use of unapproved (though legal) or unconventional herbal drugs and therapies, is in part a manifestation of the public's impatience with and resentment towards external control over their health care decisions.

Opponents next argued that even if it can be shown marijuana has medicinal benefits, there is no justification for allowing the medical use of all illicit drugs. Why not just limit medicinal use to marijuana?

Our response was to point out that many drugs once thought to be of no benefit have been found over the years to have medicinal applications. Heroin, or diacetyl-morphine, is used outside of the U.S., in hospital settings, for pain control. Government-approved research is under way at American medical schools on the use of LSD in the treatment of drug addiction. The point is, we replied, medical science is constantly searching for new agents for the easing or curing of illnesses. Our current drug policy discourages research on a vast array of potentially helpful agents. If, despite this policy, substantial evidence points to the beneficial application of an additional illicit drug, it should not be necessary for doctors to circulate petitions for a ballot initiative in order to expand the medicinal use provisions of an existing "medical marijuana" law.

Furthermore, Proposition 200 offered safeguards against abuse by requiring two concurring opinions from independent physicians. Beyond that, it required sufficient research documentation to convince a court (if necessary) that use of the drug was appropriate for that particular clinical setting. Only if these requirements were met would a patient be allowed to use the illicit drug, free from the fear of prosecution. This allowed doctors the freedom to use their judgment in a humane fashion, while preventing abuse of the law.

Finally, opponents warned that Proposition 200 would release from prison violent criminals who had plea-bargained with prosecutors down to a charge of "simple possession." But Proposition 200 allowed release of prisoners only if the Board of Executive Clemency were to determine that the release of the prisoner does not endanger society. The board has access to the prisoners' records and would not have to approve every prisoner for release. We argued that respect for justice compels us to consider the release of people serving time for an act that the people have determined no longer deserves imprisonment.

National political leaders, including Vice President Al Gore, Attorney General Janet Reno, "Drug Czar" General Barry McCaffrey, and former Presidents George Bush, Jimmy Carter, and Gerald Ford, participated in media events warning voters of the "dangers" inherent in the California and Arizona initiatives. Despite these efforts, the ballot measures easily passed—56% voting in favor in California and 65% in Arizona.

A New Metaphor for Autonomy?

Advocates for continuing our failed drug policy were not the only ones to attack these ballot measures. The medicalization initiatives also caught strong criticism from the opponents of drug prohibition.

Does "medicalization" further the autonomy of the individual—respect for the principle of self-ownership, the right to ingest and act according to one's own best judgment—as long as the rights of others are not infringed? Dr. Thomas Szasz, one of the most important, rational, and articulate thinkers in the movement to repeal drug prohibition, believes medicalization is flawed and potentially dangerous.

Szasz, professor of psychiatry at the State University of New York Health Center at Syracuse and author of such important works as *The Therapeutic State, Ceremonial Chemistry* and *Our Right To Drugs: The Case For A Free Market*, fears the emerging trend of medicalization is a potentially lethal treatment for our nation's malignant drug policy.

Szasz decries the "therapeutic state" that now rules Americans. In an interview with journalist Randy Paige in 1991, he asserted, "The imagery in our country is that the most important value is health. And in the name of health it is OK to lock up people, to beat people, to deprive them of their constitutional rights, and even to kill them. And this is led by physicians, psychiatrists, and politicians..."[2]

In the therapeutic state, unpopular behaviors have become "diseases" correctable by "treatment." Sometimes the treatment is compulsory. The Orwellian corruption of language allows people to become convinced that objective solutions exist for problems that are, in reality, subjective. Through language and the state, people attempt to avoid the fact that free will sometimes has unpleasant consequences. Writing in *The Lancet* in 1991, Szasz refers to this phenomenon as "the institutionalized denial of the tragic nature of life..."[3] The treatment of risky and unpopular behavior as a contagious disease justifies the state's coercive intervention into individual lifestyle preferences and choices. When risky behavior is viewed by the state as a disease, moral autonomy no longer exists. When government is the ultimate enforcer of personal behavior, when the state replaces the individual as the moral agent, totalitarianism is the unavoidable result.

Examples of the pervasive therapeutic state abound. The most prominent contemporary example of the state's propensity to treat risky behavior as a disease relates to the attempt by political leaders to absolve tobacco smokers of their responsibility for choosing to smoke—a choice made by individually deciding the amount of risk one is willing to accept in return for an expected benefit.

In the therapeutic state, acceptable risk is determined not by the risk taker, but by the governmental overseer. A recent absurd demonstration of the lack of respect for autonomy came in late August, 1997, when the Food and Drug Administration banned the active ingredient in Ex-Lax, phenolphthalein, after animal experiments found that repeated administration of the drug to rodents, at 30–100 times the normal daily human dose, produced an increased risk of rodent cancers. There has not been a recorded instance of cancer related to Ex-Lax use in the drug's 100 year history. Yet despite the safe track record of the drug, despite the fact that no user would consume 30–100 times the human dose unless attempting to commit a very grotesque form of suicide, the FDA decided people could not properly choose a laxative without direction from the state.

Szasz considers our therapeutic state analogous to medieval Spain's theocratic state. The people in medieval Spanish society did not believe in the separation of church and state, but rather embraced their union. In the same way, he believes our society does not believe in the separation of medicine and state, but fervently embraces their union. "The censorship of drugs follows from the latter ideology as inexorably as the censorship of books follows from the former," wrote Szasz in a 1978 article in *Reason*.[4] Analogous to the Spanish Inquisition is the practice in today's society of "pharmacologic tolerance." Government-approved drugs are tolerated or even encouraged. Drugs not officially sanctioned as therapeutic are considered worthless or dangerous. This ignores the fact that any drug has benefits as well as harmful effects, depending upon the needs and context of the user. Failure to recognize this simple fact cancels any respect for autonomy.

From Szasz's perspective, the public health model for drug policy reform can be seen only as a pernicious extension of the meddlesome therapeutic state. At least under the "old school" drug policy, drug users are regarded as having autonomy. They make choices of their own free will, but they must be punished for making choices not sanctioned by society. Under the public health approach, however, all moral autonomy is lost. An illicit drug user is "sick." He needs help. We must not punish him. Rather, we must force him to accept treatment.

Medicalization advocates like me, who are sympathetic to Szasz's perspective, believe, in this case, medicalization is a unique exception to his generally correct analysis. When applied to drug policy, medicalization is not at all an extension of the state. Rather, it represents a radical rupture with the federal government's oppressive drug war.

Tracking polls in California and Arizona during the initiatives' campaigns revealed 60% support for the ballot measures. At the same time, however, only 25% of those polled actually believed the measures would pass.

Some medicalization advocates find it helpful to view these phenomena through a post-modern lens. The focus group and tracking poll information present an example of what post-modern philosopher Michel Foucault calls subjugated knowledge. Subjugated knowledge is an implicit belief that people cannot express unless given the language to express it.

To the post-modernist, language is contextual. The focus group studies revealed there was a radical resistance to the drug war that lacked a "narrative" with which to express itself. The common "metaphors" of resistance, legalization, and decriminalization were unsatisfactory. A new vocabulary took shape as a result of the focus-group experiences. Group members repeatedly articulated that drug abuse was really more of a "medical" issue. They noted that drug treatment—even if it did not work—was a more just form of "punishment." Thus a new public health "discourse" on drugs emerged. This new discourse represented a "halfway" position between prohibition and repeal of prohibition. Years of prohibitionist propaganda made anything other than a halfway position impossible.

A very significant feature of this new discourse of medicalization is that it is not a top-down narrative of control perpetuated by the government. Instead, the people have generated a language of resistance to oppressive and ineffective policies. This discourse, therefore, is percolating up from citizens believing medical authorities can address the drug issue with more effectiveness than government bureaucrats. By contrast, the tobacco discourse fostered by the Clinton administration and subsequent political leaders has been a top-down discourse of medicalization.

Thus, in the post-modern analysis, medicalization has a different meaning—a different discourse—depending on the context in which the term is used.

Szasz's error is that he takes the term "medicalization" to mean the transfer of power from the political dictator to the medical dictator. To be sure, the post-modernist would agree that medicalization is a metaphor of control. However, Foucault would argue, there is no way "outside of" power. All human interactions involve power relations. Therefore, the only way of conceiving issues of autonomy is through empowerment. Medicalization used in the context of drug policy is actually a metaphor of empowerment.

Viewed in the context of power relations in the real world in the late 1990s, the ballot measures actually reversed statist drug control. The Arizona ballot measure allows doctors to prescribe all illicit drugs. The measure does not create another state-based bureaucracy for the distribution of the drugs, but exempts both the doctor and the patient from prosecution for using unsanctioned, socially unacceptable drugs.

Medicalization, in relation to drug policy, means doctors and patients standing against the federal government and its expansive medical-regulatory and drug control apparatus.

In supporting the medical use of marijuana and other illicit drugs, voters put the concerns of the suffering patient ahead of the concerns of political society. They rebelled against the governmental apparatus designed to approve or disqualify drugs, making the choice of drug an issue to be worked out between the patient and doctor—free from third-party interference of any kind. By medicalizing drug policy, voters reacted against the Food and Drug Administration, the Drug Enforcement Administration, and the medical-government complex. It is telling that the American Medical Association, the American Cancer Society, and several other major "establishment" groups have become integral parts of the medical-government complex opposed to the medicalization initiatives.

Reaction of the Drug-War Establishment

The defenders of the *status quo* did not readily accept the outcome of the vote on the initiatives. California's attorney general, an opponent of that state's medical marijuana initiative, begrudgingly vowed to respect the decision of the voters. Unfortunately, the same could not be said of Arizona's drug-war establishment.

Immediately after the voting results were certified, then-Governor Fife Symington, claiming that the people were fooled by a "slick campaign," announced he planned to veto the measure. When he was told by the Arizona Attorney General that it was against the Arizona constitution to veto a popular ballot initiative, the governor sought reassurance from state legislative leaders that they would "fix the flaws" in the proposition.

In April, 1997, Arizona's legislature narrowly passed two bills that effectively gutted Proposition 200. Such a legislative action was not constitutionally permissible in the state of California. Arizonans were outraged by the legislators' hubris. Polls, talk radio, and letters to the editors of Arizona newspapers demonstrated that the public viewed a ballot initiative to be an expression of the will of the people. They felt the outcome of such a vote must be respected. They considered the legislature to be trespassing on the people's domain.

Arizona's constitution states that a bill passed by the legislature does not become law until 90 days after the governor signs it. During that time, any interested party can gather the requisite number of signatures on a petition to force the bill to be referred to the people for their approval or rejection at the next regularly scheduled general election. This action effectively "stays" the legislation pending the decision of the voters.

Arizonans for Drug Policy Reform created a new campaign committee, "The People Have Spoken," and announced a campaign to refer the two bills to the people at the next general election in November, 1998. They gathered twice the number of required signatures.[5] Many who signed the petitions admitted to voting against Proposition 200 in November, 1996, but were incensed by the perceived arrogance of the political class and what they saw as its utter disregard for the popular initiative process. The legislature's attempt to gut Proposition 200 was thus derailed. The bills were put on hold pending the decision of the voters in November, 1998. That November, the voters rejected the legislature's two bills and thus reaffirmed Proposition 200 by a nearly two-to-one vote.

On a second front, the federal government also weighed in to protect the *status quo*. The federal government has no jurisdiction in the area that deals with how particular states treat convicted drug felons. It cannot prevent states from establishing "probation and treatment" programs as substitutes for incarceration for violations of state drug laws. But the "Feds" believe they can act where federal drug laws are violated. If states choose not to prosecute patients who possess illicit drugs for medical use, the federal government still reserves the right to prosecute for possessing federally prohibited drugs. It would be "bad politics" for federal law enforcement officials to round up terminal cancer, AIDS, and neurological patients and incarcerate them for possessing marijuana. So instead, in February, 1997, Drug Czar General Barry McCaffrey, Attorney General Janet Reno, Secretary of Health and Human Services Donna Shalala, and Drug Enforcement Administration Chief Thomas Constantine held a joint press conference. They announced that any doctor who prescribed marijuana for medical use pursuant to a state's "medical marijuana" law would lose the federal license needed to prescribe narcotics. In addition, the doctor would be banned from participation in Medicare (the government monopoly health insurance plan for those over age 65) and Medicaid (the government health plan for the indigent). Thus, they cast a "chilling effect" on doctors' ability to prescribe medicinal marijuana in accordance with their own state's law. This not only impacted doctors in Arizona and California, it also restrained doctors in Virginia and Connecticut, where those states' legislatures have allowed medical use of marijuana, with little national attention, since 1980. And, since 1996, this policy has cast a chilling effect on doctors in seven other states that have passed medical marijuana initiatives.

President Clinton, Attorney General Reno, and Drug Czar General McCaffrey attacked the medicalization propositions as among the most dangerous ballot measures ever approved. They promised a witch hunt of doctors who prescribe marijuana and other illicit drugs. They realized a new discourse on drugs was emerging, and it frightened them. Most troubling to them was that it was coming from the grassroots. Consider the fact that a 1998 national poll showed 69% of Americans were opposed to the federal response against the drug medicalization measures. Thus the dissent expressed by voters in Arizona and California had national resonance.

As a result of the ballot measures and the federal government's response to them, lawsuits were filed in California and in the District of Columbia. These suits challenged the entire way medicine is regulated in this country. On March 6, 1997, I became a plaintiff in one of those suits. I joined with doctors from California and Arizona, as well as Virginia and Connecticut, in the District of Columbia suit against the attorney general, drug czar, secretary of Health and Human Services, and DEA administrator. In the suit, we argued the federal response violates the First Amendment rights of doctors and patients to freely exchange scientific information. We also claimed it violates the Ninth and Tenth Amendments as well as the commerce clause in Article 1, Section 8 of the U.S. Constitution. Two years later, the judge decided in favor of the federal government. We did not appeal due to insufficient funding for our legal expenses.

A California suit, more narrowly focused on the right of a doctor to communicate information about the pros and cons of medicinal marijuana—the right of patients and doctors to freely exchange scientific information—was successful in the U.S. Court of Appeals for the Ninth Circuit in 2002. This may be helpful to doctors in states in the Far West, the Ninth Circuit's jurisdiction, if their states' medical marijuana laws are worded in a way that allows patients to use marijuana if it is "recommended"—verbally or otherwise—by a physician. In states such as Arizona, where a prescription is required, the decision is not as helpful. The Court drew a distinction between a recommendation and a prescription, viewing a prescription as more of an active form of defiance of federal laws, rather than an expression of free speech.

In 2002, Arizonans for Drug Policy Reform attempted to revise the drug policy reform act they succeeded in enacting four years earlier. The "Drug Medicalization, Prevention and Control Act of 2002" would have replaced the requirement of a doctor's prescription for medicinal marijuana with a doctor's recommendation on an application form. An applicant would have received a state-issued permit to receive two ounces of medicinal marijuana per month, to be made available at designated distribution centers operated by the Arizona Department of Public Safety, using confiscated marijuana that would otherwise be incinerated. The idea was to relieve the physician of threats from federal authorities and establish a distribution mechanism for the federally banned substance. The Department of Public Safety, it was believed, would be able to distribute marijuana from confiscated stores and thus not be in violation of federal laws against the sale or production of marijuana. (In addition, it was hoped that the act of having state police distribute marijuana would serve to further deconstruct the drug war by providing another example of its absurdity.)

Alas, the idea of having police distribute marijuana might have been a bit too much for the voters to handle—especially in light of their new predisposition, after September 11, 2001, to support the wishes of law enforcement. And the law-enforcement establishment vehemently opposed that feature of the initiative. So it was defeated, 57% to 43%. But Arizonans for Drug Policy Reform will not be deterred. We will learn from our defeats and come back with a measure that is less brazen.

To those who claim medicalization represents a major augmentation of the therapeutic state, the experiences in Arizona and California indicate medicalization of drug policy is a special case. I recall the debate I had with the libertarian community during Arizona's Proposition 200 campaign. Most libertarians opposed it on the grounds so eloquently articulated by Dr. Szasz. They believed it did nothing to mitigate the assault on liberty and autonomy perpetrated by the drug war. But the reaction of the federal government and the law enforcement community to its approval, and the overwhelming opposition of the public to that reaction, has made many of them re-examine their original positions. Any drug policy reform engendering so much outrage from the political establishment, and inciting such defiance among the grassroots, can't be all bad.

Is Medicalization a Third Way?

Over seven years have passed since the American political establishment was jolted by the California and Arizona drug policy reform bills. Unfortunately, efforts by the drug-war establishment, especially the federal government, to suppress these measures have delayed their impact. Therefore, it is impossible at this time to measure any effect of medicalization. The dogmatic resistance by the drug-war bureaucracy was predicted. Many of the most vocal opponents of medicalization have a vested interest in maintaining complete control over America's drug policy. But eventually the defenders of the *status quo* will have to yield to the reality of the drug war's failure; of the pain and damage it has caused to our youth, particularly in America's inner cities; and to the demand of the people that we try another approach.

Medicalization has been attacked by hard-line drug warriors as a stealthy attempt to legalize or decriminalize illicit drugs. Advocates of legalization or decriminalization are wary that medicalization will do nothing more than make doctors the new commandants in the war on drugs. That the opposing camps in the drug war debate both attack medicalization suggests this new reform proposal is *sui generis*.

To be sure, medicalization doesn't give us the complete personal autonomy we would get from the repeal of prohibition and the creation of a free market in drugs. Nor is it, as Drug Czar Barry McCaffrey called it, "a thinly disguised effort to legalize drugs." But the Arizona and California reform proposals generated the first popular expression to challenge the drug war in decades. Thus, medicalization might be a third way to confront the challenge of illicit drug use—one that is compatible with a society that, as it enters the 21st century, is wiser, and weary of war, but not yet ready to drop the war "cold turkey." As such, medicalization might make it easier for society to end its drug war addiction in the not-too-distant future.[6]

Notes

1. See also the following articles written by Jeffrey A. Singer. "A New Metaphor for Autonomy," *Reason*, Volume 29, Number 10, March, 1998, pages 26–27. "Drug Measure has Feds Frantic," *Arizona Republic*, March 16, 1997, pages H1–H2. Letter to the Editor: "Hazing Arizona," *Liberty*, Volume 11, Number 4, March, 1998, page 2. "Medical Use of Illicit Drugs/Keeping Faith with Medicine's Tradition," *Arizona Medicine*, Volume 7, Number 2, March, 1996, page 6.

2. Arnold S. Trebach and Kevin B. Zeese, editors, *Friedman and Szasz on Liberty and Drugs*, Washington, D.C.: Drug Policy Foundation Press, 1992, page 115.

3. Thomas Szasz, "Diagnoses are not diseases," *The Lancet*, Volume 338, December 21–28, 1991, page 1574.

4. Trebach and Zeese.

5. Hal Matter, "100,000 Sign petitions for marijuana law," *Arizona Republic*, July 17, 1997, page B1.

6. For additional background, see the following articles. Dan Baum, *Smoke and Mirrors*, New York: Little, Brown and Company, 1996. David Boaz, "A Drug-Free America—or a Free America?" University of California, *Davis Law Review*, Volume 24, 1991, pages 617–636. Dennis Cauchon, "Psychedelics take a trip back to the lab," *USA Today*, June 13, 1994, page 10A. Ernest Drucker, "Defending the Public Health Trademark," *Reason*, Volume 29, Number 10, March, 1998, page 30. Stephen B. Duke and Albert C. Gross, *America's Longest War*, New York: G.P. Putnam's Sons, 1993. Dave Fratello, "The Medical Marijuana Menace," *Reason*, Volume 29, Number 10, March, 1998, pages 27–28. Nick Gillespie, "Prescription: Drugs," *Reason*, Volume 28, Number 9, February, 1997, pages

36–39. Ethan A. Nadelmann, "Commonsense Drug Policy," *Foreign Affairs*, Volume 77, Number 1, January/February, 1998, pages 111–126. James Ostrowski, "Thinking About Drug Legalization," *Cato Institute Policy Analysis* Number 121, May 25, 1989. Thomas Szasz, "The Political Legitimatization of Quackery," *Reason*, Volume 29, Number 10, March, 1998, pages 25–26.

Ron Crickenberger, 1955–2004

Ron was the most inspirational Libertarian I ever met. Through him, I became a member of the party, ran for sheriff as a Libertarian, and won by closely following his advice. He was one of a few who could calmly explain libertarian thought and sway even those who disagreed with him.

Ron passed away of cancer on the day this book was sent to be published, January 20, 2004. I regret not having worked a bit harder to get the book out in time for Ron to see it. Please take the time to read his essay carefully and understand his message that all of us have both the right and responsibility to determine what is best for our own bodies.

Sheriff Bill Masters

19. My Arrest for Civil Disobedience

BY RON CRICKENBERGER

Ron Crickenberger served as political director of the Libertarian Party from 1997 to 2003, and he was the architect of the LP's Drug War Focus Strategy, a plan that seeks to end the drug war at the federal level by leveraging the Libertarian Party's influence on elections and policy at the local and national levels. In 2002, Crickenberger managed the congressional campaign of Carole Ann Rand that helped defeat incumbent Bob Barr over his opposition to medical marijuana.

On June 6, 2002, I was arrested for civil disobedience while protesting a federal government crackdown on medical marijuana clinics.

Nine other drug reform activists were arrested along with me. We had chained ourselves across the entrance of the Department of Justice on Pennsylvania Avenue in Washington, D.C. We read statements to the press and chanted slogans every time the police came to give us "one more warning."

Before the Federal Protection Service cut the chains and dragged us away in tight plastic handcuffs, we posted a "Cease and Desist" order on the door, demanding that the federal government end its misguided, immoral war against sick and critically ill patients who ease their suffering with medical marijuana.

Our protest in D.C. was one of 55 actions with more than 1,000 demonstrators in cities across America that day. I participated as part of my campaign for the U.S. House of Representatives, as did many other

Libertarian candidates around the country. Americans for Safe Access (ASA) coordinated the nationwide action that was designed to force Attorney General Ashcroft and the Bush administration to back off their anti-medical marijuana crusade and to grant states the right to choose and govern their own medical marijuana laws.

Between September 11, 2001, and our action, the federal government had conducted at least five raids against medical cannabis dispensaries that were completely legal under California state law. While terrorists plotted more attacks on our shores, federal officials attacked the sick and injured of our own country. They threw patients into the street, confiscated homes, and arrested caregivers. June 6 was picked as the day of action because a federal judge in California was expected to issue a ruling soon after that would effectively give the DEA a green light to escalate their raids—depriving thousands more patients of their safe, quality-controlled source of medicine.

Committing an act of civil disobedience was not an action I took lightly. I had always thought there was something inherently wrong with a strategy that required you to injure yourself just to make a point. I also recognized that, in addition to the obvious potential negative consequences for me personally, there was the potential for negative as well as positive public reaction. Since any media might well mention my position as the Libertarian Party's political director, I did not want to take an action that might reflect poorly on the party. So I sought advice from Libertarian Party Chairman Jim Lark, General Counsel Bill Hall, and Sheriff Bill Masters, as well as all of the LPHQ office staff. And of course, my partner in life, Noelle. Some of my friends advised that it was a great idea for me to get arrested—whether or not there was a good cause involved.

My Decision

As "point man" for the LP's Drug War Focus Strategy—our plan to end drug prohibition at the federal level by 2010—it is my responsibility to network with the other drug reform groups and to work with them to help implement our strategy. You can't do much more to demonstrate that you are committed to a cause than to get arrested in a civil disobedience action. So I had incentive to participate beyond just believing it was the right thing to do.

I came into the Libertarian Party over the issue of taxation. I spent most of my first years in the LP working on issues that were in the economic realm. I did not take up the issue of medical marijuana until it touched me personally.

I had long believed in drug re-legalization for both philosophical and pragmatic reasons. But I had looked on the concept of medical marijuana in much the same way that its opponents do: "Medical marijuana? Yeah, right. Nice try to work toward making it legal for you to get toked up." Despite years of LP activism, and plenty of reading on drug legalization in general, I was fairly ignorant of the remarkable medical properties of cannabis.

Then my best friend of 25 years sickened with cancer. She was on intense chemotherapy and was unable to keep any food down. She lost almost 50 pounds, more than a third of her body weight, in just a few months. She was on a "pain pump," which shot her full of heavy narcotics through an IV day and night.

Unfortunately, Gina is not a medical marijuana success story. I knew enough to have heard that marijuana could help with nausea from chemo, but not enough to really push her to try it. Back then I hadn't heard the personal testimonies that make it so clear just how absolutely remarkably marijuana works for some patients. For those who are suffering severe nausea from chemotherapy, the treatment can be as life-threatening as the disease.

And really, the word "nausea" just doesn't cut it. Nausea sounds like, "gee, my tummy's a little upset." With chemo and some AIDS medication combinations, we are talking about gut-wrenching, lying on the floor moaning and crying, dry heaves that go on for hours but seem like forever. Patients in this condition obviously cannot keep down any kind of anti-nausea medication that must be swallowed. For patients in this dire predicament, an inhaled medication is ideal.

Gina bought the government propaganda that smoking pot would further damage her already-ravaged immune system. If she hadn't believed the government's line on medical marijuana, and if her doctors or I had been more knowledgeable at the time about how wondrously effective it is for nausea during chemotherapy, it's likely that, at the least, her last days would have been a lot more bearable.

A couple of years later, I met Peter McWilliams and saw first-hand how quickly marijuana could relieve the nausea from chemo or AIDS medication "cocktails." His assertion that "one puff and the symptoms start going away" was dramatically demonstrated to me at the 1998 Libertarian Party national convention, where he spoke. I saw him going in just a few minutes from puking his guts up into the trashcan in the speakers' green room, to being able to compose himself and go onstage to give one of the most memorable speeches ever at an LP convention.

I also met Todd McCormick, who had cancer nine times before the age of ten. Watching the other kids in the cancer ward die off from malnutrition due to chemo and radiation, and seeing her son going down that same road, Todd's brave mother Ann decided to try medical marijuana for her nine-year-old. The difference was incredible. Todd was again able to regain both a healthy appetite and a positive attitude, and survive.

The radiation treatments left Todd with many of his vertebrae permanently fused, one hip that will forever be the size of a ten year old's, and permanent pain. Many patients with bone and muscular disorders that produce chronic pain find that marijuana relieves that pain even more effectively than the much stronger narcotics that would also make them dysfunctional. Todd effectively treated his pain with cannabis—until he was imprisoned for giving the same life-saving medicine to other patients.

I met Cheryl Miller, a multiple sclerosis sufferer for more than 30 years before she died in June, 2003. For the last ten years of her life, she was unable even to scratch her own nose. She found that marijuana relieved the painful symptoms and gave her more mobility than any of the legal prescriptions that modern medicine was able to provide. Marijuana is so effective for MS that more than 50% of British MS sufferers have used it to treat their symptoms—despite the drug's illegal status.

Cheryl used prescribed Marinol, the synthetic form of THC, which is one of the active ingredients in marijuana. But unlike the THC pill, marijuana contains 60 other active chemical compounds, called cannabinoids, several of which have been shown to be effective at treating pain and spasticity. Cheryl found the natural form of the medicine to be much superior to the synthetic Marinol. So she continued to use marijuana orally, despite the risk of arrest. The state of New Jersey paid for her Marinol prescription at a cost of more than $25,000 per year. If marijuana were legal, a similar year's dose would cost a few hundred dollars at most, and could be easily grown by a patient who could not afford to buy it.

Cheryl and her husband Jim believed so strongly in their right to treat Cheryl's symptoms with the best medicine possible that they engaged in civil disobedience of their own. In 1998 they were both arrested in Congressman Jim Rogan's office after Cheryl's husband fed her medicine as part of a civil disobedience action. Cheryl later helped make a commercial for Libertarian candidates to use to publicize the medical marijuana issue.

I met Elvy Mussika, who suffers from severe glaucoma. She treats it legally with marijuana, which lowers eye pressure. Since 1978, the federal government has grown, rolled, and mailed 300 marijuana cigarettes a month to a handful of patients who were accepted into the government's "compassionate use" program. Elvy is one of the last seven patients still alive in the program. Apparently the government ran out of compassion in 1992, when they closed entry into the program after an influx of applications from AIDS patients. I guess we can afford armies of armed agents to raid clinic after clinic, but just can't possibly afford "compassion" for more than seven people.

Since then, I've met dozens of medical marijuana patients who have found what is often life-saving relief from this oldest of nature's medications. Medical marijuana is frequently helpful in treating the symptoms of AIDS, glaucoma, cancer, multiple sclerosis, epilepsy, and chronic pain. Other patients and doctors have found it be very helpful for everything from arthritis to menstrual cramps.

Even the government's own studies support medical marijuana. The Institute of Medicine's 1999 report on medical marijuana stated, "Scientific data indicate the potential therapeutic value of cannabis drugs…for pain relief, control of nausea and vomiting, and appetite stimulation… Except for the harms associated with smoking, the adverse effects of marijuana use are within the range tolerated for other medications."

Having now seen what I have seen and learned what I have learned, how can I not do all I can to end the injustice of medical marijuana prohibition? When so much suffering could be relieved by so little effort on the part of our elected officials, aren't we all called to action?

Prior to deciding to participate in the civil disobedience, I checked with LP General Counsel Bill Hall, who said that Racketeer Influenced and Corrupt Organizations (RICO) law should not apply to this type of demonstration. We were on public property only and were not trying to influence any type of private business.

Other arrestees who were in similar employment situations checked with their general counsels or staff attorneys, and were also given a green light. In one case, one of the arrestees *was* the staff attorney, as well as the head of the organization—Kevin Zeese of Common Sense for Drug Policy.

I was especially glad that Kevin was planning on participating. It was psychologically easier for me to join in since two of the others to be arrested, Kevin and Bruce Mirkin of the Marijuana Policy Project, were also in their mid-forties and heads of their organizations. I do wish we had had some seniors participating, but our ages ranged from 20 to me as the elder incarcerant at 47.

Another turning point in my decision to participate was a thumbs-up from *LP News* editor Bill Winter. He is usually fairly "conservative" in how he wants to see the LP presented to the public and the press, and he felt the medical marijuana issue had progressed to such a degree of public support that nonviolent civil disobedience would be viewed in a positive light.

Civil disobedience must naturally be one of the last tactics resorted to in any effort to bring about political change. And for medical marijuana, that has certainly been the case. For decades, the government stonewalled clinical testing of the benefits of marijuana—while at the same time decrying the lack of scientific testing as a reason not to allow marijuana as medicine. The California legislature twice passed medical marijuana legislation, only to have the governor veto it. So activists collected more than a million signatures to place an initiative—Proposition 215—on the California ballot. The voters approved Proposition 215 in 1996, making medical marijuana the law of the land.

Most of the clinics in California being raided by the DEA were also operating in full cooperation with local authorities. Some of the caregivers were even officially deputized by city authorities to distribute medical marijuana under Proposition 215.

If you have done everything right to bring about social changes that everybody but the politicians are ready for, the direct action of civil disobedience can be just about the only option left.

The night before the action, I had a lot of trouble sleeping. I was quite naturally worried about what might happen the next morning. Would we actually get arrested? Would they stop us before we could even get to the door? Would the police get violent? Would they pry open our eyes and pepper spray us like they did to protesters in Oregon? When it's all over—will I look like a hero, or like a fool? Or will anybody even notice?

One of my fellow demonstrators had e-mailed me Martin Luther King, Jr.'s 1963 "Letter From a Birmingham Jail," defending the civil disobedience and direct actions of the civil-rights movement. These words struck me most of all:

> I must say to you that we have not made a single gain in civil rights without determined legal and nonviolent pressure... We know through painful experience that freedom is never voluntarily given by the oppressor; it must be demanded by the oppressed...

> Justice too long delayed is justice denied... There comes a time when the cup of endurance runs over, and men are no longer willing to be plunged into the abyss for despair. I hope, sirs, that you can understand our legitimate and unavoidable impatience.

The issue and the faces may have changed, but the desperate need for justice has not. I thought a lot about my friends Gina and Peter, cried a little for their being gone, and finalized my resolve. About 4:00 a.m. I wrote the following:

"There are some of my friends that my action today of civil disobedience will be too late to help. I take this action so that others may not suffer needlessly in the future. I take this step with all due seriousness, after deep contemplation, and in loving memory of my friends Gina Purcell and Peter McWilliams." Having made what I considered my final decision, I was able to get a couple of hours' sleep.

Action and Arrest

There were about 25 activists involved in the action—half a dozen Libertarians, the rest Democrats and Greens. We had met for planning sessions at one of the hard leftist's homes, amidst posters with slogans like "Liberate us from Capitalism." I doubt he and I are going to agree on free-market economics any time soon. But he's my ally on drug policy, so I refrained from proselytizing about Hayek and von Mises, and just talked drug reform.

The morning of the action we met at 9:00 a.m. for a few practice runs. But as soon as all of us got into the van we were going to use, something began scraping the ground as we drove. Somebody looked at it and said, "It's just the muffler strap; we can still go on." I looked again and saw it was the gas tank strap instead! It was making sparks as we drove, and the tank itself would fall off the first good bump we hit. So we were perhaps about to turn a peaceful sit-in into an unintentional suicide car bomb.

We had a tight schedule to keep, as the media were being held at a nearby Metro subway stop until we were all in place and chained. Plus, three carloads of arrestees and other demonstrators all had to arrive at the Justice Department at the same time. So there was no time to arrange for alternate transportation.

The driver hurried to beg a local repair shop to fix the van's gas tank strap quickly, while we practiced chaining ourselves to a couple of trees that were about the same distance apart as the doors of the Justice Department. She got it repaired and returned with just a few minutes to spare.

As we practiced, I ended up becoming the "point man," the one who would be first out of the van and first to be chained. And as it ended up, I would also be the one who would have to walk straight at the guard who was right in front of the door. In addition to the ten arrestees, we had four people

205

serve as "lockers" who would actually fasten the chains and locks onto the large rings on the doors of the Justice Department.

In addition to the chains, we had cushioned pipes that were covered with messages about medical marijuana. We threaded the chains through the pipes, and would hold hands to make it more difficult to separate us. We were not actually fastened to the chains, but would appear to be so. We also all had large pictures of medical marijuana patients hanging around our necks with "Patient, Not Criminal" printed on them, along with their names and medical conditions.

During the practice sessions, what appeared to be an undercover officer's car drove by three times, so we began to worry that our plans had been discovered.

The "lockers" went on ahead to scout the area once more, while we practiced getting out of the van a couple more times. We were afraid that with all of our unusual accoutrements of chains, pipes, and signs, we would make an exit from the van that looked like a scene from a *Three Stooges* movie.

When we left the practice area, the undercover car appeared again, followed us for several turns, and then disappeared.

We circled the Justice Department building once to see if there were more guards than usual, and things seemed normal—except the guard was standing directly in front of the door. In our scouting trips, the guard was usually walking around or sitting in the shade instead of directly in the doorway. We circled twice more to see if he would move a little, but no luck.

Our driver pulled to a stop on Pennsylvania Avenue and threw open the back door of the van. Heart pounding, and more adrenaline than blood flowing through me, I swung out of the van and headed straight for the door—and the guard.

It's a little difficult to be inconspicuous when you are walking really fast, chained to other people, your arm stuck inside some strange-looking multi-colored pipe, and there's a big sign around your neck—but I did my best. I tried to keep an eye on the guard without actually making eye contact. I could tell he had spotted us when I was within about 20 feet of the door—but I kept walking.

When I was about 10 feet away, the guard turned around and ran inside the building! Fifty-four seconds from the time the door opened on the van, we were all chained in. Some guards appeared on the other side of the glass door and chained it from the inside. We found out later that they had done this in demonstrations around the country, and we got a little chuckle out of the feds locking themselves in their own buildings.

A few minutes later the media and other demonstrators arrived. As the cameras began to roll, we began some chants. I've always felt kind of silly chanting at a demonstration, but I joined in.

Rob Kampia of the Marijuana Policy Project brought the waiting media from the subway and began the public statements to the press about who we were and why we were there. Those of us chained to the door began making statements in turn, although we were interrupted a couple of times when the police chief came to give us our first and second warnings. Our response to his warning was to chant even louder.

I then read the cease and desist order that was being posted on the doors of DEA offices across the country that day:

> On June 7th, 2002. The United States District Court for Northern California is expected to issue a ruling that clears the way for the Drug Enforcement Administration to raid medical marijuana dispensaries now providing services to the chronically ill in Alaska, California, Colorado, Hawaii, Maine, Nevada, Oregon, and Washington.

> While the practice is legal under state laws, the Federal Government has recently chosen to push aside local decision-making in favor of heavy-handed raids and intimidation of medical marijuana patients and providers.

> Based on the circumstance described above, we find that an emergency exists relating to safe access to medical marijuana, and that there is an immediate need to take action for reasons of preserving democracy in states that have implemented sound, safe and democratic laws.

> Unauthorized entry of U.S. medical marijuana dispensaries by federal agents in states that permit such facilities is unreasonable and contrary to the will of the more than 73% of Americans who favor safe, legal access to medical marijuana. Americans for Safe Access and others joined in solidarity with these dispensaries issue this statement as a warning. We are organized, we are strategic, we are nonviolent, and we are right—all qualities that the DEA lacks.

> IT IS HEREBY ORDERED that all persons acting under the authority of the U.S. Drug Enforcement Administration or other Federal agencies comply with State laws authorizing the

distribution of medical marijuana to seriously ill patients under the direction of their licensed medical professionals.

I pasted the order onto the door with my unchained hand—even though just putting a sticker on the door could have potentially subjected me to a destruction of federal property charge.

The chief gave us his third warning. We chanted back at him. The police began to move all the media and other demonstrators away, and out of sight of us. Knowing that the police did not want anyone to see what they were going to do to us was pretty unnerving. Why would they do that unless they were going to do something to us that was, well, painful?

They arrested Dave Guard first, the one member of our group who was not chained. Then they cut the chains on Jennifer and Leslie, two young ladies from the University of Maryland's Students For Sensible Drug Policy, and tried to drag them away. But they lay down and hung on tight. Eventually their arms were pulled out of the pipes, and they were dragged away to the paddy wagon.

They cut us away one by one and dragged us away with varying degrees of resistance. When it came my turn, Officer Williams in front of me was asking me if I was going to cooperate or be carried, at the same time the guy who was handcuffing me was making a point of jerking my shoulder around and squeezing my fingers painfully. I gave out a little "aarrrgh" and Officer Williams said, "Hey, lay off the guy." He asked me again if I was going to cooperate. My answer was, "The gentleman behind me has just convinced me not to."

If I ever do this again, I'm determined to be carried off a little more gracefully—if such a thing is possible in that situation. In the heat of the moment, I couldn't decide whether to go feet first or feet back. Plus, the very polite Officer Williams kept urging me to cooperate so that "they would not accidentally hurt me." My normal nice guy instincts to help out when someone nicely asks me for assistance were somehow still kicking in, even while the officer on my other arm continued to "make a point" by twisting my wrist and arm further.

So I ended up doing something like the Russian bent-knee dance as they carried me off, and looking pretty silly. Maybe the humorous aspect was why they picked me to show being dragged away on the local evening news.

Once in the police station, we all changed from resistance mode to persuasion, chatting up the officers about drug reform policy as if they were our old buddies. I don't think we made many points with this group, though—one of the officers even said he would arrest his own mother on her deathbed if she smoked medical marijuana. When we challenged him, he would not back off from the statement. "The law is the law."

The same officer also flatly stated police "had intelligence" about our plan, apparently confirming our suspicions that we had been followed earlier.

They handcuffed some of us very tightly. I have some existing nerve problems in my right hand, and the cuffs quickly caused my hand to go to a painful numb. One of the girls' hands was swelling and changing color, and all they would say was, "We'll loosen them soon." "Soon" ended up being about two hours for them to just cut the plastic cuffs off and put them back on a tiny bit looser.

Despite the fact that demonstrators are arrested on a regular basis in D.C., it really seemed like the police were not used to the procedure for arresting people. They fumbled over the paperwork for what seemed like forever. They did not process any one of us the same way. Some of us they searched over and over. Some of us they never searched at all. Some of us had our ties and belts and shoestrings taken. Some did not.

When they took our belts, I had a good laugh with Bruce Mirkin about "sittin' here on the group W bench," but most of the rest of our group was too young to get the Arlo Guthrie, "Alice's Restaurant" reference. One of the girls asked if it wouldn't be easier for her to take off her pants to hang herself than to use her shoestrings. She was told, "Say anything else like that and I'll take you to the psycho ward."

I guess logic equals insanity to that officer.

After about three hours at the Federal Protection Service office, we were driven across town to a D.C.-precinct holding cell. Our cuffs were finally removed after about three and a half hours.

We were charged with "incommoding," a rather unglamorous sounding crime that essentially means trespassing in order to block an entrance. We were offered the opportunity to "post and forfeit" a bond. This is essentially a "no contest" type of plea that closes out our cases. We accept, pay $50 each, and do not have to appear in court. You might think they would release us at that point. Nope.

We kept ourselves amused as best we could, telling war stories from other demonstrations, and discussing what our next steps might be. One of the highlights of the afternoon was when someone found a cockroach in the toilet. Hey, there's not much to keep you amused in a holding cell. While the Democrats and Libertarians were debating what to do—should we liberate the cockroach, or have a betting pool on how long he could swim—Adam, the Green Party guy, flushed him.

As the afternoon turned to early evening, a stream of arrestees on various traffic charges were added to our holding cell. While we had to depend on what they told us as to what they were arrested for, it all pretty much sounded like bogus driving-while-black charges. I can't imagine that I would have gotten more than a ticket for the same charges that these guys were arrested for.

It's one thing to read about the racism of the justice system. It's another thing to witness it right in front of your eyes.

One of the traffic arrestees gave us a good laugh with his take on our civil disobedience. "Damn, you mean you guys broke *into* jail?"

We started getting frustrated that we were not being processed more quickly, although you would think that we would not have been expecting efficiency and logic from our captors. The processing officers spent much of the afternoon watching *Scooby Doo* and other TV shows, instead of bothering to photograph and fingerprint us.

A little after 6:00 p.m., they let the first five of us out. The rest were released a couple of hours later.

The Results

We practiced civil disobedience specifically in order to get media attention for the issue of medical marijuana. We wanted the public to know that this is an issue so critical to so many sick people that others are willing to risk jail to bring it to the public's strong attention.

We certainly succeeded enough to declare the action a success. The biggest hits we know of were the two major news wire services, Reuters and United Press International. The *Los Angeles Times*, *The Washington Times*, and *The Washington Post* ran stories, as did many smaller newspapers. Local TV news affiliates around the country covered the demonstrations. Noelle had the rough experience of watching me being dragged away in handcuffs on the nightly news in D.C.

With all the media hits, it's safe to say we reached millions with our message.

But the federal government's war against medical marijuana patients not only continued, it escalated. One day after our action, U.S. District Judge Charles Breyer issued his expected ruling to permanently block California medical marijuana clubs from distributing the drug to patients. In the months since, the DEA raided many more medical marijuana dispensaries. But after each raid, medical marijuana activists responded with more demonstrations and civil disobedience.

On August 5, 2002, the feds raided the Wo/Men's Alliance for Medical

Marijuana in Santa Cruz. Santa Cruz Mayor Christopher Krohn and several current and former city council members responded by personally overseeing a medical marijuana giveaway on the steps of city hall. San Jose Police Chief William Lansdowne pulled his officers from the DEA task force that committed the raid—ending years of close cooperation.

States' rights to determine their own laws regarding medical practices versus the federal government's power to override voters' wishes heated up when the California Supreme Court issued a unanimous decision in *People v. Mower* affirming the right of patients to be free from prosecution under state law. The DEA responded with more raids on clinics. California's governor and attorney general spoke out against the raids. Days later, the feds raided a quadriplegic's tiny medical garden.

Can you even imagine a more appalling misuse of police resources? To go after the sick and dying in a manner certain to give sympathy to the plight of the patients must surely reflect the last gasps of prohibitionist public officials. They know their policy is doomed because they know the public has seen through the lies. Despite all the raids and propaganda, public support for medical marijuana is at an all time high. A November, 2002, *Time* poll showed 80% of the public now favors letting doctors and patients make medical choices, not the federal government. A policy contrary to the wishes of 80% of the voters cannot last much longer. But while the needless suffering and oppression of the sick continues, when there is a chance to be back on the front lines, I'll be there.

20. Restoring Federalism in Drug Policy

BY JASON P. SORENS

Jason P. Sorens, Ph.D., is lecturer of political science at Yale University and founder of the Free State Project (www.freestateproject.org).

State-federal conflict over drug policy has become increasingly intense over the past few years. Some California localities, citing the state's medical marijuana law, have even used city funds to establish marijuana dispensaries for patients and sued the federal government for raids on their facilities.

Federal drug prohibition is clearly unconstitutional, but it is even more clearly the enforced law of the land. If alcohol prohibition required a constitutional amendment, drug prohibition should have as well. Article I, Section 8 of the U.S. Constitution grants Congress no authority to establish any kind of criminal code, other than to punish treason and counterfeiting and crimes committed at sea or on federal property, and the Thirteenth Amendment forbids states from legalizing slavery. There is clearly no constitutional authorization for federally imposed limits on what a state may otherwise legalize.

To date, states have not stood up for their rights in the area of drug policy. No state government has filed a Tenth Amendment lawsuit against the federal government to protect a medical marijuana exception or any other deviation from federal government policy in the direction of leniency.

It seems to be only a matter of time before a state government is elected somewhere that has a backbone with regard to its exclusive rights over crime control. When such a government is elected, it may put pressure on the federal government through the courts.

Short of court action, however, an enlightened state legislature may exert moral pressure through the passage of a resolution. I present here a sample resolution that could be adopted by state legislatures around the country. While the resolution may not have legal force, its moral force could be considerable if adopted by three-fourths of the states (enough to ratify a constitutional amendment), or even just one-half of the states. It may also put pressure on states' attorneys general to begin defending state drug laws in court on Tenth Amendment grounds.

Proposed State Resolution

Whereas: Article I, Section 8 of the United States Constitution authorizes Congress to perform specific functions, including the punishment of counterfeiting the securities and coin of the United States, and the definition and punishment of piracies and felonies committed on the high seas; and Article III, Section 3 of the United States Constitution authorizes Congress to declare the punishment of treason; but no Article authorizes Congress a general role in crime control on the territory of any state;

Whereas: Article I, Section 10 forbids state governments from performing various tasks otherwise assigned specifically to Congress; but Amendment XIII is the only Article prohibiting states from legalizing any activity, namely slavery or involuntary servitude;

Whereas: Amendment X states that powers not delegated to the United States government by the Constitution, nor prohibited by it to the states, are reserved to the states respectively, or to the people;

Whereas: Amendment IX states that individuals enjoy extensive rights not specified in the Constitution, Amendment V states that no person shall be deprived of life, liberty, and property without due process of law, and Amendment IV states that the right of individuals to be secure from unreasonable searches and seizures shall not be violated;

Whereas: The federal government through its crime policies has continuously violated Amendments IV, V, and IX and the natural rights of American citizens through asset forfeiture policies, no-knock raids, preemptive punishment, surveillance, and other actions;

Therefore, Be It Resolved by the Legislature of [State *X*],

That: This state does affirm the value of Americans' civil liberties and its intention to uphold and enforce the full Bill of Rights;

That: State law enforcement officials shall not cooperate with federal law enforcement officials in any activity violating individual rights, in the absence of probable cause indicating criminal activity as defined by the state criminal code, including:

an initiation of, participation in, or assistance or cooperation with an inquiry, investigation, surveillance, or detention;

the recording, filing, and sharing of any intelligence information concerning a person or organization;

enforcement of immigration matters, which are entirely the responsibility of the Immigration and Naturalization Service;

collection or maintenance of information about the political, religious, or social views, associations, or activities of an individual, group, association, organization, corporation, business, or partnership; and

profiling based on race, ethnicity, citizenship, religion, or political views;

That: Where the law of the respective states with respect to private criminal acts differs from the law of the United States, unless regarding treason, counterfeiting, slavery or involuntary servitude, or piracies or felonies at sea, state law shall govern, unless state law is more stringent than the law of the United States and is held to violate the Constitution's protections of the individual;

That: Where the criminal law of any state is harmonious with the existing criminal law of the United States, it is permissible for agents of the United States to enforce federal law in that state, with the permission of that state's legislature;

That: Where the criminal law of any state is not harmonious with the existing criminal law of the United States, it is not permissible for agents of the United States to enforce the disharmonious portions of federal law in that state;

That: We do hereby exhort the United States Representatives and Senators of this state to introduce and vote in favor of legislation granting the aforementioned sections of this resolution the acceptance of the United States government and the full force of law.

Potential Impacts

This resolution stops all state cooperation with federal law enforcement in enforcing unconstitutional laws. In this part of the resolution, it would be desirable to bring in any specific protections of individual liberties mentioned in the state constitution, as well as the well-known protections in the federal constitution. The language used above is in part modeled on Alaska's resolution against the Patriot Act II.[1]

In addition, the resolution declares that federal law on drugs—or any other criminal law—is invalid in a state when it is stricter than that state's existing laws. However, it does not abolish federal criminal law, federal prisons, and federal enforcement agencies. All of these things may still exist, but they must serve the states. If this part of the resolution acquired force of law, it would not abolish the DEA; instead, it would require the DEA to work in all states by invitation. Thus, this legislation should be politically more palatable than a clean sweep of federal drug laws. Moreover, it provides a justification for a court challenge to federal laws by state government, in that federal courts have typically held that there must be overt conflict between branches of government before a constitutional ruling on the branches' limits is warranted. An example is the recent ruling of the First Circuit Court of Appeals that no suit could be brought against the President of the United States for initiating military hostilities unless there was a clear conflict between the executive and legislative branches.[2]

If passed, the above resolution has one immediate effect: it ends state cooperation with federal law enforcement in violating Americans' rights. It further makes a moral statement that federal criminal policy is currently unconstitutional, and that state law in criminal matters is superior to federal law. If this resolution were implemented, it would truly be a sweeping change. It might be more politically practical to tailor the resolution specifically to marijuana policy instead. The resolution would then have a much more limited impact politically and would have shakier grounding in terms of constitutional law, but there may be a greater chance of getting at least one state to pass it in the near term.

An America in which states could determine whether DEA and FBI agents would operate in the state, and to what purposes, would be a safer and saner America. States would be encouraged to try different drug policies, without compromising other states' right to attempt to control drugs in traditional fashion. The diversity that federalism allows would defuse mounting state-federal conflict over drug policy, and in the long run would work to undermine harsh prohibitionist policies that have promoted gang warfare, waves of petty theft, distribution of unsafe substances and delivery devices, police corruption, and other ills. In their place, a more progressive and flexible patchwork of drug management policies would arise.

Notes

1. For the text of this resolution, see www.bordc.org/Alaska-res.htm.

2. For details, see www.cnn.com/2003/LAW/03/13/antiwar.lawsuit/.

21. Out from the Shadows

BY DAVID BORDEN

David Borden is founder and executive director of StoptheDrugWar.org, the Drug Reform Coordination Network (DRCNet), in Washington, D.C.

One of the distinguishing characteristics of drug policy is the sheer scope of issues on which it has bearing. Whether the concern is health, safety, criminal justice, foreign policy, pain control, agriculture, civil liberties, housing, education, medical research, the environment, property rights, militarized policing of the borders and in our towns, or the corruption of our police forces and financial institutions, there are few aspects of policy—or of life—that the drug war doesn't touch in some way.

Because drug policy relates to so many issues, and because more funding has become available for reform activities, a diverse group of organizations has sprung up in the past decade or so. These organizations differ in focus and approach, but all work to roll back the drug war in one or more of its manifestations. Some groups advocate marijuana legalization and policy reform. Some state and national organizations seek to change sentencing laws. Other groups work to rein in the grossly abused practice of asset forfeiture. A myriad of organizations, whether central to the drug reform movement or distantly related to it, lobby Congress to stop its escalation of the Andean drug war or document the impact of the U.S. drug policy in Latin America on human rights, political stability, and the environment. An entire movement exists to legalize medical marijuana. Patient rights organizations oppose the DEA's witch hunt against doctors who prescribe narcotics for pain control. Numerous local outreach programs provide harm reduction services such as needle exchange, or distribute safety tools and information at rave parties, or advocate on behalf of such programs and their clientele. Other organizations exist to save the hemp food industry from the DEA's overreaching and to legalize industrial hemp cultivation in the U.S. Others defend the rights of methadone patients, or addicts who are pregnant, or those recovered from addiction or in recovery. Some groups fund or facilitate research into medical marijuana or psychedelics.

Several organizations take on a broad swath of drug policy issues, knitting them together into a cohesive call for changing drug policy across the board and ending the so-called "war on drugs," at least in its current form. Some groups cater to specific constituencies such as students or the families of prisoners. Some oppose specific excesses of the drug war while considering a variety of alternatives to current punitive drug policies. Some organizations, including my own, call for the complete repeal of drug prohibition, replacing it with some system—imprecisely termed "legalization"—in which adults at least will have legal access, through some reasonable route, to a legally produced and distributed supply of the drugs that they choose. Some organizations work in other countries and continents, either on a regional or global scale.

Though the punitive paradigm in drug policy remains fundamentally unchanged, these past 10 years have seen some significant developments in reform efforts. Medical marijuana has blossomed into a major national issue, due in part to several successful state ballot initiatives and the willingness of some advocates to risk their freedom by opening cooperative markets supplying marijuana to patients. A number of state legislatures, even some highly conservative ones such as in Oklahoma, have begun to roll back sentences for low-level, nonviolent drug offenders, partly because these states' budgets have been hurt by escalating prison costs. The possibility of lifting the ban on using federal AIDS prevention funds for needle exchange programs was a major issue a few years ago, though more recently the issue fell off the radar. Yet needle exchanges now operate, officially or tacitly sanctioned, in a larger number of municipalities than ever before. A number of states have passed voter initiatives shifting offenders and resources from prison to treatment.

The political shift in drug policy is starting to show. In July, 2003, two votes on the floor of the U.S. House of Representatives illustrated the progress we have made. One concerned an amendment, sponsored by Representatives Maurice Hinchey (D-NY) and Dana Rohrabacher (R-CA), to stop the DEA's raids on medical marijuana clinics by forbidding taxpayer funded interference with state medical marijuana laws. The amendment failed, but support for medical marijuana in Congress had more than doubled since the last vote on the issue five years before. The other vote concerned an amendment, offered by Representatives Jim McGovern (D-MA) and Ike Skelton (D-MO), to reduce the amount of U.S. military aid to Colombia, much of which funds the drug war. We lost that vote, too, but the margin was razor thin, a dramatic change from several years ago, when slowing down the Andean drug war seemed a far-away dream.

In many ways, then, drug reform efforts over the past 10 or so years have been a story of success, or at least of encouragement that successes seem to be on the way. But success has also led to a degree of caution among drug reform groups. The typical position statement of an organization in the drug reform movement stops short of directly calling for an end to prohibition—even when most of the group's leaders and members hold that view. Our movement has adopted as conventional wisdom the idea that we can be more effective at swaying public opinion, building bridges with mainstream social movements, and affecting legislative change if we temper our positions to be a little closer to the mainstream. For example, if a vote is coming up on medical marijuana, reform advocates may justifiably fear their opponents will tar them as "legalizers" and that such accusations may cost them political support. Some prominent drug policy reformers don't agree with full legalization, or aren't sure, or aren't comfortable with the association.

For some organizations, no doubt, the moderated approach is the right strategic choice. But that choice also comes with costs. Publicly expressed support for legalization—not just limited reform—has come from more prominent organizations and individuals than at any other time in recent memory. Officials coming out for legalization or showing an interest in discussing it include recent former governors of New Mexico (Gary Johnson, a Republican) and Minnesota (Jesse Ventura). *National Review*, the flagship publication of U.S. conservatism, called for legalization of all drugs in a cover article published in 1994. The highly respected news magazine *The Economist* has called for legalization regularly for at least as long. The ACLU board adopted a statement in 1994 calling for the "full and complete decriminalization of the use, sale, manufacture and distribution of drugs." The conservative-libertarian Cato Institute openly calls for legalization. The president of Mexico made pro-legalization statements during the last few years, as did the president of Uruguay with great force and passion. A committee of the Senate of Canada called for marijuana legalization in a 2002 report, and the committee's chairman has stated publicly he is for legalization across the board as well. A number of members of the U.S. Congress have even raised the issue.

But while some caution on the part of drug reformers is understandable, there is undeniable irony in a situation where organizations outside of the main drug policy reform movement are taking bolder positions than most drug policy reform groups take, and at a time when more public opinion leaders are willing to talk about legalization than ever before. It is true that the public at large does not yet agree with legalization. But they never will if they don't hear the case: only an end to prohibition can address the structural problems in our society such as inner city violence, which the illicit drug trade creates or worsens; only an end to prohibition can rescue addicts from the dangers and severe degradation that the circumstances created by criminalization impose on their lives.

Why should politicians or other public officials risk the heat of the legalization spotlight, if all the advocates most deeply involved with the issue and informed about it won't do so themselves? "Not quite legalization" is a very tempting escape route that many of our most capable allies are bound to follow if we consistently walk that path ourselves. Indeed, some sympathetic opinion leaders have already followed that lead and tempered their public pronouncements.

My contention is not that every group involved in drug policy reform should change its approach, whether it has been crafted by political considerations, ideology, or both. But I do believe that what now passes as conventional wisdom in the drug policy reform movement, that groups should temper their views to gain a more convincing appearance of being mainstream and respectable, is partly based on habit and assumption; there are other ways to prove our respectability. My organization, for example, has directly called for legalization since its inception 10 years ago—DRCNet is in fact the largest drug policy organization that formally takes this position—but this has not prevented us from also working effectively on incremental reforms that have mainstream support.

It was DRCNet in 1998 that launched the national campaign to repeal a new law that delays or denies federal financial aid to students because of drug convictions. We have worked on this issue with some of the largest and most well known education and civil rights groups in the country, and have garnered the largest number of legislative cosponsors for any positive drug reform before Congress. In May, 2002, 10 members of Congress spoke at a press conference we organized on the issue, the largest Congressional participation in any drug reform press conference to date.

We didn't alter our pro-legalization position to accomplish these things. We simply don't emphasize that aspect of our views while doing work on that issue. But neither do we hide it; anyone following the Web site links can easily figure out who we are and what we stand for. For the most part, organizations are willing to work with us and live with the fact that we happen to be "legalizers," so long as we are careful to stick to the issues we've agreed to partner on and not get the organizations associated with our other issues. Organizational leaders have told us this directly. The credibility of organizations that adopt a full anti-prohibitionist position, then, may depend on how such groups handle particular issues and general affairs, rather than whether they touch the supposed "third rail" of legalization.

Motivated by these concerns, in late 2001 we launched "Out from the Shadows: Ending Drug Prohibition in the 21st Century," a campaign and series of conferences to advance the antiprohibitionist perspective and help legalization advocates organize, amplify their voices, and elevate their standing. We decided to organize globally, in order to combine these voices into the largest, most impressive possible call for ending prohibition that could be mustered.

We entered into this effort understanding that not all of our usual allies would be willing and able to participate. One prominent advocate in fact withdrew his organization from the campaign after he realized we were talking about full legalization. But we were willing to pay this price to ensure the clarity of our message. Perhaps fewer organizations and opinion leaders would participate, but those who did would be clearly on record. Over time, it was our hope that, by taking this approach and sticking to it, we would foster a more comfortable political climate for others.

Out from the Shadows kicked off in October, 2002, with an institutional conference at the European Parliament, organized by members of the parliament (MEPs) connected with the Transnational Radical Party, a member of the coalition. In February, 2003, Out from the Shadows held its first major summit, organized by DRCNet, at the Autonomous University of the Yucatan in Mérida, Mexico ("Saliendo de las Sombras: Terminando de la Prohibición de las Drogas en el Siglo XXI"). Out from the Shadows Mérida, also known as the First Latin American Summit on Drug Legalization, drew 300 participants and featured the most high-level political participation of any drug reform conference in history, including legislators from five national parliaments—Mexico, Costa Rica, Bolivia, Colombia and Uruguay—as well as the European Parliament, and many other prominent leaders. A third Out from the Shadows event, organized by the Radical-affiliated International Antiprohibitionist League, took place in Washington, D.C. It included a press conference with Canada's Senator Pierre Claude Nolin, who chaired a committee of the Canadian Senate that produced a 2002 report calling for marijuana legalization.

Out from the Shadows will continue, as funding permits, to wind its way through more cities and countries—such as London, England; Vancouver, Canada; and Rio de Janeiro, Brazil—eventually coming back to the United States, but with with a growing capacity to engage political leaders and the media in a true dialogue about prohibition. A likely location for the first U.S. conference is Chicago, a city that evokes the Prohibition era partly through the pop-culture legacy of its famous gangster, Al Capone. Information on this effort, including the list of participating organizations, articles, interviews, and video footage, can be found on the Web at http://stopthedrugwar.org/shadows.

As Governor Johnson commented in the midst of his legalization crusade in late 2000, support for the drug war is a mile wide but an inch deep. Most of the public has never heard the extremely compelling arguments that exist for ending prohibition. Once they do, it's not hard to get them to consider the proposal. As terrible as so many drug war policies are, I'm optimistic about the future prospects for drug legalization, because large segments of the public are waiting to hear from us. There has never been a more effective time to work for drug policy reform.

Also Available from Accurate Press

Also Available from Accurate Press

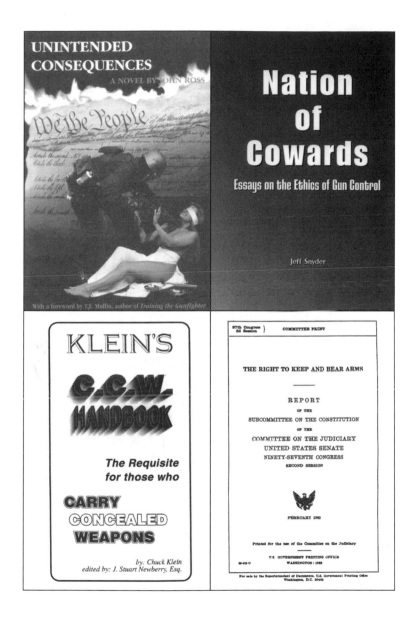

1.800.374.4049
www.accuratepress.net